Introduction *to* Buddhism

Dr. Indra Narain Singh

Prashant Publishing House
DELHI - 110094 (INDIA)

PRASHANT PUBLISHING HOUSE
C-34, 28 Foota Road, Gali No. 3
West Karawal Nagar, Delhi-110094
Phone : 9810396373, 22963970

Introduction to Buddhism

First Published : 2009

ISBN : 978-81-908282-4-6

PRINTED IN INDIA

Published by Mr. R. K. Jha M/s. Prashant Publishing House, Delhi and Printed at H.S. Offset Press, Delhi.

Acknowledgement

The present work has received encouragement, help and support from a large number of persons. It would be impossible to acknowledge my gratitude to everyone in this limited space.

I must above all especially express my idebtedness to Prof. Bhikshu Satyapal.

I wish to acknowledge with deep sense of gratitude, the unfailing encouragement and cooperation. I have received from my wife Aparajita, daughter Tanya and son Uday.

—Dr. Indra Narain Singh

Preface

Religions, it is often observed, are products of fear. This fear is in turn based on ignorance. With the dawn of wisdom and the ever-expanding horizons of knowledge, faith and confidence in religions begin to evaporate, like morning mist under the rising sun.

Not so with Buddhism. Buddhism is a result of the human quest for the ultimate truth, an aspiration for that which is the highest and noblest in life. It is based on the Buddha's wisdom, on his enlightenment, attained through the complete eradication of ignorance, fear and all other defilements from his mind. His teachings, called the Dhamma (Sanskrit: Dharma), have stood the test of time for more than twenty-five centuries.

One of the most outstanding features of Buddhism is its total independence of divine elements. It is a religion of self-help. According to Buddhism, human beings should learn to be self-reliant and to have faith in their own ability. Buddhist philosophy is anthropocentric in its outlook and practical implementation, placing man at the center of its metaphysical and ethical systems. It is a religion that insists primarily on man's own effort and perseverance to achieve his goals, be they material or spiritual, rather than prayer or wishful thinking.

— *Author*

CONTENTS

1

THE BUDDHA

On the fullmoon day of May, in the year 623 B.C., there was born in the district of Nepal an Indian Sakya Prince named Siddhattha Gotama, who was destined to be the greatest religious teacher in the world. Brought up in the lap of luxury, receiving an education befitting a prince, he married and had a son.

His contemplative nature and boundless compassion did not permit him to enjoy the fleeting material pleasures of a Royal household. He knew no woe, but he felt a deep pity for sorrowing humanity. Amidst comfort and prosperity, he realized the universality of sorrow. The palace, with all its worldly amusements, was no longer a congenial place for the compassionate prince. The time was ripe for him to depart. Realizing the vanity of sensual enjoyments, in his twenty-ninth year, he renounced all worldly pleasures and donning the simple yellow garb of an ascetic, alone, penniless, wandered forth in search of Truth and Peace.

It was an unprecedented historic renunciation; for he renounced not in his old age but in the prime of manhood, not in poverty but in plenty. As it was the belief in the ancient days that no deliverance could be gained unless one leads a life of strict asceticism, he strenuously practiced all forms of severe austerities. "Adding vigil after vigil, and penance after penance," he made a superhuman effort for six long years. His body was reduced to almost a skeleton. The more he tormented his body, the farther his goal receded from him. The painful, unsuccessful austerities which he strenuously practiced proved absolutely futile. He was now fully convinced, through personal experience, of the utter futility of self-mortification which weakened his body and resulted in lassitude of spirit.

Benefiting by this invaluable experience of his, he finally decided to follow an independent course, avoiding the two extremes of self-indulgence and self-mortification. The former retards one's spiritual progress, and the latter weakens one's intellect. The new way which he himself discovered was the Middle Path, *Majjhima Patipada,* which subsequently became one of the salient characteristics of his teaching.

One happy morning, while He was deeply absorbed in meditation, unaided and unguided by any supernatural power and solely relying on His efforts and wisdom, He eradicated all defilements, purified Himself, and, realizing things as they truly are, attained Enlightenment (Buddhahood) at the age of 35. He was not born a Buddha, but He became a Buddha by His own striving. As the perfect embodiment of all the virtues He preached, endowed with deep wisdom commensurate with His boundless compassion. He devoted the remainder of His precious life to serve humanity both by example and precept, dominated by no personal motive whatever.

After a very successful ministry of 45 long years the Buddha, as every other human being, succumbed to the inexorable law of change, and finally passed away in His 80th year, exhorting His disciples to regard His doctrine as their teacher.

The Buddha was a human being. As a man He was born, as a man He lived, and as a man His life came to an end.

Though a human being, He became an extraordinary man *(Acchariya Manussa)*, but He never arrogated to Himself divinity. The Buddha laid stress on this important point and left no room whatever for anyone to fall into the error of thinking that He was an immortal divine being. Fortunately there is no deification in the case of the Buddha. It should, however, be remarked that there was no Teacher, "ever so godless as the Buddha, yet none so god-like."

The Buddha is neither an incarnation of the Hindu God Vishnu, as is believed by some, nor is He a savior who freely saves others by His personal salvation. The Buddha exhorts His disciples to depend on themselves for their deliverance, for both purity and defilement depend on oneself. Clarifying His relationship with His followers and emphasizing the importance of self-reliance and individual striving, the Buddha plainly states: "You should exert yourselves, the Tathagatas are only teachers."

The Buddhas point out the path, and it is left for us to follow that path to obtain our purification.

"To depend on others for salvation is negative, but to depend on oneself is positive." Dependence on others means a surrender of one's effort.

In exhorting His disciples to be self-dependent the Buddha says in the *Parinibbana Sutta:* "Be ye islands unto yourselves, be ye a refuge unto yourselves, seek not for refuge in others." These significant words are self-elevating. They reveal how vital is self-exertion to accomplish one's object and, how superficial and futile it is to seek redemption through benignant saviors and to crave for illusory happiness in an after life through the propitiation of imaginary Gods or by irresponsive prayers and meaningless sacrifices.

Furthermore, the Buddha does not claim the monopoly of Buddhahood which, as a matter of fact, is not the prerogative of any specially graced person. He reached the highest possible state of perfection any person could aspire to, and without the close-fist of a teacher he revealed the only straight path that leads thereto. According to the Teaching of the Buddha anybody may aspire to that supreme state of perfection if he makes the necessary exertion. The Buddha does not condemn men by calling them wretched sinners, but, on the contrary, He gladdens them by saying that they are pure in heart at conception. In His opinion the world is not wicked but is deluded by ignorance. Instead of disheartening His followers and reserving that exalted state only to Himself, He encourages and induces them to emulate Him, for Buddhahood is latent in all. In one sense all are potential Buddhas.

One who aspires to become a Buddha is called a Bodhisatta, which, literally, means a wisdom-being. This Bodhisatta ideal is the most beautiful and the most refined course of life that has ever been presented to this ego-centric world, for what is nobler than a life of service and purity?

As a Man He attained Buddhahood and proclaimed to the world the latent inconceivable possibilities and the creative power of man. Instead of placing an unseen Almighty God over man who arbitrarily controls the destinies of mankind, and making him subservient to a supreme power, He raised the worth of mankind. It was He who taught that man can gain his deliverance and purification by his own exertion without depending on an external God or mediating priests. It was he who taught the ego-centric world the noble ideal of selfless service. It was He who revolted against the degrading caste system and taught equality of mankind and gave equal opportunities for all to distinguish themselves in every walk of life.

He declared that the gates of success and prosperity were open to all in every condition of life, high or low, saint or criminal, who would care to turn a new leaf and aspire to perfection.

Irrespective of caste, color or rank He established for both deserving men and women a democratically constituted celibate Order. He did not force His followers to be slaves either to His Teachings or to Himself but granted complete freedom of thought.

He comforted the bereaved by His consoling words. He ministered to the sick that were deserted. He helped the poor that were neglected. He ennobled the lives of the deluded, purified the corrupted lives of criminals. He encouraged the feeble, united the divided, enlightened the ignorant, clarified the mystic, guided the benighted, elevated the base, dignified the noble. Both rich and poor, saints and criminals loved Him alike. Despotic and righteous kings, famous and obscure princes and nobles, generous and stingy millionaires, haughty and humble scholars, destitute paupers, down-trodden scavengers, wicked murderers, despised courtesans — all benefited by His words of wisdom and compassion.

His noble example was a source of inspiration to all. His serene and peaceful countenance was a soothing sight to the pious eyes. His message of Peace and Tolerance was welcomed by all with indescribable joy and was of eternal benefit to every one who had the fortune to hear and practice it.

Wherever His teachings penetrated it left an indelible impression upon the character of the respective peoples. The cultural advancement of all the Buddhist nations was mainly due to His sublime Teachings. In fact all Buddhist countries like Ceylon, Burma, Thailand, Cambodia, Vietnam, Laos, Nepal, Tibet, China, Mongolia, Korea, Japan, etc., grew up in the cradle of Buddhism. Though more than 2500 years have elapsed since the passing away of this greatest

Teacher, yet his unique personality exerts a great influence on all who come to know Him.

His iron will, profound wisdom, universal love, boundless compassion, selfless service, historic renunciation, perfect purity, magnetic personality, exemplary methods employed to propagate the Teachings, and his final success — all these factors have compelled about one-fifth of the population of the world today to hail the Buddha as their supreme Teacher.

Paying a glowing tribute to the Buddha Sri Radhakrishnan states: "In Gautama the Buddha we have a master-mind from the East second to none so far as the influence on the thought and life of the human race is concerned, and, sacred to all as the founder of a religious tradition whose hold is hardly less wide and deep than any other. He belongs to the history of the world's thought, to the general inheritance of all cultivated men, for, judged by intellectual integrity, moral earnestness, and spiritual insight, He is undoubtedly one of the greatest figures in history.

In *The Three Greatest Men in History* H.G. Wells writes: "In the Buddha you see clearly a man, simple, devout, lonely, battling for light — a vivid human personality, not a myth. He too gave a message to mankind universal in character. Many of our best modern ideas are in closest harmony with it. All the miseries and discontents are due, he taught, to selfishness. Before a man can become serene he must cease to live for his senses or himself. Then he merges into a great being. Buddha in different language called men to self-forgetfulness 500 years before Christ. In some ways he is nearer to us and our needs. He was more lucid upon our individual importance and service than Christ and less ambiguous upon the question of personal immortality."

St. Hilaire remarks "The perfect model of all the virtues He preaches. His life has not a stain upon it."

Fausboll says — "The more I know of Him, the more I love Him."

A humble follower of his would say — "The more I know Him, the more I love Him; the more I love Him, the more I know Him."

The Dhamma: Is it a Philosophy?

The non-aggressive, moral and philosophical system expounded by the Buddha, which demands no blind faith from its adherents, expounds no dogmatic creeds, encourages no superstitious rites and ceremonies, but advocates a golden mean that guides a disciple through pure living and pure thinking to the gain of supreme wisdom and deliverance from all evil, is called the Dhamma and is popularly known as Buddhism.

The all-merciful Buddha has passed away, but the sublime Dhamma which He unreservedly bequeathed to humanity, still exists in its pristine purity.

Although the Master has left no written records of His Teachings, His distinguished disciples preserved them by committing to memory and transmitting them orally from generation to generation.

Immediately after His demise 500 chief Arahats versed in the Dhamma and Vinaya, held a convocation to rehearse the Doctrine as was originally taught by the Buddha. Venerable Ananda Thera, who enjoyed the special privilege of hearing all the discourses, recited the Dhamma, while the Venerable Upali recited the Vinaya. The *Tipitaka* was compiled and arranged in its present form by those Arahats of old. During the reign of the pious Sinhala King Vattagamani Abhaya, about 83 B.C., the Tipitaka was, for the first time in the history of Buddhism, committed to writing on palm leaves (ola) in Ceylon.

This voluminous *Tipitaka,* which contains the essence of the Buddha's Teaching, is estimated to be about eleven times the size of the Bible. A striking contrast between the Tipitaka and the Bible is that the former is not a gradual development like the latter.

As the word itself implies, the *Tipitaka* consists of three baskets. They are the Basket of Discipline *(Vinaya Pitaka),* the Basket of Discourses *(Sutta Pitaka),* and the Basket of Ultimate Doctrine *(Abhidhamma Pitaka).*

The *Vinaya Pitaka* which is regarded as the sheet anchor to the oldest historic celibate order — the Sangha — mainly deals with rules and regulations which the Buddha promulgated, as occasion arose, for the future discipline of the Order of monks *(Bhikkhus)* and nuns *(Bhikkunis).* It described in detail the gradual development of the *Sasana* (Dispensation). An account of the life and ministry of the Buddha is also given. Indirectly it reveals some important and interesting information about ancient history, Indian customs, arts, science, etc.

The Vinaya Pitaka consists of the five following books:

(Vibhanga):

1. *Pārājika* Pāḷi — Major Offenses
2. *Pācittiya* Pāḷi — Minor Offenses

(Khandaka):

3. *Mahāvagga* Pāḷi — Greater Section
4. *Cūllavagga* Pāḷi — Shorter Section
5. *Parivāra* Pāḷi — Epitome of the Vinaya

The *Sutta Pitaka* consists chiefly of discourses, delivered by the Buddha himself on various occasions. There are also a few discourses delivered by some of His distinguished disciples such as the Venerable Sariputta, Ananda, Moggallana, etc., included in it. It is like a book of prescriptions, as the sermons embodied therein were expounded to suit the different occasions and the temperaments of various persons. There may be seemingly contradictory statements, but they should not be misconstrued as they were opportunely uttered by the Buddha to suit a particular purpose: for instance, to the self-same question He would maintain silence (when the inquirer is merely foolishly inquisitive), or give a detailed reply when He knew the inquirer to be an earnest seeker. Most of the sermons were intended mainly for the benefit of Bhikkhus and they deal with the Holy life and with the expositions of the doctrine. There are also several other discourses which deal with both the material and moral progress of His lay followers.

This Pitaka is divided into five Nikayas or collections, viz:

1. *Dīgha Nikāya* (Collection of Long Discourses).
2. *Majjhima Nikāya* (Collection of Middle-Length Discourses).
3. *Samyuṭṭa Nikāya* (Collection of Kindred Sayings).
4. *Anguṭṭāra Nikāya* (Collection of Discourses arranged in accordance with numbers).
5. *Khuddakā Nikāya* (Smaller Collection).

The fifth is subdivided into fifteen books:

1. *Khuddaka Pātha* (Shorter texts)
2. *Dhammapada* (Way of Truth)
3. *Udāna* (Paeans of Joy)
4. *Iti Vuttaka* ("Thus said" Discourses)
5. *Sutta Nipāta* (Collected Discourses)

6. *Vimāna Vatthu* (Stories of Celestial Mansions)
7. *Peta Vatthu* (Stories of Petas)
8. *Theragāthā* (Psalms of the Brethren)
9. *Therigāthā* (Psalms of the Sisters)
10. *Jātaka* (Birth Stories)
11. *Niddesa* (Expositions)
12. *Paṭisaṁbhidā Magga* (Analytical Knowledge)
13. *Apadanā* (Lives of Arahats)
14. *Buddhavamsa* (The History of the Buddha)
15. *Cariyā Pitaka* (Modes of Conduct)

The *Abhidhamma Pitaka* is the most important and the most interesting of the three, containing as it does the profound philosophy of the Buddha's Teaching in contrast to the illuminating and simpler discourses in the Sutta Pitaka. In the *Sutta Piṭaka* is found the conventional teaching *(vohara desana)* while in the *Abhidhamma Piṭaka* is found the ultimate teaching *(paramattha-desana).*

To the wise, Abhidhamma is an indispensable guide; to the spiritually evolved, an intellectual treat; and to research scholars, food for thought. Consciousness is defined. Thoughts are analyzed and classified chiefly from an ethical standpoint. Mental states are enumerated. The composition of each type of consciousness is set forth in detail. How thoughts arise, is minutely described. Irrelevant problems that interest mankind but having no relation to one's purification, are deliberately set aside.

Matter is summarily discussed; fundamental units of matter, properties of matter, sources of matter, relationship between mind and matter, are explained.

The Abhidhamma investigates mind and matter, the two composite factors of the so-called being, to help the understanding of things as they truly are, and a philosophy has been developed on those lines. Based on that philosophy, an ethical system has been evolved, to realize the ultimate goal, Nibbāna.

The *Abhidhamma Piṭaka* consists of seven books:

1. *Dhammasaṅganī* (Classification of Dhammas)
2. *Vibhaṅga* (The book of Divisions)
3. *Kathā Vatthu* (Points of Controversy)
4. *Puggala-Paññatti* (Descriptions of Individuals)
5. *Dhatu Katha* (Discussion with reference to elements)
6. *Yamaka* (The Book of Pairs),
7. *Paṭṭhāna* (The Book of Relations)

In the Tipitaka one finds milk for the babe and meat for the strong, for the Buddha taught His doctrine both to the masses and to the intelligentsia. The sublime Dhamma enshrined in these sacred texts, deals with truths and facts, and is not concerned with theories and philosophies which may be accepted as profound truths today only to be thrown overboard tomorrow. The Buddha has presented us with no new astounding philosophical theories, nor did He venture to create any new material science. He explained to us what is within and without so far as it concerns our emancipation, as ultimately expounded a path of deliverance, which is unique. Incidentally, He has, however, forestalled many a modern scientist and philosopher.

Schopenhauer in his "World as Will and Idea" has presented the truth of suffering and its cause in a Western garb. Spinoza, though he denies not the existence of a permanent reality, asserts that all phenomenal existence is transitory. In his opinion sorrow is conquered "by finding an object of knowledge which is not transient, not ephemeral, but is immutable, permanent, everlasting." Berkeley proved that the so-called indivisible atom is a metaphysical fiction. Hume, after a relentless analysis of the mind, concluded that consciousness consists of fleeting mental states. Bergson advocates the doctrine of change. Prof. James refers to a stream of consciousness.

The Buddha expounded these doctrines of Transiency, *(Anicca)*, Sorrow *(Dukkha)*, and No-Soul *(Anatta)* some 2500 years ago while He was sojourning in the valley of the Ganges.

It should be understood that the Buddha did not preach all that He knew. On one occasion while the Buddha was passing through a forest He took a handful of leaves and said: "O Bhikkhus, what I have taught is comparable to the leaves in my hand. What I have not taught is comparable to the amount of leaves in the forest."

He taught what He deemed was absolutely essential for one's purification making no distinction between an esoteric and exoteric doctrine. He was characteristically silent on questions irrelevant to His noble mission.

Buddhism no doubt accords with science, but both should be treated as parallel teachings, since one deals mainly with material truths while the other confines itself to moral and spiritual truths. The subject matter of each is different.

The Dhamma He taught is not merely to be preserved in books, nor is it a subject to be studied from a historical or literary standpoint. On the contrary it is to be learned and put into practice in the course of one's daily life, for without practice one cannot appreciate the truth. The Dhamma is to be studied, and more to be practiced, and above all to be realized; immediate realization is its ultimate goal. As such the Dhamma is compared to a raft which is meant for the sole purpose of escaping from the ocean of birth and death *(Samsara)*.

Buddhism, therefore, cannot strictly be called a mere philosophy because it is not merely the "love of, inducing the search after, wisdom." Buddhism may approximate a philosophy, but it is very much more comprehensive.

Philosophy deals mainly with knowledge and is not concerned with practice; whereas Buddhism lays special emphasis on practice and realization.

IS IT A RELIGION?

It is neither a religion in the sense in which that word is commonly understood, for it is not "a system of faith and worship owing any allegiance to a supernatural being."

Buddhism does not demand blind faith from its adherents. Here mere belief is dethroned and is substituted by confidence based on knowledge, which, in Pali, is known as *Saddha*. The confidence placed by a follower on the Buddha is like that of a sick person in a noted physician, or a student in his teacher. A Buddhist seeks refuge in the Buddha because it was He who discovered the Path of Deliverance.

A Buddhist does not seek refuge in the Buddha with the hope that he will be saved by His personal purification. The Buddha gives no such guarantee. It is not within the power of a Buddha to wash away the impurities of others. One could neither purify nor defile another.

The Buddha, as Teacher, instructs us, but we ourselves are directly responsible for our purification.

Although a Buddhist seeks refuge in the Buddha, he does not make any self-surrender. Nor does a Buddhist sacrifice his freedom of thought by becoming a follower of the Buddha. He can exercise his own free will and develop his knowledge even to the extent of becoming a Buddha himself.

The starting point of Buddhism is reasoning or understanding, or, in other words, *Sammā-ditthi.*

To the seekers of truth the Buddha says:

"Do not accept anything on (mere) hearsay — (i.e., thinking that thus have we heard it from a long time). Do not accept anything by mere tradition — (i.e., thinking that it has thus been handed down through many generations). Do not accept anything on account of mere rumors — (i.e., by believing what others say without any investigation). Do not accept anything just because it accords with your scriptures. Do not accept anything by mere suppositions. Do not accept anything by mere inference. Do not accept anything by merely considering the reasons. Do not accept anything merely because it agrees with your pre-conceived notions. Do not accept anything merely because it seems acceptable — (i.e., thinking that as the speaker seems to be a good person his words should be accepted). Do not accept anything thinking that the ascetic is respected by us (therefore it is right to accept his word).

"But when you know for yourselves — these things are immoral, these things are blameworthy, these things are censured by the wise, these things, when performed and undertaken conduce to ruin and sorrow — then indeed do you reject them.

"When you know for yourselves — these things are moral, these things are blameless, these things are praised by the wise, these things, when performed and undertaken, conduce to well-being and happiness — then do you live acting accordingly."

These inspiring words of the Buddha still retain their original force and freshness. Though there is no blind faith, one might argue whether there is no worshiping of images etc., in Buddhism. Buddhists do not worship an image expecting worldly or spiritual favors, but pay their reverence to what it represents. An understanding Buddhist, in offering flowers and incense to an image, designedly makes himself feel that he is in the presence of the living Buddha and thereby gains inspiration from His noble personality and breathes deep His boundless compassion. He tries to follow His noble example.

The Bo-tree is also a symbol of Enlightenment. These external objects of reverence are not absolutely necessary, but they are useful as they tend to concentrate one's attention. An intellectual person could dispense with them as he could easily focus his attention and visualize the Buddha.

For our own good, and out of gratitude, we pay such external respect but what the Buddha expects from His disciple is not so much obeisance as the actual observance of His Teachings. The Buddha says — "He honors me best who practices my teaching best." "He who sees the Dhamma sees me."

With regard to images, however, Count Kevserling remarks — "I see nothing more grand in this world than the image of the Buddha. It is an absolutely perfect embodiment of spirituality in the visible domain."

Furthermore, it must be mentioned that there are not petitional or intercessory prayers in Buddhism. However much we may pray to the Buddha we cannot be saved. The Buddha does not grant favors to those who pray to Him. Instead of petitional prayers there is meditation that leads to self-control, purification and enlightenment. Meditation is neither a silent reverie nor keeping the mind blank. It is an active striving. It serves as a tonic both to the heart and the mind. The Buddha not only speaks of the futility of offering prayers but also disparages a slave mentality. A Buddhist should not pray to be saved, but should rely on himself and win his freedom.

"Prayers take the character of private communications, selfish bargaining with God. It seeks for objects of earthly ambitions and inflames the sense of self. Meditation on the other hand is self-change." — Sri Radhakrishnan

In Buddhism there is not, as in most other religions, an Almighty God to be obeyed and feared. The Buddha does not believe in a cosmic potentate, omniscient and omnipresent. In Buddhism there are no divine revelations or divine messengers. A Buddhist is, therefore, not subservient to any higher supernatural power which controls his destinies and which arbitrarily rewards and punishes. Since Buddhists do not believe in revelations of a divine being Buddhism does not claim the monopoly of truth and does not condemn any other religion. But Buddhism recognizes the infinite latent possibilities of man and teaches that man can gain deliverance from suffering by his own efforts independent of divine help or mediating priests.

Buddhism cannot, therefore, strictly be called a religion because it is neither a system of faith and worship, nor "the outward act or form by which men indicate their recognition of the existence of a God or gods having power over their own destiny to whom obedience, service, and honor are due." If, by religion, is meant "a teaching which takes a view of life that is more than superficial, a teaching which looks into life and not merely at it, a teaching which furnishes men with a guide to conduct that is in accord with this its in-look, a teaching which enables those who give it heed to face life with fortitude and death with serenity," or a system to get rid of the ills of life, then it is certainly a religion of religions.

IS BUDDHISM AN ETHICAL SYSTEM?

It no doubt contains an excellent ethical code which is unparalleled in its perfection and altruistic attitude. It deals with one way of life for the monks and another for the laity. But Buddhism is much more than an ordinary moral teaching. Morality is only the preliminary stage on the Path of Purity, and is a means to an end, but not an end in itself. Conduct, though essential, is itself insufficient to gain one's emancipation. It should be coupled with wisdom or knowledge *(pañña)*. The base of Buddhism is morality, and wisdom is its apex.

In observing the principles of morality a Buddhist should not only regard his own self but also should have a consideration for others we well — animals not excluded. Morality in Buddhism is not founded on any doubtful revelation nor is it the ingenious invention of an exceptional mind, but it is a rational and practical code based on verifiable facts and individual experience.

It should be mentioned that any external supernatural agency plays no part whatever in the moulding of the character of a Buddhist. In Buddhism there is no one to reward or punish. Pain or happiness are the inevitable results of one's actions.

The question of incurring the pleasure or displeasure of a God does not enter the mind of a Buddhist. Neither hope of reward nor fear of punishment acts as an incentive to him to do good or to refrain from evil. A Buddhist is aware of future consequences, but he refrains from evil because it retards, does good because it aids progress to Enlightenment (Bodhi). There are also some who do good because it is good, refrain from evil because it is bad.

To understand the exceptionally high standard of morality the Buddha expects from His ideal followers, one must carefully read the Dhammapada, Sigalovada Sutta, Vyaggapajja Sutta, Mangala Sutta, Karaniya Sutta, Parabhava Sutta, Vasala Sutta, Dhammika Sutta, etc.

As a moral teaching it excels all other ethical systems, but morality is only the beginning and not the end of Buddhism.

In one sense Buddhism is not a philosophy, in another sense it is the philosophy of philosophies.

In one sense Buddhism is not a religion, in another sense it is the religion of religions.

Buddhism is neither a metaphysical path nor a ritualistic path.

It is neither sceptical nor dogmatic.

It is neither self-mortification nor self-indulgence.

It is neither pessimism nor optimism.

It is neither eternalism nor nihilism.

It is neither absolutely this-worldly nor other-worldly.

It is a unique Path of Enlightenment.

The original Pali term for Buddhism is Dhamma, which, literally, means that which upholds. There is no English equivalent that exactly conveys the meaning of the Pali term.

The Dhamma is that which really is. It is the Doctrine of Reality. It is a means of Deliverance from suffering, and Deliverance itself. Whether the Buddhas arise or not the Dhamma exists. It lies hidden from the ignorant eyes of men, till a Buddha, an Enlightened One, realizes and compassionately reveals it to the world.

This Dhamma is not something apart from oneself, but is closely associated with oneself. As such the Buddha exhorts:

"Abide with oneself as an island, with oneself as a Refuge. Abide with the Dhamma as an island, with the Dhamma as a Refuge. Seek no external refuge."

SOME SALIENT FEATURES OF BUDDHISM

The foundations of Buddhism are the four Noble Truths — namely, Suffering (the *raison d'etre* of Buddhism), its cause (i.e., Craving), its end (i.e., Nibbana, the Summum Bonum of Buddhism), and the Middle Way.

What is the Noble Truth of Suffering?

"Birth is suffering, old age is suffering, disease is suffering, death is suffering, to be united with the unpleasant is suffering, to be separated from the pleasant is suffering, not to receive what one craves for is suffering, in brief the five Aggregates of Attachment are suffering."

What is the Noble Truth of the Cause of Suffering?

"It is the craving which leads from rebirth to rebirth accompanied by lust of passion, which delights now here now there; it is the craving for sensual pleasures *(Kãmatanhā)*, for existence *(Bhavatanhā)* and for annihilation *(Vibhavatanhā)*."

What is the Noble Truth of the Annihilation of Suffering?

"It is the remainderless, total annihilation of this very craving, the forsaking of it, the breaking loose, fleeing, deliverance from it."

What is the Noble Truth of the Path leading to the Annihilation of Suffering?

"It is the Noble Eightfold Path which consists of right understanding, right thoughts, right speech, right action, right livelihood, right endeavor, right mindfulness, and right concentration."

Whether the Buddhas arise or not these four Truths exist in the universe. The Buddhas only reveal these Truths which lay hidden in the dark abyss of time. Scientifically interpreted, the Dhamma may be called the law of cause and effect. These two embrace the entire body of the Buddha's Teachings.

The first three represent the philosophy of Buddhism; the fourth represents the ethics of Buddhism, based on that philosophy. All these four truths are dependent on this body itself. The Buddha states: "In this very one-fathom long body along with perceptions and thoughts, do I proclaim the world, the origin of the world, the end of the world and the path leading to the end of the world." Here the term world is applied to suffering.

Buddhism rests on the pivot of sorrow. But it does not thereby follow that Buddhism is pessimistic. It is neither totally pessimistic nor totally optimistic, but, on the contrary, it teaches a truth that lies midway between them. One would be justified in calling the Buddha a pessimist if He had only enunciated the Truth of suffering without suggesting a means to put an end to it. The Buddha perceived the universality of sorrow and did prescribe a panacea for this universal sickness of humanity. The highest conceivable happiness, according to the Buddha, is Nibbana, which is the total extinction of suffering.

The author of the article on Pessimism in the Encyclopedia Britannica writes: "Pessimism denotes an attitude of hopelessness towards life, a vague general opinion that pain and evil predominate in human affairs. The original doctrine of the Buddha is in fact as optimistic as any optimism of the West. To call it pessimism is merely to apply to it a characteristically Western principle to which happiness is impossible without personality. The true Buddhist looks forward with enthusiasm to absorption into eternal bliss."

Ordinarily the enjoyment of sensual pleasures is the highest and only happiness of the average man. There is no doubt a kind of momentary happiness in the anticipation, gratification and retrospection of such fleeting material pleasures, but they are illusive and temporary. According to the Buddha non-attachment is a greater bliss.

The Buddha does not expect His followers to be constantly pondering on suffering and lead a miserable unhappy life. He exhorts them to be always happy and cheerful, for zest *(Piti)* is one of the factors of Enlightenment.

Real happiness is found within, and is not to be defined in terms of wealth, children, honors or fame. If such possessions are misdirected, forcibly or unjustly obtained, misappropriated or even viewed with attachment, they will be a source of pain and sorrow to the possessors.

Instead of trying to rationalize suffering, Buddhism takes suffering for granted and seeks the cause to eradicate it. Suffering exists as long as there is craving. It can only be annihilated by treading the Noble Eightfold Path and attaining the supreme bliss of Nibbana.

These four Truths can be verified by experience. Hence the Buddha Dhamma is not based on the fear of the unknown, but is founded on the bedrock of facts which can be tested by ourselves and verified by experience. Buddhism is, therefore rational and intensely practical.

Such a rational and practical system cannot contain mysteries or esoteric doctrines. Blind faith, therefore, is foreign to Buddhism. Where there is no blind faith there cannot be any coercion or persecution or fanaticism. To the unique credit of Buddhism it must be said that throughout its peaceful march of 2500 years no drop of blood was shed in the name of the Buddha, no mighty monarch wielded his powerful sword to propagate the Dhamma, and no conversion was made either by force or by repulsive methods. Yet, the Buddha was the first and the greatest missionary that lived on earth.

Aldous Huxley writes: "Alone of all the great world religions Buddhism made its way without persecution censorship or inquisition."

Lord Russell remarks: "Of the great religions of history, I prefer Buddhism, especially in its earliest forms; because it has had the smallest element of persecution."

In the name of Buddhism no altar was reddened with the blood of a Hypatia, no Bruno was burnt alive.

Buddhism appeals more to the intellect than to the emotion. It is concerned more with the character of the devotees than with their numerical strength.

On one occasion Upali, a follower of Nigantha Nataputta, approached the Buddha and was so pleased with the Buddha's exposition of the Dhamma that he instantly expressed his desire to become a follower of the Buddha. But the Buddha cautioned him, saying:

"Of a verity, O householder, make a thorough investigation. It is well for a distinguished man like you to make (first) a thorough investigation."

Upali, who was overjoyed at this unexpected remark of the Buddha, said:

"Lord, had I been a follower of another religion, its adherents would have taken me round the streets in a procession proclaiming that such and such a millionaire had renounced his former faith and embraced theirs. But, Lord, Your Reverence advises me to investigate further. The more pleased am I with this remark of yours. For the second time, Lord, I seek refuge in the Buddha, Dhamma and the Sangha."

Buddhism is saturated with this spirit of free enquiry and complete tolerance. It is the teaching of the open mind and the sympathetic heart, which, lighting and warming the whole universe with its twin rays of wisdom and compassion, sheds its genial glow on every being struggling in the ocean of birth and death.

The Buddha was so tolerant that He did not even exercise His power to give commandments to His lay followers. Instead of using the imperative, He said: "It behooves you to do this — It behooves you not to do this." He commands not but does exhort.

This tolerance the Buddha extended to men, women and all living beings.

It was the Buddha who first attempted to abolish slavery and vehemently protested against the degrading caste system which was firmly rooted in the soil of India. In the Word of the Buddha it is not by mere birth one becomes an outcast or a noble, but by one's actions. Caste or color does not preclude one from becoming a Buddhist or from entering the Order. Fishermen, scavengers, courtesans, together with warriors and Brahmans, were freely admitted to the Order and enjoyed equal privileges and were also given positions of rank. Upali, the barber, for instance, was made in preference to all other the chief in matters pertaining to Vinaya discipline. The timid Sunita, the scavenger, who attained Arhatship was admitted by the Buddha Himself into the Order. Angulimala, the robber and criminal, was converted to a compassionate saint. The fierce Alavaka sought refuge in the Buddha and became a saint. The courtesan Ambapali entered the Order and attained Arhatship. Such instances could easily be multiplied from the Tipitaka to show that the portals of Buddhism were wide open to all, irrespective of caste, color or rank.

It was also the Buddha who raised the status of downtrodden women and not only brought them to a realization of their importance to society but also founded the first celibate religious order for women with rules and regulations.

The Buddha did not humiliate women, but only regarded them as feeble by nature. He saw the innate good of both men and women and assigned to them their due places in His teaching. Sex is no barrier to attaining Sainthood.

Sometimes the Pali term used to denote women is *Matugama,* which means "mother-folk" or "society of mothers." As a mother, woman holds an honorable place in Buddhism. Even the wife is regarded as "best friend" *(parama sakha)* of the husband.

Hasty critics are only making ex parte statements when they reproach Buddhism with being inimical to women. Although at first the Buddha refused to admit women into the Order on reasonable grounds, yet later He yielded to the entreaties of His foster-mother, Pajapati Gotami, and founded the Bhikkhuni Order. Just as the Arahats Sariputta and Moggallana were made the two chief disciples in the Order of monks, even so he appointed Arahats Khema and Uppalavanna as the two chief female disciples. Many other female disciples too were named by the Buddha Himself as His distinguished and pious followers.

On one occasion the Buddha said to King Kosala who was displeased on hearing that a daughter was born to him:

A woman child, O Lord of men; may prove

Even a better offspring than a male.

Many women, who otherwise would have fallen into oblivion, distinguished themselves in various ways, and gained their emancipation by following the Dhamma and entering the Order. In this new Order, which later proved to be a great blessing to many women, queens, princesses, daughters of noble families, widows, bereaved mothers, destitute women, pitiable courtesans — all, despite their caste or rank, met on a common platform, enjoyed perfect consolation and peace, and breathed that free atmosphere which is denied to those cloistered in cottages and palatial mansions.

It was also the Buddha who banned the sacrifice of poor beasts and admonished His followers to extend their loving kindness *(Metta)* to all living beings — even to the tiniest creature that crawls at one's feet. No man has the power or the right to destroy the life of another as life is precious to all.

A genuine Buddhist would exercise this loving-kindness towards every living being and identify himself with all, making no distinction whatsoever with regard to caste, color or sex.

It is this Buddhist Metta that attempts to break all the barriers which separate one from another. There is no reason to keep aloof from others merely because they belong to another persuasion or another nationality. In that noble Toleration Edict which is based on *Culla-Vyuha* and *Maha-Vyuha* Suttas, Asoka says: "Concourse alone is best, that is, all should harken willingly to the doctrine professed by others."

Buddhism is not confined to any country or any particular nation. It is universal. It is not nationalism which, in other words, is another form of caste system founded on a wider basis. Buddhism, if it be permitted to say so, is supernationalism.

To a Buddhist there is no far or near, no enemy or foreigner, no renegade or untouchable, since universal love realized through understanding has established the brotherhood of all living beings. A real Buddhist is a citizen of the world. He regards the whole world as his motherland and all as his brothers and sisters.

Buddhism is, therefore, unique, mainly owing to its tolerance, non-aggressiveness, rationality, practicability, efficacy and universality. It is the noblest of all unifying influences and the only lever that can uplift the world.

These are some of the salient features of Buddhism, and amongst some of the fundamental doctrines may be said — Kamma or the Law of Moral Causation, the Doctrine of Rebirth, Anatta and Nibbana.

KAMMA OR THE LAW OF MORAL CAUSATION

We are faced with a totally ill-balanced world. We perceive the inequalities and manifold destinies of men and the numerous grades of beings that exist in the universe. We see one born into a condition of affluence, endowed with fine mental, moral and physical qualities and another into a condition of abject poverty and wretchedness. Here is a man virtuous and holy, but, contrary to his expectation, ill-luck is ever ready to greet him.

The wicked world runs counter to his ambitions and desires. He is poor and miserable in spite of his honest dealings and piety. There is another vicious and foolish, but accounted to be fortune's darling. He is rewarded with all forms of favors, despite his shortcomings and evil modes of life.

Why, it may be questioned, should one be an inferior and another a superior? Why should one be wrested from the hands of a fond mother when he has scarcely seen a few summers, and another should perish in the flower or manhood, or at the ripe age of eighty or hundred? Why should one be sick and infirm, and another strong and healthy?

Why should one be handsome, and another ugly and hideous, repulsive to all? Why should one be brought up in the lap of luxury, and another in absolute poverty, steeped in misery? Why should one be born a millionaire and another a pauper? Why should one be born with saintly characteristics, and another with criminal tendencies? Why should some be linguists, artists, mathematicians or musicians from the very cradle? Why should some be congenitally blind, deaf and deformed? Why should some be blessed and others cursed from their birth?

These are some problems that perplex the minds of all thinking men. How are we to account for all this unevenness of the world, this inequality of mankind?

Is it due to the work of blind chance or accident?

There is nothing in this world that happens by blind chance or accident. To say that anything happens by chance, is no more true than that this book has come here of itself. Strictly speaking, nothing happens to man that he does not deserve for some reason or another.

Could this be the fiat of an irresponsible Creator?

Huxley writes:

"If we are to assume that anybody has designedly set this wonderful universe going, it is perfectly clear to me that he is no more entirely benevolent and just in any intelligible sense of the words, than that he is malevolent and unjust."

According to Einstein:

"If this being (God) is omnipotent, then every occurrence, including every human action, every human thought, and every human feeling and aspiration is also his work; how is it possible to think of holding men responsible for their deeds and thoughts before such an Almighty Being.

"In giving out punishments and rewards, he would to a certain extent be passing judgment on himself. How can this be combined with the goodness and righteousness ascribed to him."

"According to the theological principles man is created arbitrarily and without his desire and at the moment of his creation is either blessed or damned eternally. Hence man is either good or evil, fortunate or unfortunate, noble or depraved, from the first step in the process of his physical creation to the moment of his last breath, regardless of his individual desires, hopes, ambitions, struggles or devoted prayers. Such is theological fatalism." — *Spencer Lewis*

As Charles Bradlaugh says:

"The existence of evil is a terrible stumbling block to the Theist. Pain, misery, crime, poverty confront the advocate of eternal goodness and challenge with unanswerable potency his declaration of Deity as all-good, all-wise, and all-powerful."

In the words of Schopenhauer:

"Whoever regards himself as having become out of nothing must also think that he will again become nothing; for an eternity has passed before he was, and then a second eternity had begun, through which he will never cease to be, is a monstrous thought.

"If birth is the absolute beginning, then death must be his absolute end; and the assumption that man is made out of nothing leads necessarily to the assumption that death is his absolute end."

Commenting on human sufferings and God, Prof. J.B.S. Haldane writes:

"Either suffering is needed to perfect human character, or God is not Almighty. The former theory is disproved by the fact that some people who have suffered very little but have been fortunate in their ancestry and education have very fine characters. The objection to the second is that it is only in connection with the universe as a whole that there is any intellectual gap to be filled by

the postulation of a deity. And a creator could presumably create whatever he or it wanted."

Lord Russell states:

"The world, we are told, was created by a God who is both good and omnipotent. Before He created the world he foresaw all the pain and misery that it would contain. He is therefore responsible for all of it. it is useless to argue that the pain in the world is due to sin. If God knew in advance the sins of which man would be guilty, He was clearly responsible for all the consequences of those sins when He decided to create man."

In "Despair," a poem of his old age, Lord Tennyson thus boldly attacks God, who, as recorded in Isaiah, says, "I make peace and create evil." (Isaiah, xiv. 7.)

"What! I should call on that infinite love that has served us so well? Infinite cruelty, rather that made everlasting hell, Made us, foreknew us, foredoomed us, and does what he will with his own. Better our dead brute mother who never has heard us groan."

Surely "the doctrine that all men are sinners and have the essential sin of Adam is a challenge to justice, mercy, love and omnipotent fairness."

Some writers of old authoritatively declared that God created man in his own image. Some modern thinkers state, on the contrary, that man created God in his own image. With the growth of civilization man's concept of God also became more and more refined.

It is however, impossible to conceive of such a being either in or outside the universe.

Could this variation be due to heredity and environment? One must admit that all such chemico-physical phenomena revealed by scientists, are partly instrumental, but they cannot be solely responsible for the subtle distinctions and vast differences that exist amongst individuals. Yet why should identical twins who are physically alike, inheriting like genes, enjoying the same privilege of upbringing, be very often temperamentally, morally and intellectually totally different?

Heredity alone cannot account for these vast differences. Strictly speaking, it accounts more plausibly for their similarities than for most of the differences.

The infinitesimally minute chemico-physical germ, which is about 30 millionth part of an inch across, inherited from parents, explains only a portion of man, his physical foundation. With regard to the more complex and subtle mental, intellectual and moral differences we need more enlightenment. The theory of heredity cannot give a satisfactory explanation for the birth of a criminal in a long line of honorable ancestors, the birth of a saint or a noble man in a family of evil repute, for the arising of infant prodigies, men of genius and great religious teachers.

According to Buddhism this variation is due not only to heredity, environment, "nature and nurture," but also to our own kamma, or in other words, to the result of our own inherited past actions and our present deeds. We ourselves are responsible for our own deeds, happiness and misery. We build our own hells. We create our own heavens. We are the architects of our own fate. In short we ourselves are our own kamma. On one occasion a certain young man named Subha approached the Buddha, and questioned why and wherefore it was that among human beings there are the low and high states.

> *"For," said he, "we find amongst mankind those of brief life and those of long life, the hale and the ailing, the good looking and the ill-looking, the powerful and the powerless, the poor and the rich, the low-born and the high-born, the ignorant and the intelligent."*

The Buddha briefly replied: "Every living being has kamma as its own, its inheritance, its cause, its kinsman, its refuge. Kamma is that which differentiates all living beings into low and high states."

He then explained the cause of such differences in accordance with the law of moral causation. Thus from a Buddhist standpoint, our present mental, intellectual, moral and temperamental differences are mainly due to our own actions and tendencies, both past the present.

Kamma, literally, means action; but, in its ultimate sense, it means the meritorious and demeritorious volition *(Kusala Akusala Cetana).* Kamma constitutes both good and evil. Good gets good. Evil gets evil. Like attracts like. This is the law of Kamma.

As some Westerners prefer to say Kamma is "action-influence."

We reap what we have sown. What we sow we reap somewhere or some when. In one sense we are the result of what we were; we will be the result of what we are. In another sense, we are not totally the result of what we were and we will not absolutely be the result of what we are. For instance, a criminal today may be a saint tomorrow.

Buddhism attributes this variation to Kamma, but it does not assert that everything is due to Kamma.

If everything were due to Kamma, a man must ever be bad, for it is his Kamma to be bad. One need not consult a physician to be cured of a disease, for if one's Kamma is such one will be cured.

According to Buddhism, there are five orders or processes *(Niyamas)* which operate in the physical and mental realms:

i. *Kamma Niyama,* order of act and result, e.g., desirable and undesirable acts produce corresponding good and bad results.

ii. *Utu Niyama,* physical (inorganic) order, e.g., seasonal phenomena of winds and rains.

iii. *Bija Niyama,* order of germs or seeds (physical organic order); e.g., rice produced from rice-seed, sugary taste from sugar cane or honey etc. The scientific theory of cells and genes and the physical similarity of twins may be ascribed to this order.

iv. *Citta Niyama,* order of mind or psychic law, e.g., processes of consciousness *(Citta vithi),* power of mind etc.

v. *Dhamma Niyama,* order of the norm, e.g., the natural phenomena occurring at the advent of a Bodhisatta in his last birth, gravitation, etc.

Every mental or physical phenomenon could be explained by these all-embracing five orders or processes which are laws in themselves.

Kamma is, therefore, only one of the five orders that prevail in the universe. It is a law in itself, but it does not thereby follow that there should be a law-giver. Ordinary laws of nature, like gravitation, need no law-giver. It operates in its own field without the intervention of an external independent ruling agency.

Nobody, for instance, has decreed that fire should burn. Nobody has commanded that water should seek its own level. No scientist has ordered that water should consist of H_2O, and that coldness should be one of its properties. These are their intrinsic characteristics.

Kamma is neither fate nor predestination imposed upon us by some mysterious unknown power to which we must helplessly submit ourselves. It is one's own doing reacting on oneself, and so one has the possibility to divert the course of Kamma to some extent. How far one diverts it depends on oneself.

It must also be said that such phraseology as rewards and punishments should not be allowed to enter into discussions concerning the problem of Kamma. For Buddhism does not recognize an Almighty Being who rules His subjects and rewards and punishes them accordingly. Buddhists, on the contrary, believe that sorrow and happiness one experiences are the natural outcome of one's own good and bad actions. It should be stated that Kamma has both the continuative and the retributive principle.

Inherent in Kamma is the potentiality of producing its due effect. The cause produces the effect; the effect explains the cause. Seed produces the fruit; the fruit explains the seed as both are inter-related. Even so Kamma and its effect are inter-related; "the effect already blooms in the cause."

A Buddhist who is fully convinced of the doctrine of Kamma does not pray to another to be saved but confidently relies on himself for his purification because it teaches individual responsibility.

It is this doctrine of Kamma that gives him consolation, hope, self reliance and moral courage. It is this belief in Kamma "that validates his effort, kindles his enthusiasm," makes him ever kind, tolerant and considerate. It is also this firm belief in Kamma that prompts him to refrain from evil, do good and be good without being frightened of any punishment or tempted by any reward.

It is this doctrine of Kamma that can explain the problem of suffering, the mystery of so-called fate or predestination of other religions, and above all the inequality of mankind.

Kamma and rebirth are accepted as axiomatic.

Re-birth

As long as this Kammic force exists there is re-birth, for beings are merely the visible manifestation of this invisible

Kammic force. Death is nothing but the temporary end of this temporary phenomenon. It is not the complete annihilation of this so-called being. The organic life has ceased, but the Kammic force which hitherto actuated it has not been destroyed. As the Kammic force remains entirely undisturbed by the disintegration of the fleeting body, the passing away of the present dying thought-moment only conditions a fresh consciousness in another birth.

It is Kamma, rooted in ignorance and craving, that conditions rebirth. Past Kamma conditions the present birth; and present Kamma, in combination with past Kamma, conditions the future. The present is the offspring of the past, and becomes, in turn, the parent of the future.

If we postulate a past, present, and a future life, then we are at once faced with the alleged mysterious problem — "What is the ultimate origin of life?"

Either there must be a beginning or there cannot be a beginning for life.

One school, in attempting to solve the problem, postulates a first cause, God, viewed as a force or as an Almighty Being.

Another school denies a first cause for, in common experience, the cause ever becomes the effect and the effect becomes the cause. In a circle of cause and effect a first cause is inconceivable. According to the former, life has had a beginning, according to the latter, it is beginningless.

From the scientific standpoint, we are the direct products of the sperm and ovum cells provided by our parents. As such life precedes life. With regard to the origin of the first protoplasm of life, or colloid, scientists plead ignorance.

According to Buddhism we are born from the matrix of action (Kammayoni). Parents merely provide an infinitesimally small cell. As such being precedes being. At the moment of conception it is past Kamma that conditions the initial consciousness that vitalizes the fetus. It is this invisible Kammic energy, generated from the past birth that produces mental phenomena and the phenomenon of life in an already extent physical phenomenon, to complete the trio that constitutes man.

For a being to be born here a being must die somewhere. The birth of a being, which strictly means the arising of the five aggregates or psycho-physical phenomena in this present life, corresponds to the death of a being in a past life; just as, in conventional terms, the rising of the sun in one place means the setting of the sun in another place. This enigmatic statement may be better understood by imagining life as a wave and not as a straight line. Birth and death are only two phases of the same process. Birth precedes death, and death, on the other hand, precedes birth. The constant succession of birth and death in connection with each individual life flux constitutes what is technically known as *Samsara* — recurrent wandering.

What is the Ultimate Origin of Life?

The Buddha declares:

"Without cognizable end is this Samsara. A first beginning of beings, who, obstructed by ignorance and fettered by craving, wander and fare on, is not to be perceived."

This life-stream flows *ad infinitum,* as long as it is fed by the muddy waters of ignorance and craving. When these two are completely cut off, then only, if one so wishes, does the stream cease to flow, rebirth ends as in the case of the Buddhas and Arahats. An ultimate beginning of this life-stream cannot be determined, as a stage cannot be perceived when this life-force was not fraught with ignorance and craving. The Buddha has here referred merely to the beginning of the life-stream of living beings. It is left to scientists to speculate on the origin and the evolution of the universe. The Buddha does not attempt to solve all the ethical and philosophical problems that perplex mankind. Nor does He deal with theories and speculations that tend neither to edification nor to enlightenment. Nor does He demand blind faith from His adherents. He is chiefly concerned with the problem of suffering and its destruction. With but this one practical and specific purpose in view, all irrelevant side issues are completely ignored.

But how are we to believe that there is a past existence?

The most valuable evidence Buddhists cite in favor of rebirth is the Buddha, for He developed a knowledge which enabled Him to read past and future lives.

Following His instructions, His disciples also developed this knowledge and were able to read their past lives to a great extent.

Even some Indian Rishis, before the advent of the Buddha, were distinguished for such psychic powers as clairaudience, clairvoyance, thought-reading, remembering past births, etc.

There are also some persons, who probably in accordance with the laws of association, spontaneously develop the memory of their past birth, and remember fragments of their previous lives. Such cases are very rare, but those few well-attested, respectable cases tend to throw some light on the idea of a past birth. So are the experiences of some modern dependable psychics and strange cases of alternating and multiple personalities.

In hypnotic states some relate experiences of their past lives; while a few others, read the past lives of others and even heal diseases.

Sometimes we get strange experiences which cannot be explained but by rebirth.

How often do we meet persons whom we have never met, and yet instinctively feel that they are quite familiar to us? How often do we visit places, and yet feel impressed that we are perfectly acquainted with those surroundings?

The Buddha tells us:

"Through previous associations or present advantage, that old love springs up again like the lotus in the water."

Experiences of some reliable modern psychics, ghostly phenomena, spirit communications, strange alternating and multiple personalities and so on shed some light upon this problem of rebirth.

Into this world come Perfect Ones like the Buddhas and highly developed personalities. Do they evolve suddenly? Can they be the products of a single existence?

How are we to account for great characters like Buddhaghosa, Panini, Kalidasa, Homer and Plato; men of genius like Shakespeare, infant prodigies like Pascal, Mozart, Beethoven, Raphael, Ramanujan, etc.?

Heredity alone cannot account for them. "Else their ancestry would disclose it, their posterity, even greater than themselves, demonstrate it."

Could they rise to such lofty heights if they had not lived noble lives and gained similar experiences in the past? Is it by mere chance that they are been born or those particular parents and placed under those favorable circumstances?

The few years that we are privileged to spend here or, for the most five score years, must certainly be an inadequate preparation for eternity.

If one believes in the present and in the future, it is quite logical to believe in the past. The present is the offspring of the past, and acts in turn as the parent of the future.

If there are reasons to believe that we have existed in the past, then surely there are no reasons to disbelieve that we shall continue to exist after our present life has apparently ceased.

It is indeed a strong argument in favor of past and future lives that "in this world virtuous persons are very often unfortunate and vicious persons prosperous."

A Western writer says:

"Whether we believe in a past existence or not, it forms the only reasonable hypothesis which bridges certain gaps in human knowledge concerning certain facts of every day life. Our reason tells us that this idea of past birth and Kamma alone can explain the degrees of difference that exist between twins, how men like Shakespeare with a very limited experience are able to portray with marvelous exactitude the most diverse types of human character, scenes and so forth of which they could have no actual knowledge, why the work of the genius invariably transcends his experience, the existence of infant precocity, the vast diversity in mind and morals, in brain and physique, in conditions, circumstances and environment observable throughout the world, and so forth."

It should be stated that this doctrine of rebirth can neither be proved nor disproved experimentally, but it is accepted as an evidentially verifiable fact. The cause of this Kamma, continues the Buddha, is *avijjā* or ignorance of the Four Noble Truths. Ignorance is, therefore, the cause of birth and death; and its transmutation into knowingness or *vijja* is consequently their cessation. The result of this analytical method is summed up in the *Paticca Samuppada*.

Paticca Samuppada

Paticca means because of, or dependent upon: *Samuppada* "arising or origination." *Paticca Samuppada*, therefore, literally means — "Dependent Arising" or "Dependent Origination."

It must be borne in mind that *Paticca Samuppada* is only a discourse on the process of birth and death and not a theory of the ultimate origin of life. It deals with the cause of rebirth and suffering, but it does not in the least attempt to show the evolution of the world from primordial matter.

Ignorance *(Avijjā)* is the first link or cause of the wheel of life. It clouds all right understanding.

Dependent on ignorance of the Four Noble Truths arise activities *(Sankhāra)* — both moral and immoral. The activities whether good or bad rooted in ignorance which must necessarily have their due effects, only tend to prolong life's wandering. Nevertheless, good actions are essential to get rid of the ills of life.

Dependent on activities arise rebirth-consciousness *(Viññana)*. This links the past with the present.

Simultaneous with the arising of rebirth-consciousness there come into being mind and body *(Nāma-rūpa)*.

The six senses *(Salāyatana)* are the inevitable consequences of mind and body. Because of the six senses contact *(Phassa)* sets in. Contact leads to feeling *(Vedanā)*.

These five — viz., consciousness, mind and matter, six senses, contact and feeling — are the effects of past actions and are called the passive side of life.

Dependent on feeling arises craving *(Tanhā)*. Craving results in grasping *(Upādāna)*. Grasping is the cause of Kamma *(Bhāva)* which in its turn, conditions future birth *(Jāti)*. Birth is the inevitable cause of old age and death *(Jara-marana)*.

If on account of cause effect comes to be, then if the cause ceases, the effect also must cease.

The reverse order of the *Paticca Samuppada* will make the matter clear.

Old age and death are possible in and with a psychophysical organism. Such an organism must be born; therefore it pre-supposes birth. But birth is the inevitable result of past deeds or Kamma. Kamma is conditioned by grasping which is due to craving. Such craving can appear only where feeling exists. Feeling is the outcome of contact between the senses and objects. Therefore it presupposes organs of senses which cannot exist without mind and body. Where there is a mind there is consciousness. It is the result of past good and evil. The acquisition of good and evil is due to ignorance of things as they truly are.

The whole formula may be summed up thus:

Dependent on Ignorance arise Activities (Moral and Immoral)

- Activities arises Consciousness (Re-birth Consciousness)
- Consciousness arise Mind and Matter
- Mind and Matter arise the six Spheres of Sense
- 'the Six Spheres of Sense arises Contact
- Contact arises Feeling
- Feeling arises Craving
- Craving arises Grasping
- Grasping arise Actions (Kamma)
- Actions arises Rebirth
- Birth arise Decay, Death, Sorrow, Lamentation, Pain, Grief, and Despair.

Thus does the entire aggregate of suffering arise. The first two of these twelve pertain to the past, the middle eight to the present, and the last two to the future.

The complete cessation of Ignorance leads to the cessation of Activities. The cessation of Activities leads to the cessation of Consciousness.

- Consciousness leads to the cessation of mind and matter.
- Mind and Matter leads to the cessation of the six Spheres of Sense. " " " the six Spheres of Sense leads to the cessation of Contact,
- Contact leads to the cessation of Feeling.
- Feeling leads to the cessation of Craving.
- Craving leads to the cessation of Grasping.
- Grasping leads to the cessation of Actions.
- Actions leads to the cessation of Re-birth.
- Re-birth leads to the cessation of Decay, Death, Sorrow, Lamentation, Pain, Grief, and Despair.

Thus does the cessation of this entire aggregate of suffering result.

This process of cause and effect continues ad infinitum. The beginning of this process cannot be determined as it is impossible to say whence this life-flux was encompassed by nescience. But when this nescience is turned into knowledge, and the life-flux is diverted into *Nibbanadhatu*, then the end of the life process of *Samsara* comes about.

Anatta or Soul-lessness

This Buddhist doctrine of re-birth should be distinguished from the theory of re-incarnation which implies the transmigration of a soul and its invariable material rebirth. Buddhism denies the existence of an unchanging or eternal soul created by a God or emanating from a Divine Essence *(Paramatma)*. If the immortal soul, which is supposed to be the essence of man, is eternal, there cannot be either a rise or a fall. Besides one cannot understand why "different souls are so variously constituted at the outset."

To prove the existence of endless felicity in an eternal heaven and unending torments in an eternal hell, an immortal soul is absolutely necessary. Otherwise, what is it that is punished in hell or rewarded in heaven?

"It should be said," writes Bertrand Russell, "that the old distinction between soul and body has evaporated quite as much because 'matter' has lost its solidity as mind has lost its spirituality. Psychology is just beginning to be scientific. In the present state of psychology belief in immortality can at any rate claim no support from science."

Buddhists do agree with Russell when he says "there is obviously some reason in which I am the same person as I was yesterday, and, to take an even more obvious example if I simultaneously see a man and hear him speaking, there is some sense in which the 'I' that sees is the same as the 'I' that hears."

Till recently scientists believed in an indivisible and indestructible atom. "For sufficient reasons physicists have reduced this atom to a series of events. For equally good reasons psychologists find that mind has not the identity of a single continuing thing but is a series of occurrences bound together by certain intimate relations. The question of immortality, therefore, has become the question whether these intimate relations exist between occurrences connected with a living body and other occurrence which take place after that body is dead."

As C.E.M. Joad says in "The Meaning of Life," matter has since disintegrated under our very eyes. It is no longer solid; it is no longer enduring; it is no longer determined by compulsive causal laws; and more important than all, it is no longer known.

The so-called atoms, it seems, are both "divisible and destructible." The electrons and protons that compose atoms "can meet and annihilate one another while their persistence, such as it is, is rather that of a wave lacking fixed boundaries, and in process of continual change both as regards shape and position than that of a thing."

Bishop Berkeley who showed that this so-called atom is a metaphysical fiction held that there exists a spiritual substance called the soul.

Hume, for instance, looked into consciousness and perceived hat there was nothing except fleeting mental states and concluded that the supposed "permanent ego" is non-existent.

"There are some philosophers," he says, "who imagine we are every moment conscious of what we call 'ourself,' that we feel its existence and its continuance in existence and so we are certain, both of its perfect identity and simplicity. For my part, when I enter most intimately into what I call 'myself' I always stumble on some particular perception or other — of heat or cold, light or shade, love or hatred, pain or pleasure. I never catch myself... and never can observe anything but the perception... nor do I conceive what is further requisite to make me a perfect non-entity."

Bergson says, "All consciousness is time existence; and a conscious state is not a state that endures without changing. It is a change without ceasing, when change ceases it ceases; it is itself nothing but change."

Dealing with this question of soul Prof. James says — "The soul-theory is a complete superfluity, so far as accounting for the actually verified facts of conscious experience goes. So far no one can be compelled to subscribe to it for definite scientific reasons." In concluding his interesting chapter on the soul he says: "And in this book the provisional solution which we have reached must be the final word: the thoughts themselves are the thinkers."

Watson, a distinguished psychologist, states: "No one has ever touched a soul or has seen one in a test tube or has in any way come into relationship with it as he has with the other objects of his daily experience. Nevertheless to doubt its existence is to become a heretic and once might possibly even had led to the loss of one's head. Even today a man holding a public position dare not question it."

The Buddha anticipated these facts some 2500 years ago.

According to Buddhism mind is nothing but a complex compound of fleeting mental states. One unit of consciousness consists of three phases — arising or genesis *(uppāda)* static or development *(thīti),* and cessation or dissolution *(bhănga).* Immediately after the cessation stage of a thought moment there occurs the genesis stage of the subsequent thought-moment. Each momentary consciousness of this ever-changing life-process, on passing away, transmits its whole energy, all the indelibly recorded impressions to its successor.

Every fresh consciousness consists of the potentialities of its predecessors together with something more. There is therefore, a continuous flow of consciousness like a stream without any interruption. The subsequent thought moment is neither absolutely the same as its predecessor — since that which goes to make it up is not identical — nor entirely another — being the same continuity of Kamma energy. Here there is no identical being but there is an identity in process.

Every moment there is birth, every moment there is death. The arising of one thought-moment means the passing away of another thought-moment and vice versa. In the course of one life-time there is momentary rebirth without a soul.

It must not be understood that a consciousness is chopped up in bits and joined together like a train or a chain. But, on the contrary, "it persistently flows on like a river receiving from the tributary streams of sense constant accretions to its flood, and ever dispensing to the world without the thought-stuff it has gathered by the way." It has birth for its source and death for its mouth. The rapidity of the flow is such that hardly is there any standard whereby it can be measured even approximately. However, it pleases the commentators to say that the time duration of one thought-moment is even less than one-billionth part of the time occupied by a flash of lightning.

Here we find a juxtaposition of such fleeting mental states of consciousness opposed to a superposition of such states as some appear to believe. No state once gone ever recurs nor is identical with what goes before. But we worldlings, veiled by the web of illusion, mistake this apparent continuity to be something eternal and go to the extent of introducing an unchanging soul, an Atta, the supposed doer and receptacle of all actions to this ever-changing consciousness.

"The so-called being is like a flash of lightning that is resolved into a succession of sparks that follow upon one another with such rapidity that the human retina cannot perceive them separately, nor can the uninstructed conceive of such succession of separate sparks."

As the wheel of a cart rests on the ground at one point, so does the being live only for one thought-moment. It is always in the present, and is ever slipping into the irrevocable past. What we shall become is determined by this present thought-moment.

If there is no soul, what is it that is reborn, one might ask. Well, there is nothing to be re-born. When life ceases the Kammic energy re-materializes itself in another form. As Bhikkhu Silacara says: "Unseen it passes whithersoever the conditions appropriate to its visible manifestation are present. Here showing itself as a tiny gnat or worm, there making its presence known in the dazzling magnificence of a Deva or an Archangel's existence. When one mode of its manifestation ceases it merely passes on, and where suitable circumstances offer, reveals itself afresh in another name or form."

Birth is the arising of the psycho-physical phenomena. Death is merely the temporary end of a temporary phenomenon.

Just as the arising of a physical state is conditioned by a preceding state as its cause, so the appearance of psycho-physical phenomena is conditioned by cause anterior to its birth. As the process of one life-span is possible without a permanent entity passing from one thought-moment to another, so a series of life-processes is possible without an immortal soul to transmigrate from one existence to another.

Buddhism does not totally deny the existence of a personality in an empirical sense. It only attempts to show that it does not exist in an ultimate sense. The Buddhist philosophical term for an individual is *Santana,* i.e., a flux or a continuity. It includes the mental and physical elements as well.

The Kammic force of each individual binds the elements together. This uninterrupted flux or continuity of psycho-physical phenomenon, which is conditioned by Kamma, and not limited only to the present life, but having its source in the beginningless past and its continuation in the future—is the Buddhist substitute for the permanent ego or the immortal soul of other religions.

NIBBANA

This process of birth and death continues *ad infinitum* until this flux is transmuted, so to say, to Nibbanadhatu, the ultimate goal of Buddhists.

The Pali word Nibbãna is formed of *Ni* and *Vana*. *Ni* is a negative particle and *Vana* means lusting or craving. "It is called Nibbãna, in that it is a departure from the craving which is called *Vana,* lusting." Literally, Nibbana means non-attachment.

It may also be defined as the extinction of lust, hatred and ignorance, "The whole world is in flames," says the Buddha. "By what fire is it kindled? By the fire of lust, hatred and ignorance, by the fire of birth, old age, death, pain, lamentation, sorrow, grief and despair it is kindled."

It should not be understood that Nibbana is a state of nothingness or annihilation owing to the fact that we cannot perceive it with our worldly knowledge. One cannot say that there exists no light just because the blind man does not see it. In that well known story, too, the fish arguing with his friend, the turtle, triumphantly concluded that there exists no land.

Nibbana of the Buddhists is neither a mere nothingness nor a state of annihilation, but what it is no words can adequately express. Nibbãna is a Dhamma which is "unborn, unoriginated, uncreated and unformed." Hence, it is eternal *(Dhuva),* desirable *(Subha),* and happy *(Sukha).*

In Nibbana nothing is "eternalized," nor is anything "annihilated," besides suffering.

According to the Books references are made to Nibbãna as *Sopadisesa* and *Anupãdisesa.* These, in fact, are not two kinds of Nibbana, but the one single Nibbãna, receiving its name according to the way it is experienced before and after death.

Nibbana is not situated in any place nor is it a sort of heaven where a transcendental ego resides. It is a state which is dependent upon this body itself. It is an attainment (Dhamma) which is within the reach of all. Nibbāna is a supramundane state attainable even in this present life. Buddhism does not state that this ultimate goal could be reached only in a life beyond.

Here lies the chief difference between the Buddhist conception of Nibbana and the non-Buddhist conception of an eternal heaven attainable only after death or a union with a God or Divine Essence in an after-life. When Nibbana is realized in this life with the body remaining, it is called *Sopadisesa Nibbaāa-dhatu.* When an arahant attains Parinibbana, after the dissolution of his body, without any remainder of physical existence it is called *Anupadisesa Nibbāna-dhatu.*

In the words of Sir Edwin Arnold:

"If any teach Nirvana is to cease
Say unto such they lie.
If any teach Nirvana is to love
Say unto such they err."

From a metaphysical standpoint Nibbana is deliverance from suffering. From a psychological standpoint Nibbana is the eradication of egoism. From an ethical standpoint Nibbana is the destruction of lust, hatred and ignorance.

Does the arahant exist or not after death?

The Buddha replies:

"The arahant who has been released from the five aggregates is deep, immeasurable like the mighty ocean. To say that he is reborn would not fit the case. To say that he is neither reborn nor not reborn would not fit the case."

One cannot say that an arahant is reborn as all passions that condition rebirth are eradicated; nor can one say that the arahant is annihilated for there is nothing to annihilate.

Robert Oppenheimer, a scientist, writes:

"If we ask, for instance, whether the position of the electron remains the same, we must say 'no'; if we ask whether the electron's position changes with time, we must say 'no'; if we ask whether the electron is at rest, we must say 'no'; if we ask whether it is in motion, we must say 'no.'

"The Buddha has given such answers when interrogated as to the conditions of man's self after death; but they are not familiar answers from the tradition of the 17th and 18th century science."

The Path to Nibbana

How is Nibbāna to be attained?

It is by following the Noble Eight-fold Path which consists of Right Understanding *(Sammā-ditthi),* Right Thoughts *(sammā-sankappa),* Right Speech *(samma-vaca),* Right Actions *(sammā-kammanta),* Right Livelihood *(samma-ajiva),* Right Effort *(samma-vayama),* Right Mindfulness *(samma-sati),* and Right Concentration *(samma-samadhi).*

1. *Right Understanding,* which is the key-note of Buddhism, is explained as the knowledge of the four Noble Truths. To understand rightly means to understand things as they really are and not as they appear to be. This refers primarily to a correct understanding of oneself, because, as the Rohitassa Sutta states, "Dependent on this one-fathom long body with its consciousness" are all the four Truths. In the practice of the Noble Eightfold Path, Right Understanding stands at the beginning as well as at its end. A minimum degree of Right Understanding

is necessary at the very beginning because it gives the right motivations to the other seven factors of the Path and gives to them correct direction. At the culmination of the practice, Right Understanding has matured into perfect Insight Wisdom *(vipassana-pañña)*, leading directly to the Stages of Sainthood.

2. Clear vision of right understanding leads to clear thinking. The second factor of the Noble Eight-fold Path is therefore, *Right Thoughts (samma-sankappa)*, which serves the double purpose of eliminating evil thoughts and developing pure thoughts. Right Thoughts, in this particular connection, are three fold. They consist of:

   i. Nekkhamma — Renunciation of worldly pleasures or the virtue of selflessness, which is opposed to attachment, selfishness, and possessiveness;

   ii. Avyapada — Loving-kindness, goodwill, or benevolence, which is opposed to hatred, ill-will, or aversion; and

   iii. Avihimsa — Harmlessness or compassion, which is opposed to cruelty and callousness.

3. Right Thoughts lead to *Right Speech*, the third factor. This includes abstinence from falsehood, slandering, harsh words, and frivolous talk.

4. Right Speech must be followed by *Right Action* which comprises abstinence from killing, stealing and sexual misconduct.

5. Purifying his thoughts, words and deeds at the outset, the spiritual pilgrim tries to purify his *livelihood* by refraining from the five kinds of trade which are forbidden to a lay-disciple. They are trading in arms, human beings, animals for slaughter, intoxicating drinks and drugs, and poisons.

For monks, wrong livelihood consists of hypocritical conduct and wrong means of obtaining the requisites of monk-life.

6. *Right Effort* is fourfold, namely:
   i. the endeavor to discard evil that has already arisen;
   ii. the endeavor to prevent the arising of unarisen evil;
   iii. the endeavor to develop unarisen good;
   iv. the endeavor to promote the good which has already arisen.
7. *Right Mindfulness* is constant mindfulness with regard to body, feelings, thoughts, and mind-objects.
8. Right Effort and Right Mindfulness lead to *Right Concentration.* It is the one-pointedness of mind, culminating in the Jhanas or meditative absorptions.

Of these eight factors of the Noble Eightfold Path the first two are grouped under the heading of Wisdom *(pañña),* the following three under Morality *(sila),* and the last three under Concentration *(samădhi).*

But according to the order of development the sequence is as follows:

I. Morality *(sila)*
- Right Speech
- Right Action
- Right Livelihood

II. Concentration *(samădhi)*
- Right Effort
- Right Mindfulness
- Right Concentration

III. Wisdom *(pañña)*

- Right Understanding
- Right Thoughts
- Morality *(sila)* is the first stage on this path to Nibbana.

Without killing or causing injury to any living creature, man should be kind and compassionate towards all, even to the tiniest creature that crawls at his feet. Refraining from stealing, he should be upright and honest in all his dealings. Abstaining from sexual misconduct which debases the exalted nature of man, he should be pure. Shunning false speech, he should be truthful. Avoiding pernicious drinks that promote heedlessness, he should be sober and diligent.

These elementary principles of regulated behavior are essential to one who treads the path to Nibbana. Violation of them means the introduction of obstacles on the path which will obstruct his moral progress. Observance of them means steady and smooth progress along the path.

The spiritual pilgrim, disciplining thus his words and deeds, may advance a step further and try to control his senses. While he progresses slowly and steadily with regulated word and deed and restrained senses, the Kammic force of this striving aspirant may compel him to renounce worldly pleasures and adopt the ascetic life. To him then comes the idea that,

"A den of strife is household life,
And filled with toil and need;
But free and high as the open sky
Is the life the homeless lead."

It should not be understood that everyone is expected to lead the life of a Bhikkhu or a celibate life to achieve one's goal. One's spiritual progress is expedited by being a Bhikkhu although as a lay follower one can become an arahant. After attaining the third state of Sainthood, one leads a life of celibacy.

Securing a firm footing on the ground of morality, the progressing pilgrim then embarks upon the higher practice of Samadhi, the control and culture of the mind — the second stage on this Path.

Samadhi — is the "one-pointedness of the mind." It is the concentration of the mind on one object to the entire exclusion of all irrelevant matter.

There are different subjects for meditation according to the temperaments of the individuals. Concentration on respiration is the easiest to gain the one-pointedness of the mind. Meditation on loving-kindness is very beneficial as it is conducive to mental peace and happiness.

Cultivation of the four sublime states — loving-kindness *(Metta),* compassion *(Karunā),* sympathetic joy *(Mudita),* and equanimity *(Upekkhā)* — is highly commendable.

After giving careful consideration to the subject for contemplation, he should choose the one most suited to his temperament. This being satisfactorily settled, he makes a persistent effort to focus his mind until he becomes so wholly absorbed and interested in it, that all other thoughts get ipso facto excluded from the mind. The five hindrances to progress — namely, sense-desire, hatred, sloth and torpor, restlessness and brooding and doubts are then temporarily inhibited. Eventually he gains ecstatic concentration and, to his indescribable joy, becomes enwrapt in Jhana, enjoying the calmness and serenity of a one-pointed mind.

When one gains this perfect one-pointedness of the mind it is possible for one to develop the five Supernormal Powers *(Abhiñña):* Divine Eye *(Dibbacakkhu),* Divine Ear

(Dibhasota), Reminiscence of past births *(Pubbeniva-sanussati-ñana).* Thought Reading *(Paracitta vijañana)* and different Psychic Powers *(Iddhividha).* It must not be understood that those supernormal powers are essential for Sainthood.

Though the mind is now purified there still lies dormant in him the tendency to give vent to his passions, for by concentration, passions are lulled to sleep temporarily. They may rise to the surface at unexpected moments.

Both Discipline and Concentration are helpful to clear the Path of its obstacles but it is Insight *(Vipassana Pañña)* alone which enables one to see things as they truly are, and consequently reach the ultimate goal by completely annihilating the passions inhibited by Samadhi. This is the third and the final stage on the Path of Nibbana.

With his one-pointed mind which now resembles a polished mirror he looks at the world to get a correct view of life. Wherever he turns his eyes he sees nought but the Three Characteristics —*Aniccā* (transiency), *Dukkha* (sorrow) and *anattā* (soul-lessness) standing out in bold relief. He comprehends that life is constantly changing and all conditioned things are transient. Neither in heaven nor on earth does he find any genuine happiness, for every form of pleasure is a prelude to pain. What is transient is therefore painful, and where change and sorrow prevail there cannot be a permanent immortal soul.

Whereupon, of these three characteristics, he chooses one that appeals to him most and intently keeps on developing Insight in that particular direction until that glorious day comes to him when he would realize Nibbana for the first time in his life, having destroyed the three Fetters — self-illusion *(Sakkāyā-diṭṭhi),* doubts *(Vicikicchā),* indulgence in (wrongful) rites and ceremonies *(Silabbataparamasa).*

At this stage he is called a *Sotapanna* (stream-winner)— one who has entered the stream that leads to Nibbana. As he has not eradicated all Fetters he is reborn seven times at the most.

Summoning up fresh courage, as a result of this glimpse of Nibbana, the Pilgrim makes rapid progress and cultivating deeper Insight becomes a *Sakadagami* (onnce-returner) by weakening two more Fetters — namely Sense-desire *(Kamaraga)* and ill-will *(Patigha)*. He is called a Sakadagami because he is reborn on earth only once in case he does not attain Arhatship.

It is in the third state of Sainthood — *Anagama* (never-returner) that he completely discards the aforesaid two Fetters. Thereafter, he neither returns to this world nor does he seek birth in the celestial realms, since he has no more desire for sensual pleasures. After death he is reborn in the "Pure Abodes" *(Suddhavasa)* a congenial Brahma plane, till he attains Arhatship.

Now the saintly pilgrim, encouraged by the unprecedented success of his endeavors, makes his final advance and, destroying the remaining Fetters — namely, lust after life in Realms of Forms *(Ruparaga)* and Formless Realms *(Aruparaga)*, conceit *(Mana)*, restlessness *(Uddhacca)*, and ignorance *(Avijjā)* — becomes a perfect Saint: an arahant, a **Worthy** One.

Instantly he realizes that what was to be accomplished has been done, that a heavy burden of sorrow has been relinquished, that all forms of attachment have been totally annihilated, and that the Path to Nibbana has been trodden. The Worthy One now stands on heights more than celestial, far removed from the rebellious passions and defilements of the world, realizing the unutterable bliss of Nibbana and like many an arahant of old, uttering that paean of joy:

"Goodwill and wisdom, mind by method trained,

The highest conduct on good morals based,
This maketh mortals pure, not rank or wealth."

As T.H. Huxley states — "Buddhism is a system which knows no God in the Western sense, which denies a soul to man, which counts the belief in immortality a blunder, which refuses any efficacy to prayer and sacrifice, which bids men to look to nothing but their own efforts for salvation, which in its original purity knew nothing of vows of obedience and never sought the aid of the secular arm: yet spread over a considerable moiety of the world with marvelous rapidity— and is still the dominant creed of a large fraction of mankind."

CONCENTRATION ON RESPIRATION

Anapana Sati

Anapana Sati is mindfulness on respiration. *Ana* means inhalation and *Apana* exhalation.

Concentration on the breathing process leads to one-pointedness of the mind and ultimately to Insight which enables one to attain Sainthood or Arhatship.

The Buddha also practiced concentration on respiration before He attained Enlightenment.

This harmless concentration may be practiced by any person irrespective of religious beliefs. Adopting a convenient posture, keep the body erect. Place the right hand over the left hand. Eyes may be closed or half-closed.

Easterners generally sit cross-legged with the body erect. They sit placing the right foot on the left thigh and the left foot on the right thigh. This is the full position. Sometimes they adopt the half position, that is by simply placing the right foot on the left thigh or the left foot on the right thigh.

When the triangular position is assumed the whole body is well-balanced.

Those who find the cross-legged posture too difficult may sit comfortably in a chair or any other support sufficiently high to rest the legs on the ground.

It is of no importance which posture one may adopt provided the position is easy and relaxed.

Head should not be drooping. Neck should be straightened so that the nose may be in a perpendicular line with the navel.

Buddhas usually adopt the full lotus position. They sit with half closed eyes looking not more than a distance of three and half feet.

Before the practice, bad air from the lungs should be breathed out slowly through the mouth and then the mouth should be closed.

Now inhale through the nostrils normally, without strain, without force. Mentally count one. Exhale and count two. Inhale and count three. Count up to ten constantly concentrating on the breathing process without thinking of anything else. While doing so one's mind may wander. But one need not be discouraged. Gradually one may increase the number of series — say five series of ten.

Later, one may inhale and pause for a moment, concentrating merely on inhalation without counting. Exhale and pause for a moment. Thus inhale and exhale concentrating on respiration. Some prefer counting as it aide concentration while others prefer not to count. What is essential is concentration and not counting, which is secondary.

When one practices this concentration one feels very peaceful, light in mind and body. After practicing for a certain period a day might come when one may realize that this so-called body is supported by mere breath and that body perishes when breathing ceases. One fully realizes impermanence. Where there is change there cannot be a permanent entity or an immortal soul. Insight can then be developed to attain Arhatship.

It is clear that the object of this concentration on respiration is not merely to gain one-pointedness but also to cultivate Insight to obtain deliverance from suffering.

In some discourses this simple and harmless method of respiration is described as follows:

"Mindfully he inhales; mindfully he exhales.

1. When making a long inhalation he knows: 'I make a long inhalation'; when making a long exhalation he knows; 'I make a long exhalation.'
2. When making a short inhalation he knows: ' I make a short inhalation'; when making a short exhalation he knows: 'I make a short exhalation.'
3. Clearly perceiving the entire breathing process (i.e., the beginning, middle and end), 'I will inhale; thus he trains himself; clearly perceiving the entire breathing process, 'I will exhale'; thus he trains himself.
4. Calming the respiration, 'I will inhale'; thus he trains himself; calming the respirations, 'I will exhale'; thus he trains himself. "

Meditation on Loving-kindness

Metta

Be still and peaceful. Recite three times — *Nammo Buddhaya* — (Honor to the Buddha) Recite three times — *Araham* — (The Pure One)

Recite:

Buddham saranam gacchami — (I go to the Buddha for refuge)

Dhamman saranam gacchami — (I go to the Dhamma for refuge)

Sangham saranam gacchami — (I go to the Sangha for refuge)

Think thus:

My mind is temporarily pure, free from all impurities; free from lust, hatred and ignorance; free from all evil thoughts

My mind is pure and clean. Like a polished mirror is my stainless mind.

As a clean and empty vessel is filled with pure water I now fill my clean heart and pure mind with peaceful and sublime thoughts of boundless loving-kindness over-flowing compassion, sympathetic joy and perfect equanimity.

I have now washed my mind and heart of anger, ill will, cruelty, violence, jealousy, envy, passion and aversion.

Think ten times:

May I be well and happy!

May I be free from suffering, disease, grief, worry and anger!

May I be strong, self-confident, healthy and peaceful!

Think thus:

Now I charge every particle of my system, from head to foot, with thoughts of boundless loving-kindness and compassion. I am the embodiment of loving-kindness and compassion. My whole body is saturated with loving-kindness and compassion. I am a stronghold, a fortress of loving-kindness and compassion. I am nothing but loving-kindness and compassion. I have sublimated myself, elevated myself, ennobled myself.

Think ten times:

May I be well and happy!

May I be free from suffering, disease, grief, worry and anger!

May I be strong, self-confident, healthy and peaceful!

Think:

Mentally I create an aura of loving-kindness around me. By means of this aura, I cut off all negative thoughts, hostile vibrations. I am not affected by the evil vibrations of others. I return good for evil, loving-kindness for anger, compassion for cruelty, sympathetic joy for jealously. I am peaceful and well-balanced in mind. Now I am a fortress of loving-kindness, a stronghold of morality.

What I have gained I now give unto others.

Think of all your near and dear ones at home, individually or collectively, and fill them with thoughts of loving-kindness and wish them peace and happiness, repeating May all beings be well and happy!...

Then think of all seen and unseen beings, living near and far, men, women, animals and all living beings, in the East, West, North, South, above and below, and radiate boundless loving-kindness, without any enmity or obstruction, towards all, irrespective of class, creed, color or sex.

Think that all are your brothers and sisters, fellow-beings in the ocean of life. You identify with all. You are one with all.

Repeat ten times, "May all beings be well and happy," and wish them all peace and happiness.

In the course of your daily life try to translate your thoughts into action as occasion demands.

Perfections

Parami

1. May I be generous and helpful! *(Dana* — Generosity)
2. May I be well-disciplined and refined in manners! May I be pure and clean in all my dealings! May my thoughts, words and deeds be pure! *(Sila* — Morality)
3. May I not be selfish and self-possessive but selfless and disinterested! May I be able to sacrifice my pleasure for the sake of others! *(Nekkhamma* — Renunciation)
4. May I be wise and be able to see things as they truly are! May I see the light of Truth and lead others from darkness to light! May I be enlightened and be able to enlighten others! May I be able to give the benefit of my knowledge to others! *(Panna* — Wisdom)
5. May I be energetic, vigorous and persevering! May I strive diligently until I achieve my goal! May I be fearless in facing dangers and courageously surmount all obstacles! May I be able to serve others to the best of my ability! *(Viriya* — Energy)
6. May I be ever patient! May I be able to bear and forbear the wrongs of others! May I ever be tolerant and see the good and beautiful in all! *(Khanti* — Patience)
7. May I ever be truthful and honest! May I not hide the truth to be polite! May I never swerve from the path of Truth! *(Sacca* — Truthfulness)
8. May I be firm and resolute and have an iron will! May I be soft as a flower and firm as a rock! May I ever be high-principled! *(Adhitthana* — Determination)

9. May I ever be kind, friendly and compassionate! May I be able to regard all as my brothers and sisters and be one with all! (*Metta* — Loving-kindness)

10. May I ever be calm, serene, unruffled and peaceful! May I gain a balanced mind! May I have perfect equanimity! (*Upekkha* — Equanimity)

May I serve to be perfect!

May I be perfect to serve!

2

BUDDHISM AND SOCIAL ACTION

THE FUNDAMENTALS

Buddhism and the New Global Society

It is the manifest suffering and folly in the world that invokes humane and compassionate social action in its many different forms. For Buddhists this situation raises fundamental and controversial questions. And here, also, Buddhism has implications of some significance for Christians, humanists and other non-Buddhists.

By "social action" we mean the many different kinds of action intended to benefit mankind. These range from simple individual acts of charity, teaching and training, organized kinds of service, "Right Livelihood" in and outside the helping professions, and through various kinds of community development as well as to political activity in working for a better society.

Buddhism is a pragmatic teaching which starts from certain fundamental propositions about how we experience the world and how we act in it. It teaches that it is possible to transcend this sorrow-laden world of our experience and is concerned first and last with ways of achieving that transcendence. What finally leads to such transcendence is what we call Wisdom. The enormous literature of Buddhism is not a literature of revelation and authority. Instead, it uses ethics and meditation, philosophy and science, art and poetry to point a Way to this Wisdom. Similarly, Buddhist writing on social action, unlike secular writings, makes finite proposals which must ultimately refer to this Wisdom, but which also are arguable in terms of our common experience.

In the East, Buddhism developed different schools of "traditions," serving the experiences of different cultures, ranging from Sri Lanka through Tibet and Mongolia to Japan. Buddhism may thus appear variously as sublime humanism, magical mysticism, poetic paradox and much else. These modes of expression, however, all converge upon the fundamental teaching, the "perennial Buddhism." This pamphlet is based upon the latter, drawing upon the different oriental traditions to present the teachings in an attempt to relate them to our modern industrial society.

From the evidence of the Buddha's discourses, or suttas in the Digha Nikaya, it is clear that early Buddhists were very much concerned with the creation of social conditions favorable to the individual cultivation of Buddhist values. An outstanding example of this, in later times, is the remarkable "welfare state" created by the Buddhist emperor, Asoka (B.C. 274-236). Walpola Rahula stated the situation — perhaps at its strongest — when he wrote that "Buddhism arose in India as a spiritual force against social injustices, against degrading superstitious rites, ceremonies and sacrifices; it denounced the tyranny of the caste system and advocated the equality of all men; it emancipated woman and gave her complete spiritual freedom." (Rahula, 1978). The Buddhist scriptures do indicate the general direction of Buddhist social thinking, and to that extent they are *suggestive* for our own times. Nevertheless it would be pedantic, and in some cases absurd, to apply directly to modern industrial society social prescriptions detailed to meet the needs of social order which flourished twenty-three centuries ago. The Buddhist householder of the Sigalovada Sutta experienced a different way of life from that of a computer consultant in Tokyo or an unemployed black youth in Liverpool. And the conditions which might favor their cultivation of the Middle Way must be secured by correspondingly different — and more complex — social, economic and political strategies.

It is thus essential to attempt to distinguish between perennial Buddhism on the one hand and, on the other, the specific social prescriptions attributed to the historical Buddha which related the basic, perennial teaching to the specific conditions of his day. We believe that it is unscholarly to transfer the scriptural social teaching *uncritically* and with careful qualification to modern societies, or to proclaim that the Buddha was a democrat and an internationalist. The modern terms "democracy" and "internationalism" did not exist in the sense in which we understand them in the emergent feudal society in which the Buddha lived. Buddhism is ill-served in the long run by such special pleading. On the other hand, it is arguable that there are democratic and internationalist *implications* in the basic Buddhist teachings.

In the past two hundred years society in the West has undergone a more fundamental transformation than at any period since Neolithic times, whether in terms of technology or the world of ideas. And now in the East while this complex revolution is undercutting traditional Buddhism, it is also stimulating oriental Buddhism; and in the West it is creating problems and perceptions to which Buddhism seems particularly relevant. Throughout its history Buddhism has been successfully reinterpreted in accordance with different cultures, whilst at the same time preserving its inner truths. Thus has Buddhism spread and survived.

The historic task of Buddhists in both East and West in the twenty-first century is to interpret perennial Buddhism in terms of the needs of industrial man and woman in the social conditions of their time, and to demonstrate its acute and urgent relevance to the ills of that society. To this great and difficult enterprise Buddhists will bring their traditional boldness and humility. For certainly this is no time for clinging to dogma and defensiveness.

Social Action and the Problem of Suffering

In modern Western society, humanistic social action, in its bewildering variety of forms, is seen both as the characteristic way of relieving suffering and enhancing human well-being and, at the same time, as a noble ideal of service, of self-sacrifice, by humanists of all faiths.

Buddhism, however, is a humanism in that it rejoices in the possibility of a true freedom as something inherent in human nature. For Buddhism, the ultimate freedom is to achieve full release from the root causes of all suffering: greed, hatred and delusion, which clearly are also the root causes of all social evils. Their grossest forms are those which are harmful to others. To weaken, and finally eliminate them in oneself, and, as far as possible, in society, is the basis of Buddhist ethics. And here Buddhist social action has its place.

The experience of suffering is the starting point of Buddhist teaching and of any attempt to define a distinctively *Buddhist* social action. However, misunderstanding can arise at the start, because the Pali word *dukkha,* which is commonly translated simply as "suffering," has a much wider and more subtle meaning. There is, of course, much gross, objective suffering in the world *(dukkha-dukkha),* and much of this arises from poverty, war, oppression and other social conditions. We cling to our good fortune and struggle at all costs to escape from our bad fortune.

This struggle may not be so desperate in certain countries which enjoy a high material standard of living spread relatively evenly throughout the population. Nevertheless, the material achievements of such societies appear somehow to have been "bought" by social conditions which breed a profound sense of insecurity and anxiety, of restlessness and inner confusion, in contrast to the relatively stable and ordered society in which the Buddha taught.

Lonely, alienated industrial man has unprecedented opportunities for living life "in the context of equipment," as the philosopher Martin Heidegger so aptly put it. He has a highly valued freedom to make meaning of his life from a huge variety of more or less readily available forms of consumption or achievement — whether career building, home making, shopping around for different world ideologies (such as Buddhism), or dedicated social service. When material acquisition palls, there is the collection of new experiences and the clocking up of new achievements. Indeed, for many their vibrating busyness becomes itself a more important self-confirmation that the goals to which it is ostensibly directed. In developing countries to live thus, "in the context of equipment," has become the great goal for increasing numbers of people. They are watched sadly by Westerners who have accumulated more experience of the disillusion and frustration of perpetual non-arrival.

Thus, from the experience of social conditions there arises both physical and psychological suffering. But more fundamental still is that profound sense of unease, of anxiety or *angst*, which arises from the very transience *(anicca)* of life *(viparinama-dukkha)*. This angst, however conscious of it we may or may not be, drives the restless search to establish a meaningful self-identity in the face of a disturbing awareness of our insubstantiality *(anatta)*. Ultimately, life is commonly a struggle to give meaning to life — and to death. This is so much the essence of the ordinary human condition and we are so very much *inside* it, that for much of the time we are scarcely aware of it. This *existential* suffering is the distillation of all the various conditions to which we have referred above — it is the human condition itself.

Buddhism offers to the individual human being a religious practice, a Way, leading to the transcendence of suffering. Buddhist social action arises from this practice and contributes to it. From suffering arises desire to end suffering. The secular humanistic activist sets himself the endless task of *satisfying* that desire, and perhaps hopes to end social suffering by constructing utopias. The Buddhist, on the other hand, is concerned *ultimately* with the *transformation* of desire. Hence he contemplates and experiences social action in a fundamentally different way from the secular activist. This way will not be readily comprehensible to the latter, and has helped give rise to the erroneous belief that Buddhism is indifferent to human suffering. One reason why the subject of this pamphlet is so important to Buddhists is that they will have to start here if they are to begin to communicate effectively with non-Buddhist social activists. We should add, however, that although such communication may not be easy on the intellectual plane, at the level of feelings shared in compassionate social action experience together, there may be little difficulty.

We have already suggested one source of the widespread belief that Buddhism is fatalistic and is indifferent to humanistic social action. This belief also appears to stem from a misunderstanding of the Buddhist law of Karma. In fact, there is no justification for interpreting the Buddhist conception of karma as implying quietism and fatalism. The word karma (Pali: *kamma)* mean volitional action in deeds, words and thoughts, which may be morally good or bad. To be sure, our actions are *conditioned* (more or less so), but they are not inescapably *determined*. Though human behavior and thought are too often governed by deeply ingrained habits or powerful impulses, still there is always the potentiality of freedom — or, to be more exact, of a relative freedom of choice. To widen the range of that freedom is the primary task of Buddhist mind training and meditation.

The charge of fatalism is sometimes supported by reference to the alleged "social backwardness" of Asia. But this ignores the fact that such backwardness existed also in the West until comparatively recent times. Surely, this backwardness and the alleged fatalistic acceptance of it stem from the specific social and political conditions, which were too powerful for would-be reformers to contend with. But apart from these historic facts, it must be stressed here that the Buddha's message of compassion is certainly not indifferent to human suffering in any form; nor do Buddhists think that social misery cannot be remedied, at least partly. Though Buddhist realism does not believe in the Golden Age of a perfect society, nor in the permanence of social conditions, yet Buddhism strongly believes that social imperfections can be reduced, by the reduction of greed, hatred and ignorance, and by compassionate action guided by wisdom.

From the many utterances of the Buddha, illustrative of our remarks, two may be quoted here:

"He who has understanding and great wisdom does not think of harming himself or another, nor of harming both alike. He rather thinks of his own welfare, of that of others, of that of both, and of the welfare of the whole world. In that way one shows understanding and great wisdom." — Anguttara Nikaya (Gradual Sayings) Fours, No. 186

"By protecting oneself (e.g., morally), one protects others; by protecting others, one protects oneself." — Samyutta

Nikaya (Kindred Sayings), 47; Satipatthana Samy., No. 19 In this section we have introduced the special and distinctive quality of Buddhist social action. In the remainder of Part One we shall explore this quality further, and show how it arises naturally and logically from Buddhist teaching and practice.

The Weight of Social Karma

Individual karmic behavior patterns are created by the struggles of the individual human predicament. They condition the behavior of the individual and, in traditional Buddhist teaching, the subsequent rounds of birth and rebirth. We suggest, however, that this karmic inheritance is *also* expressed as *social* karma. Specific to time and place, different social cultures arise, whether of a group, a community, a social class or a civilization. The young are socialized to their inherited culture. Consciously and unconsciously they assimilate the norms of the approved behavior — what is good, what is bad, and what is "the good life" for that culture.

The social karma — the establishment of conditioned behavior patterns — of a particular culture is and is not the aggregate of the karma of the individuals who comprise the culture. Individuals share common institutions and belief systems, but these are the results of many different wills, both in the past and the present, rather than the consequence of any single individual action. It is, however, individual karmic action that links the individual to these institutions and belief systems. Each individual is a light-reflecting jewel in Indra's net, at the points where time and space intersect. Each reflects the light of all and all of each. This is the mysticism of sociology or the sociology of mysticism!

Human societies, too, suffer the round of birth and rebirth, of revolution and stability. Each age receives the collective karmic inheritance of the last, is conditioned by it, and yet also struggles to refashion it. And within each human society, institutions, social classes, and subcultures, as well as individuals, all struggle to establish their identity and perpetuate their existence.

Capitalist industrial society has created conditions of extreme impermanence, and the struggle with a conflict-creating mood of dissatisfaction and frustration. It would be difficult to imagine any social order for which Buddhism is more relevant and needed. In these conditions, egotistical enterprise, competitive conflict, and the struggle for status become great social virtues, while, in fact, they illustrate the import of the three root-causes of suffering — greed, hatred, and delusion.

"These cravings," argues David Brandon, "have become cemented into all forms of social structures and institutions. People who are relatively successful at accumulating goods and social position wish to ensure that the remain successful... Both in intended and unintended ways they erect barriers of education, finance and law to protect their property and other interests... These structures and their protective institutions continue to exacerbate and amplify the basic human inequalities in housing, health care, education and income. They reward and encourage greed, selfishness, and exploitation rather than love, sharing and compassion. Certain people's life styles, characterized by greed and overconsumption, become dependent on the deprivation of the many. The oppressors and oppressed fall into the same trap of continual craving" (Brandon, 1976, 10-11). It should be added that communist revolution and invasion have created conditions and social structures which no less, but differently, discourage the spiritual search.

Thus we see that modern social organization may create conditions of life which not only give rise to "objective," non-volitionally caused suffering, but also tend to give rise to "subjective," volitionally caused karmic suffering, because they are more *likely* to stimulate negative karmic action than do other kinds of social organization.

Thus, some of us are born into social conditions which are more likely to lead us into following the Buddhist way than others. An unskilled woman factory worker in a provincial factory town is, for example, less likely to follow the Path than a professional person living in the university quarter of the capital city.

A property speculator, wheeling and dealing his samsaric livelihood anywhere is perhaps even less *likely* than either of them to do so. However, all three *may* do so. Men and women make their own history, but they make it under specific karmic conditions, inherited from previous generations *collectively*, as well as individually. The struggle is against nurture, as well as nature, manifested in the one consciousness. "The present generation are living in this world under great pressure, under a very complicated system, amidst confusion. Everybody talks about peace, justice, equality but in practice it is very difficult. This is not because the individual person is bad but because the overall environment, the pressures, the circumstances are so strong, so influential" (Dalai Lama, 1976, p. 17).

In short, Buddhist social action is justified ultimately and above all by the existence of social as well as individual karma. Immediately it is simply concerned with relieving suffering; ultimately, in creating social conditions which will favor the ending of suffering through the individual achievement of transcendent wisdom. But is it enough, to take a beautiful little watering can to a flower dying in sandy, sterile soil? This will satisfy only the waterer. But if we muster the necessary plows, wells, irrigation systems and organized labor, what then will become of the spiritual life amongst all this busyness and conflict? We must next consider this fundamental question.

Is not a Buddhist's prime task to work on him- or herself?

Answer: YES and NO

Buddhism is essentially pragmatic. Buddhism is, in one sense, something that one does. It is a guide to the transformation of individual experience. In the traditional Buddhist teaching, the individual sets out with a karmic inheritance of established volitions, derived from his early life, from earlier lives and certainly from his social environment, a part of his karmic inheritance. Nevertheless, the starting point is the *individual* experiencing of life, here and now.

Our train of argument began with the anxiety, the profound sense of unease felt by the individual in his naked experience of life in the world when not masked by busyness, objectives, diversions and other confirmations and distractions. Buddhism teaches that all suffering, whether it be anxiety, or more explicitly karmic, brought-upon-ourselves-suffering, or "external" suffering, accidental and inevitable through war, disease, old age and so on — arise ultimately from the deluded belief in a substantial and enduring self. In that case, what need has the individual Buddhist for concern for other individuals, let alone for social action since his prime task is to work on himself in order to dissolve this delusion? Can he only *then* help others?

The answer to these questions is both yes and no. This does not mean half-way between yes and no. It means yes and no. It means that the answer to these fundamental questions of Buddhist social action cannot ultimately be logical or rational. For the Buddhist Middle Way is not the middle *between* two extremes, but the Middle Way which *transcends* the two extremes in a "higher" unity.

Different traditions of Buddhism offer different paths of spiritual practice. But all depend ultimately upon the individual becoming more deeply aware of the nature of his experience of the world, and especially of other people and hence of himself and of the nature of the self. "To learn the way of the Buddha is to learn about oneself. To learn about oneself is to forget oneself. To forget oneself is to experience the world as pure object — to let fall one's own mind and body and the self-other mind and body" (Zen Master Dogen: *Shobogenzo).* Meditation both reveals and ultimately calms and clarifies the choppy seas and terrifying depths of the underlying emotional life. All the great traditions of spiritual practice, Buddhist — and non-Buddhist — emphasize the importance of periods of withdrawal for meditation and reflection. Their relative importance is not our present concern. However, in all Buddhist traditions the training emphasizes a vigilant mindfulness of mental feelings in the course of active daily life, as well as in periods of withdrawal. It all advocates the parallel development of habitual forms of ethical behavior *(sila).*

"We need not regard life as worth [either] boycotting or indulging in. Life situations are the food of awareness and mindfulness... We wear out the shoe of *samsara* by walking on it through the practice of meditation" (Chogyam Trungpa, 1976, p. 50). The same message comes across forcefully in the Zen tradition: "For penetrating to the depths of one's true nature... nothing can surpass the practice of Zen in the midst of activity... The power or wisdom obtained by practicing Zen in the world of action is like a rose that rises from the fire. It can never be destroyed. The rose that rises from the midst of flames becomes all the more beautiful and fragrant the nearer the fire rages" (Zen Master Hakuin, 1971, p. 34).

It is open to us, if we wish, to extend our active daily life to include various possible forms of social action. This offers a strong immediate kind of experience to which we can give our awareness practice. Less immediately, it serves to fertilize our meditation — "dung for the field of bodhi." Thirdly, it offers wider opportunities for the cultivation of *sila* — the habituation to a selfless ethic.

The above remarks are about *taking* social action. They refer to the potential benefits of social action for individual practice. They are less "reasons" for social action than reasons why a Buddhist should not desist from social action. The mainspring of Buddhist social action lies elsewhere; it arises from the heart of a ripening compassion, however flawed it still may be by ego needs. This is *giving* social action, with which we shall be concerned in the next section.

Social action as a training in self-awareness (and compassionate awareness of others) may be a discipline more appropriate to some individual temperaments, and, indeed, to some cultures and times, than to others. We are not concerned with advocating it for all Buddhists, but simply to suggesting its legitimacy for such as choose to follow it. For Buddhism has always recognized the diversity of individual temperaments and social cultures that exist, and has offered a corresponding diversity of modes of practice.

Buddhist Social Action as Heartfelt Paradox

As we have noted, the significance of social action as mindfulness training is, of course, incidental to that profound compassionate impulse which more — or less — leads us to seek the relief of the suffering of others. Our motives may be mixed, but to the extent that they are truly selfless they do manifest our potential for Awakening and our relatedness to all beings.

Through our practice, both in the world and in withdrawn meditation, the delusion of a struggling self becomes more and more transparent, and the conflicting opposites of good and bad, pain and pleasure, wealth and poverty, oppression and freedom are seen and understood in a Wisdom at once serene and vigilant. This Wisdom partakes of the sensitivity of the heart as well as the clarity of thought.

In this Wisdom, in the words of R.H. Blyth, things are beautiful — but not desirable; ugly — but not repulsive; false — but not rejected. What is inevitable, like death, is accepted without rage; what may not be, like war, is the subject of action skillful and the more effective because, again, it is not powered and blinded by rage and hate. We may recognize an oppressor and resolutely act to remove the oppression, but we do not hate him. Absence of hatred, disgust, intolerance or righteous indignation within us is itself a part of our growth towards enlightenment *(bodhi)*.

Such freedom from negative emotions should not be mistaken for indifference, passivity, compromise, loving our enemy instead of hating him, or any other of these relativities. This Wisdom transcends the Relativities which toss us this way and that. Instead, there is an awareness, alert and dispassionate, of an infinitely complex reality, but always an awareness free of despair, of self-absorbing aggression, or of blind dogma, an awareness free to act or not to act.

Buddhists have their preferences, and in the face of such social cataclysms as genocide and nuclear war, they are strong preferences, but they are not repelled into quietism by them. What has been said above has to be cultivated to perfection by one following the Bodhisattva ideal. We are inspired by it, but very few of us can claim to live it. Yet we shall never attain the ideal by turning our backs upon the world and denying the compassionate Buddha nature in us that reaches out to suffering humanity, however stained by self love those feelings may be. Only through slowly

"Wearing out the shoe of *samsara*" in whatever way is appropriate to us can we hope to achieve this ideal, and not through some process of incubation.

This Great Wisdom *(prajna)* exposes the delusion, the folly, sometimes heroic, sometimes base, of human struggle in the face of many kinds of suffering. This sense of folly fuses with the sense of shared humanity in the form of compassion *(karuna)*. Compassion is the everyday face of Wisdom.

In individual spiritual practice though, some will incline to a Way of Compassion and others to a Way of Wisdom, but finally the two faculties need to be balanced, each complementing and ripening the other.

He who clings to the Void

And neglects Compassion

Does not reach the highest stage.

But he who practices only Compassion

Does not gain release from the toils of existence. —
(Saraha, 1954)

To summarize: Buddhist or non-Buddhist, it is our common humanity, our "Buddha nature," that moves us to compassion and to action for the relief of suffering. These stirrings arise from our underlying relatedness to all living things, from being brothers and sisters one to another. Buddhist spiritual practice, whether at work or in the meditation room, ripens alike the transcendental qualities of Compassion and Wisdom.

Social action starkly confronts the actor with the sufferings of others and also confronts him with his own strong feelings which commonly arise from such experience, whether they be feelings of pity, guilt, angry partisanship or whatever. Social action is thus a powerful potential practice for the follower of the Way, a "skillful means" particularly relevant to modern society. Finally, it is only some kind of *social* action that can be an effective and relevant response to the weight of *social* karma which oppresses humanity and which we all share.

THE ACTION

Giving and Helping

All social action is an act of giving *(dana),* but there is a direct act which we call charitable action, whether it be the UNESCO Relief Banker's Order or out all night with the destitutes' soup kitchen. Is there anything about Buddhism that should make it less concerned actively to maintain the caring society than is Christianity or humanism? "Whoever nurses the sick serves me," said the Buddha. In our more complex society does this not include the active advancement and defense of the principles of a national health service?

The old phrase "as cold as charity" recalls numerous possibilities for self-deception in giving to others and in helping them. Here is opportunity to give out goodness in tangible form, both in our own eyes and those of the world. It may also be a temptation to impose our own ideas and standards from a position of patronage. David Brandon, who has written so well on the art of helping, reminds us that "respect is seeing the Buddha nature in the other person. It means perceiving the superficiality of positions of moral authority. The other person is as good as you. However untidy, unhygienic, poor, illiterate and bloody-minded he may seem, he is worthy of your respect. He also has autonomy and purpose. He is another form of nature" (Brandon, 1976, p. 59).

There are many different ways in which individual Buddhists and their organizations can give help and relieve suffering. However, "charity begins at home." If a Buddhist group or society fails to provide human warmth and active caring for all of its members in their occasional difficulties and troubles — though always with sensitivity and scrupulous respect for privacy — where then is its Buddhism? Where is the Sangha?

In our modern industrial society there has been on the one hand a decline in personal and voluntary community care for those in need and, on the other, too little active concern for the quality and quantity of institutional care financed from the public purse that has to some extent taken its place. One facet of this which may be of particular significance for Buddhists, is a failure to recognize adequately and provide for the needs of the dying. In recent years there has been a growing awareness of this problem in North America and Europe, and a small number of hospices have been established by Christian and other groups for terminally ill people. However, only a start has been made with the problem. The first Buddhist hospice in the West has yet to be opened. And, less ambitiously, the support of regular visitors could help many lonely people to die with a greater sense of dignity and independence in our general hospitals.

Teaching

Teaching is, of course, also a form of giving and helping. Indeed, one of the two prime offenses in the Mahayana code of discipline is that of withholding the wealth of the Dharma from others. Moreover, teaching the Dharma is one of the most valuable sources of learning open to a Buddhist.

Here we are concerned primarily with the teaching of the Dharma to newcomers in Buddhism, and with the general publicizing of Buddhism among non-Buddhists.

Buddhism is by its very nature lacking in the aggressive evangelizing spirit of Christianity or Islam. It is a pragmatic system of sustained and systematic self-help practice, in which the teacher can do no more than point the way and, together with fellow Buddhists, provide support, warmth and encouragement in a long and lonely endeavor. There is here no tradition of instant conversion and forceful revelation for the enlightenment experience, however sudden, depends upon a usually lengthy period of careful cultivation. Moreover, there is a tolerant tradition of respect for the beliefs and spiritual autonomy of non-Buddhists.

Nevertheless, a virtue may be cultivated to a fault. Do we not need to find a middle way between proselytizing zeal and aloof indifference? Does not the world cry out for a Noble Truth that "leads to the cessation of suffering"? The task of teaching the Dharma also gives individual Buddhists an incentive to clarify their ideas in concise, explicit everyday terms. And it requires them to respond positively to the varied responses which their teaching will provoke in others.

It will be helpful to treat the problem on two overlapping levels, and to distinguish between (a) publicizing the Dhamma, and (b) introductory teaching for enquirers who interest has thus been awakened.

At both the above levels activity is desirable both by a central body of some kind and by local groups (in many countries there will certainly be several "central bodies," representing different traditions and tendencies). The central body can cost-effectively produce for local use introductory texts and study guides, speakers' notes, audiocassettes, slide presentations and "study kits" combining all of these different types of material.

It has the resources to develop correspondence courses such as those run by the Buddhist Society in the United Kingdom which offer a well-tried model. And it will perhaps have sufficient prestige to negotiate time on the national radio and television network.

Particularly in Western countries there are strong arguments for organizations representing the different Buddhist traditions and tendencies to set up a representative Buddhist Information and Liaison Service for propagating fundamental Buddhism and some first introductions to the different traditions and organizations. It would also provide a general information clearing house for all the groups and organizations represented. It could be financed and controlled through a representative national Buddhist council which, with growing confidence between its members and between the different Buddhist organizations which they represented, might in due course take on additional functions. Certainly in the West there is the prospect of a great many different Buddhist flowers blooming, whether oriental or new strains developed in the local culture. This is to be welcomed, but the kind of body we propose will become a necessity to avoid confusion for the outsider and to work against any tendency to sectarianism of a kind from which Buddhism has been relatively free.

Local groups will be able to draw upon the publicity and teaching resources of national centers and adapt these to the needs of local communities. Regular meetings of such groups may amount to no more than half a dozen people meeting in a private house. Sensitively handled it would be difficult to imagine a better way of introducing a newcomer to the Dharma. Such meetings are worthy of wide local publicity. A really strong local base exists where there is a resident Buddhist community of some kind, with premises convenient for meetings and several highly committed workers. Unfortunately, such communities will, understandably, represent a particular Buddhist tradition or tendency, and this exclusiveness may be less helpful to the newcomer than a local group in which he or she may have the opportunity to become acquainted with the different Buddhist traditions represented in the membership and in the program of activity. In many countries the schools provide brief introductions to the world's great religions. Many teachers do not feel sufficiently knowledgeable about introducing Buddhism to their pupils and may be unaware of suitable materials even where these do exist. There may be opportunities here for local groups, and certainly the Information Service suggested above would have work to do here.

Finally, the method of introductory teaching employed in some Buddhist centers leaves much to be desired both on educational grounds and as Buddhist teaching. The Buddha always adapted his teaching to the particular circumstances of the individual learner; he sometimes opened with a question about the enquirer's occupation in life, and built his teaching upon the answer to this and similar questions. True learning and teaching has as its starting point a problem or experience posed by the learner, even if this be no more than a certain ill-defined curiosity. It is there that teacher and learner must begin. The teacher starts with the learner's thoughts and feelings and helps him or her to develop understanding and awareness. This is, of course, more difficult than a standard lecture which begins and ends with the teacher's thoughts and feelings, and which may in more sense than one leave little space for the learner. It will exclude the teacher from any learning.

It follows that unless the teacher is truly inspiring, the "Dharma talk" is best used selectively: to introduce and stimulate discussion or to summarize and consolidate what has been learned. Dharma teachers must master the arts of conducting open discussion groups, in which learners can gain much from one another and can work through an emotional learning situation beyond the acquisition of facts about Buddhism. Discussion groups have become an important feature of many lay Buddhist and social action organizations in different parts of the world. They are the heart, for example, of the Japanese mass organization Rissho Kosei Kai, which explores problems of work, the family and social and economic problems.

POLITICAL ACTION: THE CONVERSION OF ENERGY

Political power may manifest and sustain social and economic structures which breed both material deprivation and spiritual degradation for millions of men and women. In many parts of the world it oppresses a wide range of social groupings — national and racial minorities, women, the poor, homosexuals, liberal dissidents, and religious groups. Ultimately, political power finds its most terrible expression in war, which reaches now to the possibility of global annihilation.

For both the oppressors and the oppressed, whether in social strife or embattled nations, karmic delusion is deepened. Each group or nation emphasizes its differences, distinguishing them from its opponents; each projects its own short-comings upon them, makes them the repository of all evil, and rallies round its own vivid illusions and blood-warming hates. Collective hating, whether it be the raised fist, or prejudice concealed in a quiet community, is a heady liquor. Allied with an ideology, hate in any form will not depart tomorrow or next year. Crowned with delusive idealism, it is an awesome and murderous folly. And even when victory is achieved, the victors are still more deeply poisoned by the hate that carried them to victory. Both the revolution and the counter-revolution consume their own children. Buddhism's "Three Fires" of delusion *(moha),* hatred and ill-will *(dosa),* and greed and grasping, *(lobha),* surely burn nowhere more fiercely.

Contrariwise, political power may be used to fashion and sustain a society whose citizens are free to live in dignity and harmony and mutual respect, free of the degradation of poverty and war. In such a society of good heart *all* men and women find encouragement and support in making, if they will, the best use of their human condition in the practice of wisdom and compassion. This is the land of good karma — not the end of human suffering, but the beginning of the end, the bodhisattva-land, the social embodiment of sila.

This is not to be confused with the belief common among the socially and politically oppressed that if power could be seized (commonly by an elite claiming to represent them), then personal, individual, "ideological" change will inevitably follow. This absolutely deterministic view of conditioning (which Marx called "vulgar Marxism"), is as one-sided as the idea of a society of "individuals" each struggling with only his own personal karma in a private bubble hermetically sealed off from history and from other people.

Political action thus involves the Buddhist ideal of approaching each situation without prejudice but with deserved circumspection in questions of power and conflict, social oppression and social justice. These social and political conflicts are the great public samsaric driving energies of our life to which an individual responds with both aggression and self-repression. The Buddha Dharma offers the possibility of transmuting the energies of the individual into Wisdom and Compassion. At the very least, in faith and with good heart, a start can be made.

Buddhists are thus concerned with political action, first, in the direct relief of non-volitionally caused suffering now and in the future, and, secondly, with the creation of social karmic conditions favorable to the following of the Way that leads to the cessation also of volitionally-caused suffering, the creation of a society of a kind which tends to the ripening of wisdom and compassion rather than the withering of them. In the third place, political action, turbulent and ambiguous, is perhaps the most potent of the "action meditations."

It is perhaps because of this potency that some Buddhist organizations ban political discussion of any kind, even at a scholarly level, and especially any discussion of social action. There are circumstances in which this may be a sound policy. Some organizations and some individuals may not wish to handle such an emotionally powerful experience which may prove to be divisive and stir up bad feeling which cannot be worked upon in any positive way. This division would particularly tend to apply to "party politics." On the other hand, such a discussion may give an incomparable opportunity to work through conflict to a shared wisdom. Different circumstances suggest different "skillful means," but a dogmatic policy of total exclusion is likely to be ultimately unhelpful.

In this connection it is worth noting that any kind of social activity which leads to the exercise of power or conflict may stir up "the fires" in the same way as overtly political activity. Conflict within a Buddhist organization is cut from the same cloth as conflict in a political assembly and may be just as heady, but the Buddhist context could make such an activity a much more difficult and delusive meditation subject. The danger of dishonest collusion may be greater than that of honest collusion (to borrow one of the Ven. Sangharakshita's aphorisms). The dogmatism and vehemence with which some Buddhists denounce and proscribe all political involvement is the same sad attitude as the dogmatism and vehemence of the politicians which they so rightly denounce.

To be lost in revolution or reform or conservatism is to be lost in *samsara* and the realm of the angry warrior, deluded by his power and his self-righteousness. To turn one's back upon all this is to be lost in an equally false idea of *nirvana* — the realm of the gods no less deluded by spiritual power and righteousness, "You do not truly speak of fire if your mouth does not get burnt."

Effective social action on any but the smallest scale will soon involve the Buddhist in situations of power and conflict, of "political" power. It may be the power of office in a Buddhist organization. It may be the unsought for leadership of an action group protesting against the closing of an old people's day care center. It may be the organizing of a fund-raising movement to build a Buddhist hospice for care of the dying. It may be membership of a local government council with substantial welfare funds. It may be joining an illegal dissident group. In all these cases the Buddhist takes the tiger — his own tiger — by the tail. Some of the above tigers are bigger than others, but all are just as fierce. Hence a Buddhist must be mindful of the strong animal smell of political power and be able to contain and convert the valuable energy which power calls up. A sharp cutting edge is given into his hands. Its use we must explore in the sections which follow.

BUDDHIST POLITICAL THEORY AND POLICY

Buddhism and politics meet at two levels — theory and practice. Buddhism has no explicit body of social and political theory comparable to its psychology or metaphysics. Nevertheless, a Buddhist political theory can be deduced primarily from basic Buddhism, from Dharma. Secondly, it can be deduced from the general orientation of scriptures which refer explicitly to a bygone time. We have already argued, however, that this can be done only in a limited and qualified way. Whatever form it may take, Buddhist political theory like other Buddhist "theory" is just another theory. As it stands in print, it stands in the world of the conditioned; it is of *samsara*. It is its potential, its spiritual implications, which make it different from "secular" theory. When skillfully practiced, it becomes a spiritual practice. As always, Buddhist "theory" is like a label on a bottle describing the contents which sometimes is mistaken for the contents by zealous label-readers. In that way we can end up with a lot of politics and very little Buddhism.

This is not to decry the value of a Buddhist social and political theory — only its misuse. We have only begun to apply Buddhism as a catalyst to the general body of Western social science and most of the work so far has been in psychology. Such work in allied fields could be extremely helpful to Buddhists and non-Buddhists alike.

The writings of some Buddhists from Sri Lanka, Burma and elsewhere offer interesting examples of attempts to relate Buddhism to nationalism and Marxism (not to be confused with communism). Earlier in the century Anagarika Dharmapala stressed the social teaching of the Buddha and its value in liberating people from materialistic preoccupations. U Nu, the eminent Burmese Buddhist statesman, argued that socialism follows naturally from the ethical and social teachings of the Buddha, and another Burmese leader, U Ba Swe, held that Marxism is relative truth, Buddhism absolute truth. This theme has been explored more recently in Trevor Ling's book "Buddha, Marx and God," (2nd ed., Macmillan, London 1979) and Michal Edwarde's "In the Blowing out of a Flame" (Allen & Unwin 1976). Both are stimulating and controversial books. E.F. Schumacher's celebrated book "Small is Beautiful" (Blond & Briggs, London 1973) has introduced what he terms "Buddhist economics" and its urgent relevance to the modern world to many thousand of non-Buddhists. Of this we shall say more in a later section on the Buddhist "good society."

Buddhist social and political theory and policy can only be mentioned in passing in this pamphlet, although we have earlier introduced the idea of "social karma" as of central importance. We are, instead, concerned here with problems and questions arising in the practice of social and political work by Buddhists and the nature of that work.

CONFLICT AND PARTISANSHIP

The Buddhist faced with political thought, let alone political action, is straightaway plunged in the turbulent stream of conflict and partisanship and right and wrong.

Let the reader, perhaps prompted by the morning newspaper, select and hold in his mind some particular controversial public issue or public figure. Now, how does your Buddhism *feel,* please? (No, not what does your Buddhism *think!)* How does it feel when, again, some deeply held conviction is roughly handled at a Buddhist meeting or in a Buddhist journal? "The tears and anguish that follow arguments and quarrels," said the Buddha, "the arrogance and pride and the grudges and insults that go with them are all the result of one thing. They come from having preferences, from holding things precious and dear. Insults are born out of arguments and grudges are inseparable with quarrels." (Kalahavivada-sutta, trans. H. Saddhatissa, 1978, para. 2) Similarly, in the words of one of the Zen patriarchs: "The conflict between longing and loathing is the mind's worse disease" (Seng Ts'an, 1954).

In all our relationships as Buddhists we seek to cultivate a spirit of openness, cooperation, goodwill and equality. Nonetheless, we may not agree with another's opinions, and, in the final analysis, this divergence could have to do even with matters of life and death. But hopefully we shall be mindful and honest about how we think and, with what we feel, and how our opponent thinks and feels. In such controversies, are we each to confirm our own ego? Or each to benefit from the other in the search for wise judgment? Moreover, in the words of the Dalai Lama, "when a person criticizes you and exposes your faults, only then are you able to discover your faults and make amends.

So your enemy is your greatest friend because he is the person who gives you the test you need for your inner strength, your tolerance, your respect for others... Instead of feeling angry with or hatred towards such a person, one should respect him and be grateful to him" (Dalai Lama, 1976, p. 9). We are one with our adversary in our common humanity; we are two in our divisive conflict. We should be deluded if we were to deny either — if we were to rush either to compromise or to uncompromising struggle. Our conflict and our humanity may be confirmed or denied at any point along that line of possibilities which links the extremes, but ultimately it will be resolved in some other, less explicit sense. Sangharakshita expresses this paradox in his observation that "it is not enough to sympathize with something to such an extent that one agrees with it. If necessary, one must sympathize to such an extent that one disagrees" (Sangharakshita, 1979, p. 60).

Zen Master Dogen advised that "when you say something to someone he may not accept it, but do not try to make him understand it rationally. Don't argue with him; just listen to his objections, until he himself finds something wrong with them." Certainly we shall need much time and space for such wisdom and compassion as may inform us in such situations. If we do fight, may our wisdom and compassion honor both our adversary and ourselves, whether in compromise, victory or defeat.

And so,

"On how to sing

The frog school and the skylark school

Are arguing."

— *(Shiki, 1958, p. 169)*

AMBIGUITY, COMPLEXITY, UNCERTAINTY

Our "Small Mind" clings to delusions of security and permanence. It finds neither of these in the world where, on the contrary, it experiences a sense of ambiguity, complexity and uncertainty which it finds intolerable, and which make it very angry when it is obliged to confront them. Small Mind prefers to see social, economic and political phenomena in terms of black and white, or "Left and Right." It likes to take sides, and it clings to social dogmas both sophisticated and simple. ("The rich/poor are always selfish/idle.")

To the extent that we have achieved "Big Mind" we perceive with equanimity what Small Mind recoils from as intolerable. We are freer *to see the world as it is* in all the many colors of the rainbow, each merging imperceptibly into the next. In place of clinging to a few black, white and gray compartments, scrutiny is freed, encouraged by the Buddha's discriminating and differentiating attitude. (Vibhajjavada; see Wheel: No. 238/240, Anguttara Anthology, Part II, pp. 59 ff.)

We shall not be surprised then that the personal map which guides the Wise through social and political realities may turn out to be disturbingly unconventional. Their reluctance readily to "take sides" arises not from quietism or an attachment to a compromise or a belief in the "unreality" of conflict, as is variously the case with those guided by mere rules. On the contrary, they may not even sit quietly, throwing soothing generalizations into the ring, as is expected of the religious. This seemingly uncomfortable, seemingly marginal stance simply reflects a reality which is experienced with equanimity.

However, it does not require much equanimity to discover the deeper truths which underlie many current conventional truths. Conventional politics, for example, run from "left," to "right," from radicals through liberals and conservatives to fascists. Some radicals are, for example, as dogmatic and authoritarian in practice as fascists, and to their ultimate detriment they hate no less mightily. And, again, some conservatives are equally dogmatic because of an awareness of the subtle, organic nature of society and hence the danger of attempts at "instant" restructuring.

Similarly an ideology such as Marxism may be highly complex but has been conveniently oversimplified even by quite well educated partisans, both those "for" and those "against" the theory. The present Dalai Lama is one of those who have attempted to disentangle "an authentic Marxism" which he believes is not without relevance to the problems of a feudal theocracy of the kind that existed in Tibet, from "the sort one sees in countless countries claiming to be Marxist," but which are "mixing up Marxism and their national political interests and also their thirst for world hegemony" (Dalai Lama, 1979).

The Wise person sees clearly because he does not obscure his own light; he does not cast the shadow of himself over the situation. However, even an honest perception of complexity commonly paralyzes action with, "Yes, that's all very well, but...," "On the other hand it is also true that...." Contemplative wisdom is a precious thing, but true Wisdom reveals itself in positive action — or "in-action." Though a person may, through Clear Comprehension of Purpose *(satthaka-sampajanna),* keep loyal to the social ideal, his Clear Comprehension of (presently absent) Suitability may counsel in-action, or just "waiting."

In a social action situation the complexity and ambiguity to which we refer is strongly felt as ethical quandary, uncertainty as to what might be the best course of action. Even in small organizations all power is potentially corrupting; the power wielded is soon lost in a thicket of relative ethics, of means and ends confused, of greater and lesser evils, of long term and short term goals. This is not a "game." It is the terrible reality of power, wealth and suffering in the world, and the confusing of good and delusion. It cannot be escaped; it can only be suffered through. We cannot refuse life's most difficult problems because we have not yet attained to Wisdom. We simply have to do our mindful and vigilant best, without guilt or blame. That is all we have to do.

VIOLENCE AND NON-VIOLENCE

The First Precept of Buddhism is to abstain from taking life. But it must be made clear that the Buddhist "Precepts" are not commandments; they are "good resolutions," sincere aspirations voluntarily undertaken. They are signposts. They suggest to us how the truly Wise behave, beyond any sense of self and other.

Evil springs from delusion about our true nature as human beings, and it takes the characteristic forms of hatred, aggression and driving acquisitiveness. These behaviors feed upon themselves and become strongly rooted, not only in individuals but in whole cultures. Total war is no more than their most spectacular and bloody expression. In Buddhism the cultivation of *sila* (habitual morality) by attempting to follow the Precepts is an aspiration toward breaking this karmic cycle. It is a first step towards dissolving the egocentricity of headstrong willfulness, and cultivating heartfelt awareness of others. The Precepts invite us to loosen the grip, unclench the fist, and to aspire to open-handedness and open-heartedness. Whether, and to what extent, he keeps the Precepts is the responsibility of each individual. But he needs to be fully aware of what he is doing.

The karmic force of violent behavior will be affected by the circumstances in which it occurs. For example, a "diminished responsibility" may be argued in the case of conscripts forced to kill by an aggressive government. And there is surely a difference between wars of conquest and wars of defense. Ven. Walpola Rahula described a war of national independence in Sri Lanka in the 2nd century BC conducted under the slogan "Not for kingdom but for Buddhism," and concludes that "to fight against a foreign invader for national independence became an established Buddhist tradition, since freedom was essential to the spiritual as well as the material progress of the community" (Rahula, 1978, p. 117). We may deplore the historic destruction of the great Indian Buddhist heritage in the middle-ages, undefended against the Mongol and Muslim invaders. It is important to note, however, that "according to Buddhism there is nothing that can be called a 'just war' — which is only a false term coined and put into circulation to justify and excuse hatred, cruelty, violence and massacre" (Rahula, 1967, 84).

It is an unfortunate fact, well documented by eminent scholars such as Edward Conze and Trevor Ling, that not only have avowedly Buddhist rulers undertaken violence and killing, but also monks of all traditions in Buddhism. Nonetheless, Buddhism has no history of specifically *religious wars,* that is, wars fought to impose Buddhism upon reluctant believers.

Violence and killing are deeply corrupting in their effect upon all involved, and Buddhists will therefore try to avoid direct involvement in violent action or in earning their living in a way that, directly or indirectly, does violence. The Buddha specifically mentioned the trade in arms, in living beings and flesh.

The problem is whether, in today's "global village" we are not all in some degree responsible for war and violence to the extent that we refrain from any effort to diminish them. Can we refrain from killing a garden slug and yet refrain, for fear of "political involvement," from raising a voice against the nuclear arms race or the systematic torture of prisoners of conscience in many parts of the world?

These are questions which are disturbing to some of those Buddhists who have a sensitive social and moral conscience. This is understandable. Yet, a well-informed Buddhist must not forget that moral responsibility, or karmic guilt, originate from a volitional and voluntary act *affirming* the harmful character of the act. If that affirmation is absent, neither the responsibility for the act, not karmic guilt, rest with those who, through some form of pressure, participate in it.

A slight guilt, however, might be involved if such participants yield too easily even to moderate pressure or do not make use of "escape routes" existing in these situations. But failure to protest publicly against injustice or wrong-doings does not necessarily constitute a participation in evil. Voices of protest should be raised when there is a chance that they are heard.

But "voices in the wilderness" are futile, and silence, instead, is the better choice. It is futile, indeed, if a few well-meaning heads try to run against walls of rock stone that may yield only to bulldozers. It is a sad fact that there are untold millions of our fellow-humans who do affirm violence and use it for a great variety of reasons (though not "reasonable reasons"!). They are unlikely to be moved by our protests or preachings, being entirely obsessed by divers fanaticisms or power urges. This has to be accepted as an aspect of existential suffering. Yet there are still today some opportunities and nations where a Buddhist can and should work for the cause of peace and reducing violence in human life. No efforts should be spared to convince people that violence does not solve problems or conflicts.

The great evil of violence is its separation unto death of us and them, of "my" righteousness and "your" evil. If you counter violence with violence you will deepen that separation through thoughts of bitterness and revenge. The Dhammapada says: "Never by hatred is hatred appeased, but it is appeased by kindness. This is an eternal truth" (I, 5) Buddhist non-violent social action *(avihimsa, ahimsa)* seeks to communicate, persuade and startle by moral example. "One should conquer anger through kindness, wickedness through goodness, selfishness through charity, and falsehood through truthfulness" (Dhammapada, XVII, 3).

The Buddha intervened personally on the field of battle, as in the dispute between the Sakyas and Koliyas over the waters of the Rohini. Since that time, history has provided us with a host of examples of religiously inspired non-violent social action, skillfully adapted to particular situations. These are worthy of deep contemplation.

Well known is Mahatma Gandhi's non-violent struggle against religious intolerance and British rule in India, and also the Rev. Martin Luther King's black people's civil rights movement in the United States. A familiar situation for many people today is the mass demonstration against authority, which may be conducted either peacefully or violently. As Robert Aitken Roshi has observed, "the point of disagreement, even the most fundamental disagreement, is still more superficial than the place of our common life." He recalls the case of a friend who organized an anti-nuclear demonstration at a naval base passing through a small town in which virtually every household had at least one person who gained his livelihood by working at the base. Consequently, when the friend visited every single house before the demonstration he hardly expected to win the people over to his cause. But he did convince them that he was a human being who was willing to listen to them and who had faith in them as human beings. "We finally had our demonstration, with four thousand people walking through this tiny community, nobody resisted us, nobody threw rocks. They just stood and watched" *(The Ten Directions,* Los Angeles Zen Center, 1 (3) September 1980, p. 6).

And yet again, situations may arise in which folly is mutually conditioned, but where we must in some sense take sides in establishing the ultimate responsibility. If we do not speak out then, we bow only to the conditioned and accept the endlessness of suffering and the perpetuation of evil karma. The following lines were written a few days after Archbishop Oscar Romero, of the Central American republic of El Salvador, had been shot dead on the steps of his chapel. Romero had roundly condemned the armed leftist rebel factions for their daily killings and extortions. However, he also pointed out that these were the reactions of the common people being used as "a production force under the management of a privileged society... The gap between poverty and wealth is the main cause of our trouble... And sometimes it goes further: It is the hatred in the heart of the worker for his employer... If I did not denounce the killings and the way the army removes people and ransacks peasants' homes I should be acquiescing in the violence" *(Observer* newspaper (London), March 30, 1980).

Finally there is the type of situation in which the truly massive folly of the conflict and of the contrasting evils may leave nothing to work with and there is space left only for personal sacrifice to bear witness to that folly. Such was the choice of the Buddhist monks who burnt themselves to death in the Vietnam war — surely one of the most savage and despairing conflicts of modern times, in which a heroic group of Buddhists had for some time struggled in vain to establish an alternative "third force."

The Good Society

The social order to which Buddhist social action is ultimately directed must be one that minimizes non-volitionally caused suffering, whether in mind or body, and which also offers encouraging conditions for its citizens to see more clearly into their true nature and overcome their karmic inheritance. The Buddhist way is, with its compassion, its equanimity, its tolerance, its concern for self-reliance and individual responsibility, the most promising of all the models for the New Society which are an on offer.

What is needed are political and economic relations and a technology which will:

(a) Help people to overcome ego-centeredness, through co-operation with others, in place of either subordination and exploitation or the consequent sense of "righteous" struggle against all things.

(b) Offer to each a freedom which is conditional only upon the freedom and dignity of others, so that individuals may develop a self-reliant responsibility rather than being the conditioned animals of institutions and ideologies. (See "Buddhism and Democracy," Bodhi Leaves No. B. 17)

The emphasis should be on the undogmatic acceptance of a diversity of tolerably compatible material and mental "ways," whether of individuals or of whole communities. There are no short cuts to utopia, whether by "social engineering" or theocracy. The good society towards which we should aim should simply provide a means, an environment, in which different "ways," appropriate to different kinds of people, may be cultivated in mutual tolerance and understanding. A prescriptive commonwealth of saints is totally alien to Buddhism.

(c) The good society will concern itself primarily with the material and social conditions for personal growth, and only secondarily and dependently with material production. It is noteworthy that the 14th Dalai Lama, on his visit to the West in 1973, saw "nothing wrong with material progress provided man takes precedence over progress. In fact it has been my firm belief that in order to solve human problems in all their dimensions we must be able to combine and harmonize external material progress with inner mental development." The Dalai Lama contrasted the "many problems like poverty and disease, lack of education" in the East with the West, in which "the living standard is remarkably high, which is very important, very good." Yet he notes that despite these achievements there is "mental unrest," pollution, overcrowding, and other problems. "Our very life itself is a paradox, contradictory in many senses; whenever you have too much of one thing you have problems created by that. You always have extremes and therefore it is important to try and find the middle way, to balance the two" (Dalai Lama, 1976, pp. 10, 14, 29).

(d) E.F. Schumacher has concisely expressed the essence of Buddhist economics as follows:

"While the materialist is mainly interested in goods, the Buddhist is mainly interested in liberation. But Buddhism is 'The Middle Way' and therefore in no way antagonistic to physical well-being...

The keynote of Buddhist economics is simplicity and non-violence. From an economist's point of view, the marvel of the Buddhist way of life is the utter rationality of its pattern — amazingly small means leading to extraordinarily satisfying results" (Schumacher, 1973, p. 52).

Schumacher then outlines a "Buddhist economics" in which production would be based on a middle range technology yielding on the one hand an adequate range of material goods (and no more), and on the other a harmony with the natural environment and its resources. (See also Dr. Padmasiri de Silva's pamphlet *The Search for a Buddhist Economics,* in the series, Bodhi Leaves, No. B. 69)

The above principles suggest some kind of diverse and politically decentralized society, with co-operative management and ownership of productive wealth.

It would be conceived on a human scale, whether in terms of size and complexity of organization or of environmental planning, and would use modern technology selectively rather than being used by it in the service of selfish interests.

In Schumacher's words, "It is a question of finding the right path of development, the Middle Way, between materialist heedlessness and traditionalist immobility, in short, of finding 'Right Livelihood.'"

Clearly, all the above must ultimately be conceived on a world scale. "Today we have become so interdependent and so closely connected with each other that without a sense of universal responsibility, irrespective of different ideologies and faiths, our very existence or survival would be difficult" (Dalai Lama, 1976, pp. 5, 28). This statement underlines the importance of Buddhist internationalism and of social policy and social action conceived on a world scale.

The above is not offered as some kind of blueprint for utopia. Progress would be as conflict-ridden as the spiritual path of the ordinary Buddhist — and the world may never get there anyway. However, Buddhism is a very practical and pragmatic kind of idealism, and there is, as always, really no alternative but to try.

ORGANIZING SOCIAL ACTION

A systematic review of the different kinds of Buddhist organization for social action which have appeared in different parts of the world is beyond the scope of this pamphlet. Some considerable research would be required, and the results would merit at least a separate pamphlet.

Later we shall introduce three contrasting movements which are in some sense or others examples of Buddhist social action. Each is related more or less strongly to the particular social culture in which it originated, and all should therefore be studied as illustrative examples-in-context and not necessarily as export models for other countries. They are, however, very suggestive, and two of the three have spread beyond their country of origin.

MAINTAINING BALANCE

Social action needs to be organized and practiced in such a way as to build upon its potential for spiritual practice and to guard against its seductions. Collective labor with fellow-Buddhists raises creative energy, encourages positive attitudes and engenders a strong spirit of fellowship. The conflicts, disagreements, obstacles, and discouragements which will certainly be met along the way offer rich meditation experiences and opportunity for personal growth, so long as scrupulous mindfulness is sustained.

The meditator will learn as much about himself in a contentious meeting as he will in the meditation hall. Both kinds of experience are needed, and they complement one another. Social action is a great ripener of compassion (for self as well as for others), out of the bitterness of the experiences which it commonly offers. Yet, like nothing else, it can stir up the partisan emotions and powerfully exult the opinionated ego. The busy, patronizing evangelist not only gives an undercover boost to his own ego; he also steals another person's responsibility for himself. However, these dangers are, comparatively speaking, gross and tangible when set against the no less ego-enhancing seduction of Other-Worldliness and dharma-ridden pietism. Such "spiritual materialism," as Chogyam Trungpa calls it, has long been recognized as the ultimate and most elusive kind of self-deception which threatens the follower of the spiritual path.

The seduction lies in being carried away by our good works, in becoming subtly attached to the new goals and enterprises we have set ourselves, so that no space is left in our busily structured hours in which some saving strength of the spirit can abide. Here is opportunity to learn how to dance with time — "the river in which we go fishing," as Thoreau called it, instead of neatly packaging away our lives in it, or letting it dictate us. And in committee lies the opportunity of slowly turning the hot, lusty partisanship of self-opinionated confirmation into the kind of space and dialogue in which we can communicate, and can even learn to love our most implacable opponents.

It is therefore important that both the individual and the group set aside regular periods for meditation, with periods of retreat at longer intervals. It is important also that experience and the feel of the social action project should as far as possible be shared openly within the Buddhist group.

In our view, the first social action of the isolated Buddhist is not to withhold the Dharma from the community in which he or she lives. However modest one's own understanding of the Dharma, there is always some first step that can be taken and something to be learned from taking that step. Even two or three can be a greater light to one another, and many forms of help are often available from outside such as working together through a correspondence course, for example, or listening to borrowed audiocassettes. For the reasons given earlier it is important that social action projects should, where possible, be undertaken by a Buddhist *group* rather than each individual "doing his own thing." And since the Buddhist group will, in most Western countries, be small and isolated, it is important that the work be undertaken in co-operation with like-minded non-Buddhists. This will both use energies to better effect since social action can be very time- and energy-consuming, and create an even better learning situation for all involved. Forms of social action which are high on explicit giving of service and low on conflict and power situations will obviously be easier to handle and to "give" oneself to, though still difficult in other respects. For example, organizing and participating in a rota of visits to lonely, long-stay hospital patients would contrast, in this respect, with involvement in any kind of local community development project.

SPIRITUAL CENTERS: EXAMPLE AND OUTREACH

In this section we are concerned with the significance of Buddhist residential communities both as manifestations and examples of the "good society" and as centers of social outreach (mainly, though not solely, in the form of teaching the Dharma). We may distinguish four possible kinds of activity here.

In the *first* place, any healthy spiritual community does, by its very existence, offer to the world a living example not only of the Good Life but also of the Good Society. Certain spiritual values are made manifest in its organization and practice in a way not possible in print or in talk. On the other hand, the purely contemplative and highly exclusive community can do this only in some limited, special and arguable sense.

In the *second* place, where the members of such a community undertake work as a community economically

("Right Livelihood"), then to that extent the community becomes a more realistic microcosm of what has to be done in the wider world and a more realistic model and example of how it might best be done.

Thirdly, such communities are commonly teaching and training communities. This may be so in formal terms, in that they offer classes and short courses and also longer periods of training in residence, in which the trainees become veritable community members. And it may be true in terms of the "openness" of the community to outsiders who wish for the present to open up their communication with the community through some participation in work, ritual, teaching, meditation.

Fourthly, the community might involve itself in various kinds of outside community service, development or action beyond that of teaching, and beyond the necessarily commercial services which may sustain the community's "Right Livelihood." Examples might be running a hospice for the terminally ill, providing an information and advice center on a wide range of personal and social problems for the people of the local community, and assisting — and maybe leading — in various aspects of a socially deprived local community. The spiritual community thus becomes more strongly a community within a community. In this kind of situation would the spiritual community draw strength from its service to the social, the "lay" community, creating an upward spiral of energy? Or would the whole scheme founder through the progressive impoverishment and corruption of the spiritual community in a vicious downward spiral?

In the Eastern Buddhist monastic tradition the first and third aspects (above) are present. In contrast to Christian monasticism, monks are not necessarily expected to be monks for life, and the monasteries may have an important function as seminaries and as long and short stay teaching and training centers. On the other hand, economically such communities are commonly strongly sustained by what is predominantly Buddhist society. In the West there are now similar communities in all the main Buddhist traditions. Although these are to some extent sustained also by lay Buddhist contributions, their income from training and teaching fees may be important. And whether it is or not, it is clear that their actual and potential training and teaching role is likely to be very important in non-Buddhist societies in which there is a growing interest in Buddhism. A good example is the Manjusri Institute in the United Kingdom, which is now seeking official recognition for the qualifications which it awards, and which could eventually become as much part of the national education system as, say, a Christian theological college. Such an integration of Buddhist activity into the pattern of national life in the West is, of course, most welcome, and opens up many new opportunities for making the Dharma more widely understood.

The above developments may be compared with the communities which form the basis of the Friends of the Western Buddhist Order (FWBO). In these, our second aspect (above), that of Right Livelihood, is found, in addition to the first and third.

The FWBO was founded in 1967 in the United Kingdom by the Ven. Maha Sthavira Sangharakshita, a Londoner who spent twenty years in India as a Buddhist monk and returned with the conviction that the perennial Buddhism always expresses itself anew in each new age and culture. The FWBO is concerned with building what it calls the "New Society" in the minds and practice of its members. Opening the FWBO's London Buddhist Center, Ven. Sangharakshita was reported as saying that the New Society was a spiritual community composed of individuals who are "truly human beings: self-aware, emotionally positive people whose energies flow freely and spontaneously, who accept responsibility for their own growth and development, in particular by providing three things: firstly, a residential spiritual community; secondly, a co-operative Right Livelihood situation; and thirdly a public center, offering classes, especially in meditation" (Marichi, 1979).

The FWBO does in fact follow a traditional Mahayana spiritual practice, but within this framework it does have, as the quotation above suggests, a strong Western flavor. This owes much to the eleven co-operatives by which many of the eighteen autonomous urban communities support themselves. These businesses are run by teams of community members as a means of personal and group development. They include a printing press, graphic design business, photographic and film studio, metalwork forge, and shops and cafes.

Membership of the communities (which are usually single sex), varies between four and thirty people, and often the community members pool their earnings in a "common purse." The FWBO comprises Order members, Mitras (who have made some initial commitment) and Friends (supporters in regular contact). Each community is autonomous and has its own distinctive character. Attached to communities are seven Centers, through which the public are offered talks, courses and instruction in meditation. Regular meetings of Chairmen of Centers and other senior Order members, supported by three central secretariats, are planned for the future, but it is not intended to abridge the autonomy of the constituent communities, each of which is a separately registered legal body.

The FWBO is growing very rapidly, not only in the United Kingdom but also overseas, with branches in Finland, the Netherlands, New Zealand, Australia, the USA, and, interestingly, in India, where a sustained effort is being made to establish centers.

COMMUNITY SERVICES AND DEVELOPMENT

We refer in this section to the fourth aspect distinguished early, namely, various possible kinds of service and support which may be given by organized Buddhists to the local community in which they live. The FWBO does not undertake this kind of activity (see previous section for examples), and in fact there do not appear to be any *major* examples of it in the West.

Arguably if this kind of work is undertaken at all, it might more likely be initiated by a non-residential "lay" Buddhist group, whose members as householders and local workers may have strong roots in their town or neighborhood. As an example of what can be achieved by a relatively small group of this kind, we quote the following (from *The Middle Way,* 54 (3) Autumn 1979, p. 193):

"The Harlow Buddhist Society have recently opened Dana House, a practical attempt to become involved with the ordinary people of the town and their problems. The new center... has four regular groups using it. The first is an after-care service for those who have been mentally or emotionally ill. The center is there for those in need of friendship and understanding. The second group is a psychotherapy one, for those with more evident emotional problems. It is run by an experienced group leader and a psychologist who can be consulted privately. The third group is a 'beginners' meditation class based on the concept of 'Right Understanding.' The fourth group is the Buddhist group, which is not attached to any particular school of Buddhism.

"Peter Donahoe writes: 'We have endeavored to provide a center which can function in relation to a whole range

of different needs, a place of charity and compassion, where all are welcomed regardless of race, color, sex or creed, welcomed to come to terms with their suffering in a way which is relative to each individual.'"

However, on the whole, it is only in the East, in societies in which Buddhist culture is predominant or important, that there are sufficiently committed Buddhists to play a part in extensive community service and development projects. For example, in Japan there are several such movements and we shall refer in the next section to one example — Soka Gakkai, a movement which also plays a number of other roles. We must first, however, turn our attention to a pre-eminent example of a Buddhist-inspired movement for community development, the Sarvodaya Shramadana Movement of Sri Lanka.

"Sarvodaya" means "awakening of all" and "Shramadana" means "sharing of labor," making a gift of time, thought and energy. This well describes what is basically a village self-help movement, inspired by Buddhist principles and founded in 1958 as part of a general national awakening. It is now by far the largest non-governmental, voluntary organization in Sri Lanka.

The Movement learned in its earlier days how very important non-economic factors are in community development, and its projects combine spiritual-cultural with socioeconomic development. "One important element that cannot be improved upon in Buddhist villages in particular is the unique place of the temple and the Buddhist monk, the one as the meeting place, the other as the chief exponent of this entire process." (All quotations are from the pamphlet *Ethos and Work Plan,* published by the Movement.) Founded on traditional culture, Sarvodaya Shramadana is ultimately "a nonviolent revolutionary movement for changing man and society." At the same time it aims to retain the best in the traditional social and cultural fabric of the community.

Village development projects are undertaken on the initiative of the villagers themselves. To begin with the community is made aware of the historic causes that led to the impoverishment and disintegration of the community and of its cultural and traditional values. Economic regeneration is only possible if there is a restoration of social values within the village. It is emphasized that the community itself must take the initiative in removing obstacles to development and in learning the new skills needed to carry through a change of program. The volunteers brought in to help serve only as a catalyst. Action is focused initially on Shramadana Camps in which villagers and outside volunteers work together upon some community project such as a road or irrigation channel. The experience of such Camps helps to develop a sense of community. Local leaders, working through village groups of farmers, of youth, of mothers and others, emerge to take increasing responsibility for a more or less comprehensive development program. This may include pre-school care for the under-fives, informal education for adults, health care programs, and community kitchens, with co-operation with State agencies as appropriate. By 1980, Sarvodaya was reaching 3,500 villages and was running 1,185 pre-schools.

Essential to these community development programs in Sarvodaya Shramadana's system of Development Education programs, operating through six Institutes and through the Gramodaya centers each of which co-ordinates development work in some twenty to thirty villages. The movement also provides training in self-employment for the youth who compose the largest sector of the unemployed. Although the main thrust of activity has been in rural areas, the Movement is also interested in urban community development where conditions are favorable and there is local interest.

The main material support for the movement comes from the villagers themselves, although financial and material assistance has also been received from overseas.

It is argued that the basic principles of Sarvodaya Shramadana can be adapted to developed as well as developing countries, and Sarvodaya groups are already active in West Germany, the Netherlands, Japan and Thailand. "The rich countries also have to helped to change their purely materialistic outlook and strike a balance, with spiritual values added to the materialistic values of their own communities so that together all can build a new One World social order."

POLITICAL ACTION AND MASS MOVEMENTS

Although there may be exceptional circumstances in certain countries, as a general rule there are strong arguments against Buddhist groups explicitly aligning themselves with any political party. It is not just that to do so would be irrelevantly divisive. As we have noted in section 2.6 (above), there are deeper, underlying social and political realities which cross-cut the conventional political spectrum of left, right and center.

Nevertheless, Buddhism, like other great religious systems, inevitably has political implications. To some extent these seem to be relatively clear, and in other senses they are arguable and controversial. Religion has its own contribution to make to politics and, ultimately, it is the only contribution to politics that really matters. It has failed both politically and as religion it falls either into the extreme of being debased by politics or of rejecting any kind of political involvement as a kind of fearful taboo. The fear of creating dissension among fellow Buddhists is understandable, but if Buddhists cannot handle conflict in a positive and creative way, then who can?

On closer examination we shall find that it is not "politics" that requires our vigilance so much as the problems of power and conflict inherent in politics. Indeed, a better use of the term "political" would be to describe any kind of power and conflict situation. In this sense a Buddhist organization may be more intensely and unhappily "political" in managing its spiritual and practical affairs than if and when its members are discussing such an "outside" matter as conventional politics. Indeed, any such discussion of social and political questions may be banned by a Buddhist society which may be in fact intensely political in terms of underlying power and conflict with which its members have not really come to terms. All kinds of organizations have problems of power and conflict and derive their positive dynamism from the good management of these, but the dangers of self-delusion seem to be greater in religious bodies.

When we meet Buddhists and get to know them, we find that even when they do not express explicit opinions on political and social matters, it is clear from other things they say that some are inclined to a conservative "establishment" stance, some are of a radical inclination, and others more dissident still. Since the diversities of THIS and THAT exist everywhere else in the conditioned world, even Buddhists cannot pretend to exclude themselves from such disturbing distinctions. This is not really in question. What is in question is their ability to handle their differences *openly* and with Buddhist maturity. And, as we have tried to show earlier, this maturity implies a progressive diminution of emotional attachment to views of THIS and THAT, so that we no longer need either in order to sustain our identity in the world and have in some sense transcended our clinging by a higher understanding. We still carry THIS or THAT, but lightly and transparently and manageably — without ego-weight. If we did not still carry them, how could we feel the Compassion for *samsara,* for ourselves as well as others?

Alan Watts wrote a suitably controversial little pamphlet on this subject, entitled *Beat Zen, Square Zen and Zen* (City Lights Books, San Francisco, 1959). The following passage may be found helpful to our present discussion; what the author has to say about Zen is surely no less applicable to Buddhism as a whole. Watts argues that the Westerner who wishes to understand Zen deeply "must understand his own culture so thoroughly that he is no longer swayed by its premises unconsciously. He must really have come to terms with the Lord God Jehovah and with his Hebrew-Christian conscience so he can take it or leave it without fear or rebellion. He must be free of the itch to justify himself. Lacking this, his Zen will be either 'beat' or 'square,' either a revolt from the culture and social order or a new form of stuffiness and respectability. For Zen is above all the liberation of the mind from conventional thought and this is something utterly different from rebellion against convention, on the one hand, or adapting foreign conventions, on the other."

In the West, individual Buddhists have been particularly attracted to pacifist, disarmament, and environmentalist movements and parties. These movements have profound concerns, which, arguably, undercut the expediencies of conventional party politics. On the other hand, are they not made the more attractive by a certain political innocence, as yet uncorrupted and unblessed by the realities of power? And do they not also underestimate the karma of power and property?

However, in Western and other non-Buddhist countries Buddhist political action of any kind is little more than speculative. Buddhists are few in number, and their energies are necessarily fully occupied with learning and teaching.

Teaching is the major form of social action and we have already discussed certain social action implications of the spiritual community. Social action at most verges upon certain possible kinds of service to the wider community or even participation in community development. We have already suggested the merit of such enterprises. But as to politics, using the word conventionally, in the West and at the present time, that can be no more than a matter for *discussion* in Buddhist groups. As always, individual Buddhists and perhaps informal groups will decide for themselves about political *action* or inaction.

However, in countries where there are strong Buddhist movements, well rooted in society, some kind of political stance and action seems unavoidable and, indeed, logical and natural, though conventional party political alignments may generally be avoided.

For example, Sarvodaya Shramadana's success at the higher levels of village self-development depends on "the extent that unjust economic arrangements such as ownership of means of production, e.g., land in the hands of a few, administrative system and political power structures, are changed in such a way that the village masses become the true masters of their own selves and their environment. That the present government has gone very far in this direction is amply demonstrated when one examines the radical measures that have already been taken" (Sarvodaya Shramadana pamphlet *Ethos and Work Plan,* p. 31).

For large and explicitly Buddhist movements filing a variety of different roles, from the devotional to the so-called "New Religions" which have become particularly important in Japan in the post-war period. (Some mention has already been made of the small discussion groups which are a notable feature of Rissho-Kosei-Kai — The "Society for Establishing Righteousness and Family Relations".) With their strong emphasis on pacifism, brotherly love, and mutual aid, these organizations have done much to assist the recovery of the Japanese people from the trauma of military aggression and the nuclear explosions which terminated it.

Soka Gakkai (literally, "Value Creation Society") is perhaps the most striking of these Japanese Buddhist socio-political movements. It is a lay Buddhist organization with over fifteen million adherents, associated with the Nichiren-Sho-Shu sect.

Soka Gakkai has an ambitious education and cultural program, and has founded its own university, high school and hospital. It also has a political party, Komeito — the "Clean Government Party," which as early as 1967 returned twenty-five parliamentary candidates to the Japanese lower house, elected with five percent of the national vote. The party has continued to play an important part in Japanese political life, basing itself on "the principles of Buddhist democracy" and opposition to rearmament. Soka Gakkai is a populist movement, militant, evangelical and well organized, pledged to "stand forever on the side of the people" and to "devote itself to carrying out the movement for the human revolution" (President Daisaku Ikeda). More specifically, its political achievements have included a successful confrontation with the mineowners of Hokkaido.

Attitudes to Soka Gakkai understandably differ widely. It has been criticized by some for its radicalism and by others for its conservatism; certainly it has been criticized on the grounds of dogmatism and aggressiveness. Certainly it is imbued with the nationalist fervor of Nichiren, the 13th century Buddhist monk who inspired it. Although it has some claims to missionary work in other countries, Soka Gakkai appears to have a more distinctive national flavor than the other social action groups we have looked at and to be less suitable for export.

UNIVERSAL RESPONSIBILITY AND THE GOOD HEART

Elsewhere we have already quoted the words of the Dalai Lama emphasizing the active global responsibility of Buddhists, and the importance above all of what he calls "Universal Responsibility and the Good Heart." In all countries will be found non-Buddhists, whether religionists or humanists, who share with us a non-violent, non-dogmatic and non-sectarian approach to community and world problems, and with whom Buddhists can work in close cooperation and with mutual respect.

This is part of the "Good Heart" to which the Dalai Lama refers. "I believe that the embracing of a particular religion like Buddhism does not mean the rejection of another religion or one's own community. In fact it is important that those of you who have embraced Buddhism should not cut yourself off from your own society; you should continue to live within your own community and with its members. This is not only for your sake but for others' also, because by rejecting your community you obviously cannot benefit others, which actually is the basic aim of religion" (Dalai Lama, 1976).

Mr. Emilios Bouratinos and his colleagues of the Buddhist Society of Greece have framed certain farsighted proposals for the "rehumanization of society" which have Buddhist inspiration but which seek to involve non-Buddhist ideological groups with the aim of reaching some common ground with them on the organization of society. Mr. Bouratinos argues that Buddhists should address themselves "to all people somehow inspired from within — whether they be religionists or not. This is indispensable, for we Buddhists are a tiny minority in the West and yet we must touch the hearts of many if this world is to survive in some meaningful fashion" (Letter to the author, 15 May 1980).

CONCLUSION

Certainly in the West many Buddhists will maintain that it is necessary to take one step at a time, and that for the present our individual and collective action must go into the inner strengthening of our faith and practice.

They would doubtless agree on the importance of teaching the Dharma, which we have characterized as one of the important forms of social action, but they would argue that the seduction of other kinds of social action, and the drain of energy, are greater than the opportunities which it can afford for "wearing out the shoe of *samsara*." They would argue that the best way to help other people is by personal example.

This pamphlet concedes some possible truth to the above position but also offers a wide range of evidence to the contrary, to which in retrospect the reader may now wish to return.

Whatever we may feel about it, certainly the debate is a worthwhile one since, as we have seen, it points to the very heart of Buddhism — the harmony, or creative equilibrium, of Wisdom and Compassion. And as in all worthwhile debates, the disagreement, and, still more, the possible sense of disagreeableness which it engenders, offers each of us a valuable meditation.

The needs and aptitudes of individual differ, and our debate will also appear differently to readers in different countries with different cultural backgrounds. Though we are brothers and sisters to one another, as Buddhists each must light his or her own way. To the enquiring reader who has little knowledge of Buddhism and yet who has managed to stay with me to the end, I offer my apologies if I have sometimes seemed to forget him and if my explanations have proved inadequate. For:

"This is where words fail: for what can words tell
Of things that have no yesterday, tomorrow or today?"
— *Tseng Ts'an*

To a world knotted in hatreds and aggression and a host of follies, grand and mean, heroic and base, Buddhism offers a unique combination of unshakable equanimity and a deeply compassionate practical concern. And so may we tread lightly through restless experience, riding out defeats and discouragements, aware always of the peace at the heart of things, of the freedom that is free of nothing.

3

BUDDHISM: A METHOD OF MIND TRAINING

When you hear something about Buddhism in the daily news you usually think of it having a background of huge idols and yellow-robed monks, with a thick atmosphere of incense fumes. You never feel that there is anything in it for you, except, maybe, an exotic spectacle.

But is that all there is in Buddhism? Do the news photographers take pictures of the real Buddhism? Do the glossy magazines show you the fundamentals, or only the externals?

Let us see, then, what Buddhism really is, Buddhism as it was originally expounded and as it still exists underneath the external trappings and trimmings.

Although generally regarded as a religion, Buddhism is basically a method of cultivating the mind. It is true that, with its monastic tradition and its emphasis on ethical factors, it possesses many of the surface characteristics that Westerners associate with religion. However, it is not theistic, since it affirms that the universe is governed by impersonal laws and not by any creator-god; it has no use for prayer, for the Buddha was a teacher and not a god; and it regards devotion not as a religious obligation but as a means of expressing gratitude to its founder and as a means of self-development. Thus it is not a religion at all from these points of view.

Again, Buddhism knows faith only in the sense of confidence in the way recommended by the Buddha. A Buddhist is not expected to have faith or to believe in anything merely because the Buddha said it, or because it is written in the ancient books, or because it has been handed down by tradition, or because others believe it. He may, of course, agree with himself to take the Buddha-doctrine as a working hypothesis and to have confidence in it; but he is not expected to accept anything unless his reason accepts it. This does not mean that everything can be demonstrated rationally, for many points lie beyond the scope of the intellect and can be cognized only by the development of higher faculties. But the fact remains that there is no need for blind acceptance of anything in the Buddha-doctrine.

Buddhism is a way of life based on the training of the mind. Its one ultimate aim is to show the way to complete liberation from suffering by the attainment of the Unconditioned, a state beyond the range of the normal untrained mind. Its immediate aim is to strike at the roots of suffering in everyday life.

All human activity is directed, either immediately or remotely, towards the attainment of happiness in some form or other; or, to express the same thing in negative terms, all human activity is directed towards liberation from some kind of unsatisfactoriness or dissatisfaction. Dissatisfaction, then, can be regarded as the starting point in human activity, with happiness as its ultimate goal.

Dissatisfaction, the starting point in human activity, is also the starting point in Buddhism; and this point is expressed in the formula of the Four Basic Statements, which set out the fact of dissatisfaction, its cause, its cure, and the method of its cure. The First Basic Statement can be stated thus:

Dissatisfaction is Inescapable in En-self-ed Life

In its original meaning, the word which is here rendered as "dissatisfaction" and which is often translated as "suffering" embraces the meanings not only of pain, sorrow, and displeasure, but also of everything that is unsatisfactory, ranging from acute physical pain and severe mental anguish to slight tiredness, boredom, or mild disappointment.

Sometimes the term is rendered as "dissatisfaction" or "unsatisfactoriness"; in some contexts these are perhaps more accurate, while at other times the word "suffering" is more expressive. For this reason we shall use both "suffering" and "dissatisfaction" or "unsatisfactoriness" according to context.

In some translations of the original texts it is stated that birth is suffering, sickness is suffering, old age is suffering, and pleasure is suffering. In English, this last statement fails to make sense; but if we restate it as "pleasure is unsatisfactory" it becomes more readily understandable, for all pleasure is impermanent and is eventually succeeded by its opposite, and from this point of view at least it is unsatisfactory.

Now the Buddha-doctrine teaches that dissatisfaction or suffering is inescapable in en-self-ed life; and the term "en-self-ed life" needs some explanation. In brief, the doctrine teaches that the self, considered as a fixed, unchanging eternal soul, has no reality.

The central core of every being is not an unchanging soul but a life-current, an ever-changing stream of energy which is never the same for two consecutive seconds. The self, considered as an eternal soul, therefore, is a delusion, and when regarded from the ultimate standpoint it has no reality; and it is only within this delusion of selfhood that ultimate suffering can exist. When the self-delusion is finally transcended and the final enlightenment is attained, the ultimate state which lies beyond the relative universe is reached. In this ultimate state, the Unconditioned, suffering is extinguished; but while any element of selfhood remains, even though it is a delusion, suffering remains potentially within it.

We must understand, then, that the First Basic Statement does not mean that suffering is inescapable; it means that suffering is inescapable in enselfed life, or while the delusion of selfhood remains.

We can now move on to the Second Basic Statement, which says:

The Origin of Dissatisfaction is Craving

If you fall on a slippery floor and suffer from bruises, you say that the cause of your suffering is the slippery floor. In an immediate sense you are right, of course, and to say that the cause of your bruises is craving fails to make sense.

But the Second Statement does not refer to individual cases or to immediate causes. It means that the integrating force that holds together the life-current is self-centered craving; for this life-current — this self-delusion — contains in itself the conditions for suffering, while the slippery floor is merely an occasion for suffering. It is obviously impossible, by the nature of the world we live in, to cure suffering by the removal of all the occasions for suffering; whereas it is possible in Buddhism to strike at its prime or fundamental cause. Therefore the Third Basic Statement states:

Liberation May be Achieved by Destroying Craving

It is self-centered craving that holds together the forces which comprise the life-current, the stream of existence which we call the self; and it is only with self-delusion that unsatisfactoriness or suffering can exist. By the destruction of that which holds together the delusion of the self, the root cause of suffering is also destroyed.

The ultimate aim of Buddhist practice, then, is to annihilate the self. This is where a great deal of misunderstanding arises, and naturally so; but once it is realized that to annihilate the self is to annihilate a delusion, this misunderstanding disappears.

When the delusion is removed, the reality appears; so that to destroy delusion is to reveal the reality. The reality cannot be discovered while the delusion of self continues to obscure it. Now what is this reality which appears when the delusion is removed?

The ultimate reality is the Unconditioned, called also the Unborn, the Unoriginated, the Uncreated, and the Uncompounded. We can, inadequately and not very accurately, describe it as a positive state of being.

It is characterized by supreme bliss and complete freedom from suffering and is so utterly different from ordinary existence that no real description of it can be given. The Unconditioned can be indicated — up to a point — only by stating what it is not; for it is beyond words and beyond thought.

Hence, in the Buddhist texts, the Unconditioned is often explained as the final elimination from one's own mind, of greed, hatred and delusion. This, of course, also implies the perfection of the opposite positive qualities of selflessness, loving-kindness, and wisdom. The attainment of the Unconditioned is the ultimate aim of all Buddhist practice, and is the same as complete liberation from dissatisfaction or suffering. This brings us to the last of the Four Basic Statements:

The Way of Liberation is the Noble Eightfold Path

The eight factors of the path are these:

1. Right understanding, a knowledge of the true nature of existence.
2. Right thought, thought free from sensuality, ill-will and cruelty.
3. Right speech, speech without falsity, gossip, harshness, and idle babble.
4. Right action, or the avoidance of killing, stealing and adultery.
5. Right livelihood, an occupation that harms no conscious living being.
6. Right effort, or the effort to destroy the defilements of the mind and to cultivate wholesome qualities.
7. Right mindfulness, the perfection of the normal faculty of attention.
8. Right concentration, the cultivation of a collected, focused mind through meditation.

Now you will see that in this Noble Eightfold Path there is nothing of an essentially religious nature; it is more a sort of moral psychology.

But in the East as well as in the West people as a whole demand external show of some sort, and — on the outside at least — the non-essentials have assumed more importance than the essentials.

While some external features in the practice of Buddhism must of necessity vary according to environment, the essential and constant characteristics of that practice are summed up in the following outline of the Noble Eightfold Path, the Middle Way between harmful extremes, as taught by the Buddha.

Although it is convenient to speak of the various aspects of the eightfold path as eight steps, they are not to be regarded as separate steps, taken one after another. On the contrary, each one must be practiced along with the others, and it might perhaps be better to think of them as if they were eight parallel lanes within the one road rather than eight successive steps.

The first step of this path, right understanding, is primarily a matter of seeing things as they really are — or at least trying to do so without self-deceit or evasion. In another sense, right understanding commences as an intellectual appreciation of the nature of existence, and as such it can be regarded as the beginning of the path; but, when the path has been followed to the end, this merely intellectual appreciation is supplanted by a direct and penetrating discernment of the principles of the teaching first accepted intellectually. While right understanding can be regarded as the complete understanding of the Buddha doctrine, it is based on the recognition of three dominating characteristics of the relative universe, of the universe of time, form and matter. These three characteristics can briefly be set out in this way:

1. Impermanence: All things in the relative universe are unceasingly changing.
2. Dissatisfaction: Some degree of suffering or dissatisfaction is inherent in en-selfed life, or in life within the limitations of the relative universe and personal experience.
3. Egolessness: No being — no human being or any other sort of being — possesses a fixed, unchanging, eternal soul or self. Instead, every being consists of an ever-changing current of forces, an ever-changing flux of material and mental phenomena, like a river which is always moving and is never still for a single second.

The self, then, is not a static entity but an ever-changing flux. This dynamic concept of existence is typical of deeper Buddhist thought; there is nothing static in life, and since it is ever-flowing you must learn to flow with it.

Another aspect of right understanding is the recognition that the universe runs its course on the basis of a strict sequence of cause and effect, or of action and reaction, a sequence just as invariable and just as exact in the mental or moral realm as in the physical. In accordance with this law of moral action and reaction all morally good or wholesome will actions eventually bring to the doer happiness at some time, while unwholesome or morally bad will-actions bring suffering to the doer.

The effects of wholesome and unwholesome will-actions — that is to say, the happiness and suffering that result from them — do not generally follow immediately; there is often a considerable time-lag, for the resultant happiness and suffering can arise only when appropriate conditions are present. The results may not appear within the present lifetime. Thus at death there is normally a balance of "merit" which has not yet brought about its experience of happiness; and at the same time there is also a balance of "demerit" which has not yet given rise to the suffering which is to be its inevitable result.

After death, the body disintegrates, of course, but the life-current continues, not in the form of an unchanging soul, but in the form of an ever-changing stream of energy. Immediately after death a new being commences life to carry on this life current; but the new being is not necessarily a human being, and the instantaneous rebirth may take place on another plane of existence. But in any case, the new being is a direct sequel to the being that has just died.

Thus the new being becomes an uninterrupted continuation of the old being, and the life-current is unbroken. The new being inherits the balance of merit built up by the old being, and this balance of merit will inevitably bring happiness at some future time. At the same time, the new being inherits the old being's balance of demerit, which will bring suffering at some time in the future.

In effect, in the sense of continuity, the new being is the same as the old being. In just the same way — that is, in the sense of continuity only — an old man is the same as the young man he once was, the young man is the same as the boy he once was, and the boy is the same as the baby he once was. But the identity of the old man with the young man, and with the boy, and with the baby, is due only to continuity; there is no other identity.

Everything in the universe changes from day to day and from moment to moment, so that every being at this moment is a slightly different being from that of the moment before; the only identity is due to continuity. In the same way, the being that is reborn is different from the previous one that died; but the identity due to continuity remains as before.

These teachings are basic to the Buddha-doctrine — the illusory nature of the self, the law of action and reaction in the moral sphere, and the rebirth of the life-forces — but there is no need for anyone to accept anything that does not appeal to his reason. Acceptance of any particular teaching is unimportant; what is important is the continual effort to see things as they really are, without self-deceit or evasion.

So much for a brief outline of the doctrine under the heading of right understanding. The second step, right thought or aim, is a matter of freeing the intellectual faculties from adverse emotional factors, such as sensuality, ill-will, and cruelty, which render wise and unbiased decisions impossible.

Right speech, right action, and right livelihood together make up the moral section of the path, their function being to keep the defilements of the mind under control and to prevent them from reaching adverse expression. These defilements, however, cannot be completely eradicated by morality alone, and the other steps of the path must be applied to cleanse the mind completely of its defilements.

Now in the next step — right effort — we enter the sphere of practical psychology, for right effort in this context means effort of will. In other words, the sixth step of the path is self-discipline, the training of the will in order to prevent and overcome those states of mind that retard development, and to arouse and cultivate those that bring about mental progress.

The seventh step of the path is also one of practical psychology; this is the step called right mindfulness, and it consists of the fullest possible development of the ordinary faculty of attention. It is largely by the development of attention — expanded and intensified awareness — that the mind can eventually become capable of discerning things as they really are.

The primary function of the seventh step, right mindfulness, is to develop an increasing awareness of the unreality of the self. However, it functions also by continually improving the normal faculty of attention, thus equipping the mind better to meet the problems and stresses of the workaday world.

In the Buddha-way, mindfulness consists of developing the faculty of attention so as to produce a constant awareness of all thoughts that arise, all words that are spoken, and all actions that are done, with a view to keeping them free from self-interest, from emotional bias, and from self-delusion.

Right mindfulness has many applications in the sphere of everyday activities. For example, it can be employed to bring about a sharpened awareness, a clear comprehension, of the motives of these activities, and this clear comprehension of motive is extremely important.

In right concentration, the last of the eight steps, the cultivation of higher mind-states — up to the meditative absorptions — is undertaken, and these higher mind-states serve to unify, purify, and strengthen the mind for the achievement of liberating insight.

In this ultimate achievement the delusion of selfhood, with its craving and suffering, is transcended and extinguished.

This penetrating insight is the ultimate goal of all Buddhist practices, and with it comes a direct insight into the true nature of life, culminating in realization of the Unconditioned. While the Unconditioned is the extinction of self, it is nevertheless not mere non-existence or annihilation, for the extinction of self is nothing but the extinction of a delusion. Every description of the Unconditioned must fail, for it lies not only beyond words but beyond even thought; and the only way to know it is to follow the Noble Eightfold Path to its end.

This, then, is the original Buddhism; this is the Buddhism of the Noble Eightfold Path, of the path that leads from the bondage of self to liberating insight into reality.

Going for Refuge

The act of going for refuge marks the point where one commits oneself to taking the Dhamma, or the Buddha's teaching, as the primary guide to one's life. To understand why this commitment is called a "refuge," it's helpful to look at the history of the custom.

In pre-Buddhist India, going for refuge meant proclaiming one's allegiance to a patron — a powerful person or god — submitting to the patron's directives in hopes of receiving protection from danger in return. In the early years of the Buddha's teaching career, his new followers adopted this custom to express their allegiance to the Buddha, Dhamma, and Sangha, but in the Buddhist context this custom took on a new meaning.

Buddhism is not a theistic religion — the Buddha is not a god — and so a person taking refuge in the Buddhist sense is not asking for the Buddha personally to intervene to provide protection. Still, one of the Buddha's central teachings is that human life is fraught with dangers — from greed, anger, and delusion — and so the concept of refuge is central to the path of practice, in that the practice is aimed at gaining release from those dangers. Because the mind is the source both of the dangers and of release, there is a need for two levels of refuge: external refuges, which provide models and guidelines so that we can identify which qualities in the mind lead to danger and which to release; and internal refuges, i.e., the qualities leading to release that we develop in our own mind in imitation of our external models. The internal level is where true refuge is found.

Although the tradition of going to refuge is an ancient practice, it is still relevant for our own practice today, for we are faced with the same internal dangers that faced people in the Buddha's time. We still need the same protection as they.

When a Buddhist takes refuge, it is essentially an act of taking refuge in the doctrine of karma: It's an act of submission in that one is committed to living in line with the principle that actions based on skillful intentions lead to happiness, while actions based on unskillful intentions lead to suffering; it's an act of claiming protection in that, by following the teaching, one hopes to avoid the misfortunes that bad karma engenders. To take refuge in this way ultimately means to take refuge in the quality of our own intentions, for that's where the essence of karma lies.

The refuges in Buddhism — both on the internal and on the external levels — are the Buddha, Dhamma, and Sangha, also known as the Triple Gem. They are called gems both because they are valuable and because, in ancient times, gems were believed to have protective powers. The Triple Gem outdoes other gems in this respect because its protective powers can be put to the test and can lead further than those of any physical gem, all the way to absolute freedom from the uncertainties of the realm of aging, illness, and death.

The Buddha, on the external level, refers to Siddhattha Gotama, the Indian prince who renounced his royal titles and went into the forest, meditating until he ultimately gained Awakening. To take refuge in the Buddha means, not taking refuge in him as a person, but taking refuge in the fact of his Awakening: placing trust in the belief that he did awaken to the truth, that he did so by developing qualities that we too can develop, and that the truths to which he awoke provide the best perspective for the conduct of our life.

The Dhamma, on the external level, refers to the path of practice the Buddha taught to this followers. This, in turn, is divided into three levels: the words of his teachings, the act of putting those teachings into practice, and the attainment of Awakening as the result of that practice. This three-way division of the word "Dhamma" acts as a map showing how to take the external refuges and make them internal: learning about the teachings, using them to develop the qualities that the Buddha himself used to attain Awakening, and then realizing the same release from danger that he found in the quality of Deathlessness that we can touch within.

The word Sangha, on the external level, has two senses: conventional and ideal. In its ideal sense, the Sangha consists of all people, lay or ordained, who have practiced the Dhamma to the point of gaining at least a glimpse of the Deathless. In a conventional sense, Sangha denotes the communities of ordained monks and nuns. The two meanings overlap but are not necessarily identical. Some members of the ideal Sangha are not ordained; some monks and nuns have yet to touch the Deathless. All those who take refuge in the Buddha, Dhamma, and Sangha become members of the Buddha's four-fold assembly *(parisa)* of followers: monks, nuns, male lay devotees, and female lay devotees. Although there's a widespread belief that all Buddhist followers are members of the Sangha, this is not the case. Only those who are ordained are members of the conventional Sangha; only those who have glimpsed the Deathless are members of the ideal Sangha. Nevertheless, any followers who don't belong to the Sangha in either sense of the word still count as genuine Buddhists in that they are members of the Buddha's *parisa*.

When taking refuge in the external Sangha, one takes refuge in both senses of the Sangha, but the two senses provide different levels of refuge. The conventional Sangha has helped keep the teaching alive for more than 2,500 years. Without them, we would never have learned what the Buddha taught. However, not all members of the conventional Sangha are reliable models of behavior. So when looking for guidance in the conduct of our lives, we must look to the living and recorded examples provided by the ideal Sangha. Without their example, we would not know (1) that Awakening is available to all, and not just to the Buddha; and (2) how Awakening expresses itself in real life.

On the internal level, the Buddha, Dhamma, and Sangha are the skillful qualities we develop in our own minds in imitation of our external models. For instance, the Buddha was a person of wisdom, purity, and compassion. When we develop wisdom, purity, and compassion in our own minds, they form our refuge on an internal level. The Buddha tasted Awakening by developing conviction, persistence, mindfulness, concentration, and discernment. When we develop these same qualities to the point of attaining Awakening too, that Awakening is our ultimate refuge. This is the point where the three aspects of the Triple Gem become one: beyond the reach of greed, anger, and delusion, and thus totally secure.

READINGS

'Indeed, the Blessed One [the Buddha] is worthy and rightly self-awakened, consummate in knowledge and conduct, well-gone, an expert with regard to the cosmos, unexcelled as a trainer for those people fit to be tamed, the Teacher of divine and human beings, awakened, blessed.'

'The Dhamma is well-expounded by the Blessed One, to be seen here and now, timeless, inviting verification, pertinent, to be realized by the wise for themselves.'

'The Sangha of the Blessed One's disciples who have practiced well... who have practiced straight-forwardly... who have practiced methodically... who have practiced masterfully — in other words, the four types of noble disciples when taken as pairs, the eight when taken as individual types — they are the Sangha of the Blessed One's disciples: worthy of gifts, worthy of hospitality, worthy of offerings, worthy of respect, the incomparable field of merit for the world.' — A X.92

BUDDHA

[The Buddha speaks:] I lived in refinement, utmost refinement, total refinement. My father even had lotus ponds made in our palace: one where red-lotuses bloomed, one where white lotuses bloomed, one where blue lotuses bloomed, all for my sake. I used no sandalwood that was not from Varanasi. My turban was from Varanasi, as were my tunic, my lower garments, and my outer cloak. A white sunshade was held over me day and night to protect me from cold, heat, dust, dirt, and dew.

I had three palaces: one for the cold season, one for the hot season, one for the rainy season. During the four months of the rainy season I was entertained in the rainy-season palace by minstrels without a single man among them, and I did not once come down from the palace. Whereas the servants, workers, and retainers in other people's homes are fed meals of lentil soup and broken rice, in my father's home the servants, workers, and retainers were fed wheat, rice, and meat.

Even though I was endowed with such fortune, such total refinement, the thought occurred to me: "When an untaught, run-of-the-mill person, himself subject to aging, not beyond aging, sees another who is aged, he is horrified, humiliated, and disgusted, oblivious to himself that he too is subject to aging, not beyond aging. If I — who am subject to aging, not beyond aging — were to be horrified, humiliated, and disgusted on seeing another person who is aged, that would not be fitting for me." As I noticed this, the [typical] young person's intoxication with youth entirely dropped away.

Even though I was endowed with such fortune, such total refinement, the thought occurred to me: "When an untaught, run-of-the-mill person, himself subject to illness, not beyond illness, sees another who is ill, he is horrified, humiliated, and disgusted, oblivious to himself that he too is subject to illness, not beyond illness. And if I — who am subject to illness, not beyond illness — were to be horrified, humiliated, and disgusted on seeing another person who is ill, that would not be fitting for me." As I noticed this, the healthy person's intoxication with health entirely dropped away.

Even though I was endowed with such fortune, such total refinement, the thought occurred to me: "When an untaught, run-of-the-mill person, himself subject to death, not beyond death, sees another who is dead, he is horrified, humiliated, and disgusted, oblivious to himself that he too is subject to death, not beyond death. And if I — who am subject to death, not beyond death — were to be horrified, humiliated, and disgusted on seeing another person who is dead, that would not be fitting for me." As I noticed this, the living person's intoxication with life entirely dropped away. — A III.38

The Quest for Awakening

Before my Awakening, when I was still an unawakened Bodhisatta, being subject myself to birth, aging, illness, death, sorrow, and defilement, I sought [happiness in] what was subject to birth, aging, illness, death, sorrow, and defilement. The thought occurred to me: "Why am I, being subject myself to birth... defilement, seeking what is subject to birth... defilement? What if I... were to seek the unborn, unaging, unailing, undying, sorrowless, undefiled, unsurpassed security from bondage: Unbinding."

So at a later time, when I was still young, black-haired, endowed with the blessings of youth in the first stage of life, I shaved off my hair and beard — though my parents wished otherwise and were grieving with tears on their faces — and I put on the ochre robe and went forth from the home life into homelessness.

Having gone forth in search of what might be skillful, seeking the unexcelled state of sublime peace, I went to where Alara Kalama was staying and, on arrival, said to him: "I want to practice in this doctrine and discipline."

When this was said, he replied to me, "You may stay here. This doctrine is such that a wise person can soon enter and dwell in his own teacher's knowledge, having realized it for himself through direct knowledge."

I quickly learned the doctrine. As far as mere lip-reciting and repetition, I could speak the words of knowledge, the words of the elders, and I could affirm that I knew and saw— I, along with others.

I thought: "It isn't through mere conviction alone that Alara Kalama declares, 'I have entered and dwell in this Dhamma, having realized it directly for myself.' Certainly he dwells knowing and seeing this Dhamma." So I went to him and said, "To what extent do you declare that you have entered and dwell in this Dhamma?" When this was said, he declared the dimension of nothingness.

I thought: "Not only does Alara Kalama have conviction, persistence, mindfulness, concentration, and discernment. I, too, have conviction, persistence, mindfulness, concentration, and discernment.

Suppose I were to endeavor to realize for myself the Dhamma that Alara Kalama declares he has entered and dwells in..." So it was not long before I entered and dwelled in that Dhamma, having realized it for myself through direct knowledge. I went to him and said, "Friend Kalama, is this the extent to which you have entered and dwell in this Dhamma, having realized it for yourself through direct knowledge?"

"Yes..."

"This is the extent to which I, too, have entered and dwell in this Dhamma, having realized it for myself through direct knowledge."

"It is a gain for us, a great gain for us, that we have such a companion in the holy life... As I am, so are you; as you are, so am I. Come friend, let us now lead this community together."

In this way did Alara Kalama, my teacher, place me, his pupil, on the same level with himself and pay me great honor. But the thought occurred to me, "This Dhamma leads not to disenchantment, to dispassion, to cessation, to stilling, to direct knowledge, to Awakening, nor to Unbinding, but only to reappearance in the dimension of nothingness." So, dissatisfied with that Dhamma, I left. — M 26

"Now, Aggivessana, these three similes — spontaneous, never before heard — appeared to me. Suppose there were a wet, sappy piece of timber lying in the water, and a man were to come along with an upper fire-stick, thinking, 'I'll light a fire. I'll produce heat.' Now what do you think? Would he be able to light a fire and produce heat by rubbing the upper fire-stick in the wet, sappy timber lying in the water?"

"No, Master Gotama..."

"So it is with any priest or contemplative who does not live withdrawn from sensuality in body and mind, and whose desire, infatuation, urge, thirst, and fever for sensuality is not relinquished and stilled within him: Whether or not he feels painful, racking, piercing feelings due to his striving [for Awakening], he is incapable of knowledge, vision, and unexcelled self-awakening...

"Then a second simile — spontaneous, never before heard — appeared to me. Suppose there were a wet, sappy piece of timber lying on land far from water, and a man were to come along with an upper fire-stick, thinking, 'I'll light a fire. I'll produce heat.' Now what do you think? Would he be able to light a fire and produce heat by rubbing the upper fire-stick in the wet, sappy timber lying on land?"

"No, Master Gotama..."

"So it is with any priest or contemplative who lives withdrawn from sensuality in body only, but whose desire, infatuation, urge, thirst, and fever for sensuality is not relinquished and stilled within him: Whether or not he feels painful, racking, piercing feelings due to his striving, he is incapable of knowledge, vision, and unexcelled self-awakening...

"Then a third simile — spontaneous, never before heard — appeared to me. Suppose there were a dry, sapless piece of timber lying on land far from water, and a man were to come along with an upper fire-stick, thinking, 'I'll light a fire. I'll produce heat.' Now what do you think? Would he be able to light a fire and produce heat by rubbing the upper fire-stick in the dry, sapless timber lying on land?"

"Yes, Master Gotama..."

"So it is with any priest or contemplative who lives withdrawn from sensuality in body and mind, and whose desire, infatuation, urge, thirst, and fever for sensuality is relinquished and stilled within him: Whether or not he feels painful, racking, piercing feelings due to his striving, he is capable of knowledge, vision, and unexcelled self-awakening...

"I thought: 'Suppose that I, clenching my teeth and pressing my tongue against the roof of my mouth, were to beat down, constrain, and crush my mind with my awareness'... So, just as if a strong man, seizing a weaker man by the head or the throat or the shoulders would beat him down, constrain and crush him, in the same way I beat down, constrained, and crushed my mind with my awareness. As I did so, sweat poured from my armpits. But although tireless persistence was aroused in me, and unmuddled mindfulness established, my body was aroused and uncalm because of the painful exertion. But the painful feeling that arose in this way did not invade my mind or remain.

"I thought: 'Suppose I were to become absorbed in the trance of non-breathing.' So I stopped the in-breaths and out-breaths in my nose and mouth. As I did so, there was a loud roaring of winds coming out my earholes, just like the loud roar of winds coming out of a smith's bellows... So I stopped the in-breaths and out-breaths in my nose and mouth and ears. As I did so, extreme forces sliced through my head, just as if a strong man were slicing my head open with a sharp sword... Extreme pains arose in my head, just as if a strong man were tightening a turban made of tough leather straps around my head... Extreme forces carved up my stomach cavity, just as if a butcher or his apprentice were to carve up the stomach cavity of an ox... There was an extreme burning in my body, just as if two strong men, grabbing a weaker man by the arms, were to roast and broil him over a pit of hot embers. But although tireless persistence was aroused in me, and unmuddled mindfulness established, my body was aroused and uncalm because of the painful exertion. But the painful feeling that arose in this way did not invade my mind or remain.

"Devas, on seeing me, said, 'Gotama the contemplative is dead.' Other devas said, 'He isn't dead, he's dying.' Others said, 'He's neither dead nor dying, he's an arahant, for this is the way arahants live.'

"I thought: 'Suppose I were to practice going altogether without food.' Then devas came to me and said, 'Dear sir, please don't practice going altogether without food. If you go altogether without food, we'll infuse divine nourishment in through your pores, and you will survive on that.' I thought, 'If I were to claim to be completely fasting while these devas are infusing divine nourishment in through my pores, I would be lying.' So I dismissed them, saying, 'Enough.'

"I thought: 'Suppose I were to take only a little food at a time, only a handful at a time of bean soup, lentil soup, vetch soup, or pea soup.' So I took only a little food at a time, only handful at a time of bean soup, lentil soup, vetch soup, or pea soup. My body became extremely emaciated. Simply from my eating so little, my limbs became like the jointed segments of vine stems or bamboo stems... My backside became like a camel's hoof... My spine stood out like a string of beads... My ribs jutted out like the jutting rafters of an old, run-down barn... The gleam of my eyes appeared to be sunk deep in my eye sockets like the gleam of water deep in a well... My scalp shriveled and withered like a green bitter gourd, shriveled and withered in the heat and the wind... The skin of my belly became so stuck to my spine that when I thought of touching my belly, I grabbed hold of my spine as well; and when I thought of touching my spine, I grabbed hold of the skin of my belly as well... If I urinated or defecated, I fell over on my face right there... Simply from my eating so little, if I tried to ease my body by rubbing my limbs with my hands, the hair — rotted at its roots — fell from my body as I rubbed...

"I thought: 'Whatever priests or contemplatives in the past have felt painful, racking, piercing feelings due to their striving, this is the utmost. None have been greater than this. Whatever priests or contemplatives in the future... in the present are feeling painful, racking, piercing feelings due to their striving, this is the utmost. None is greater than this. But with this racking practice of austerities I have not attained any superior human state, any distinction in knowledge or vision worthy of the noble ones. Could there be another path to Awakening?'

"I thought: 'I recall once, when my father the Sakyan was working, and I was sitting in the cool shade of a rose-apple tree, then — quite withdrawn from sensuality, withdrawn from unskillful mental qualities — I entered and remained in the first jhana: rapture and pleasure born from withdrawal, accompanied by directed thought and evaluation. Could that be the path to Awakening?' Then, following on that memory, came the realization: 'That is the path to Awakening... So why am I afraid of that pleasure that has nothing to do with sensuality, nothing to do with unskillful mental qualities?' I thought: 'I am no longer afraid of that pleasure... but it is not easy to achieve that pleasure with a body so extremely emaciated...' So I took some solid food: some rice and porridge.

Now five monks had been attending on me, thinking, 'If Gotama, our contemplative, achieves some higher state, he will tell us.' But when they saw me taking some solid food — some rice and porridge — they were disgusted and left me, thinking, 'Gotama the contemplative is living luxuriously. He has abandoned his exertion and is backsliding into abundance.'

"So when I had taken solid food and regained strength, then — quite withdrawn from sensuality, withdrawn from unskillful mental qualities, I entered and remained in the first jhana: rapture and pleasure born from withdrawal, accompanied by directed thought and evaluation.

But the pleasant feeling that arose in this way did not invade my mind or remain. With the stilling of directed thoughts & evaluations, I entered and remained in the second jhana: rapture and pleasure born of composure, unification of awareness free from directed thought and evaluation — internal assurance... With the fading of rapture I remained in equanimity, mindful and alert, and physically sensitive of pleasure. I entered and remained in the third jhana, of which the Noble Ones declare, 'Equanimous and mindful, he has a pleasurable abiding.'... With the abandoning of pleasure and pain — as with the earlier disappearance of elation and distress — I entered and remained in the fourth jhana: purity of equanimity and mindfulness, neither pleasure nor pain. But the pleasant feeling that arose in this way did not invade my mind or remain.

"When the mind was thus concentrated, purified, bright, unblemished, rid of defilement, pliant, malleable, steady, and attained to imperturbability, I directed it to the knowledge of recollecting my past lives. I recollected my manifold past lives, i.e., one birth, two... five, ten... fifty, a hundred, a thousand, a hundred thousand, many eons of cosmic contraction, many eons of cosmic expansion, many eons of cosmic contraction and expansion: 'There I had such a name, belonged to such a clan, had such an appearance. Such was my food, such my experience of pleasure and pain, such the end of my life. Passing away from that state, I re-arose there. There too I had such a name, belonged to such a clan, had such an appearance. Such was my food, such my experience of pleasure and pain, such the end of my life. Passing away from that state, I re-arose here.' Thus I remembered my manifold past lives in their modes and details.

"This was the first knowledge I attained in the first watch of the night. Ignorance was destroyed; knowledge arose; darkness was destroyed; light arose — as happens in one who is heedful, ardent, and resolute. But the pleasant feeling that arose in this way did not invade my mind or remain.

"When the mind was thus concentrated, purified, bright, unblemished, rid of defilement, pliant, malleable, steady, and attained to imperturbability, I directed it to the knowledge of the passing away and reappearance of beings. I saw — by means of the divine eye, purified and surpassing the human — beings passing away and re-appearing, and I discerned how they are inferior and superior, beautiful and ugly, fortunate and unfortunate in accordance with their kamma: 'These beings — who were endowed with bad conduct of body, speech, and mind, who reviled the noble ones, held wrong views and undertook actions under the influence of wrong views — with the break-up of the body, after death, have re-appeared in the plane of deprivation, the bad destination, the lower realms, in hell. But these beings — who were endowed with good conduct of body, speech and mind, who did not revile the noble ones, who held right views and undertook actions under the influence of right views — with the break-up of the body, after death, have re-appeared in the good destinations, in the heavenly world.' Thus — by means of the divine eye, purified and surpassing the human — I saw beings passing away and re-appearing, and I discerned how they are inferior and superior, beautiful and ugly, fortunate and unfortunate in accordance with their kamma.

"This was the second knowledge I attained in the second watch of the night. Ignorance was destroyed; knowledge arose; darkness was destroyed; light arose — as happens in one who is heedful, ardent, and resolute. But the pleasant feeling that arose in this way did not invade my mind or remain.

"When the mind was thus concentrated, purified, bright, unblemished, rid of defilement, pliant, malleable, steady, and attained to imperturbability, I directed it to the knowledge of the ending of the mental effluents *(asava)*. I discerned, as it had come to be, that 'This is stress... This is the origination of stress... This is the cessation of stress... This is the way leading to the cessation of stress... These are effluents... This is the origination of effluents... This is the cessation of effluents... This is the way leading to the cessation of effluents.' My heart, thus knowing, thus seeing, was released from the effluent of sensuality, released from the effluent of becoming, released from the effluent of ignorance. With release, there was the knowledge, 'Released.' I discerned that 'Birth is ended, the holy life fulfilled, the task done. There is nothing further for this world.'

"This was the third knowledge I attained in the third watch of the night. Ignorance was destroyed; knowledge arose; darkness was destroyed; light arose — as happens in one who is heedful, ardent, and resolute. But the pleasant feeling that arose in this way did not invade my mind or remain." — M 36

Through the round of many births
without reward,
without rest,
seeking the house builder.
Painful is birth again
and again.
House builder, you're seen!
You will not build a house again.
All your rafters broken,
the ridge pole destroyed,
gone to the Unformed, the mind
has attained the end of craving.

— *Dhp 153-54*

The Buddha's Passing Away

Now at that time Subhadda the Wanderer was staying in Kusinara. He heard that 'Tonight, in the last watch of the night, the total Unbinding of Gotama the contemplative will take place.' Then this thought occurred to him, 'I have heard the elder wanderers, teachers of teachers, saying that only once in a long, long time do Tathagatas — worthy ones, rightly self-awakened — appear in the world. Tonight, in the last watch of the night, the total Unbinding of Gotama the contemplative will take place. Now there is a doubt that has arisen in me, but I have faith that he could teach me the Dhamma in such a way that I might abandon that doubt.'

So he went to the Mallan Sal Tree grove and, on arrival, said to Ven. Ananda, 'I have heard the elder wanderers, teachers of teachers, saying that only once in a long, long time do Tathagatas — worthy ones, rightly self-awakened — appear in the world. Tonight, in the last watch of the night, the total Unbinding of Gotama the contemplative will take place. Now there is a doubt that has arisen in me, but I have faith that he could teach me the Dhamma in such a way that I might abandon that doubt. It would be good, Ven. Ananda, if you would let me see him.'

When this was said, Ven. Ananda said to him, 'Enough, friend Subhadda. Do not bother the Blessed One. The Blessed One is tired.'

For a second time... For a third time, Subhadda the Wanderer said to Ven. Ananda, '...It would be good, Ven. Ananda, if you would let me see him.'

For a third time, Ven. Ananda said to him, 'Enough, friend Subhadda. Do not bother the Blessed One. The Blessed One is tired.'

Now, the Blessed One heard the exchange between Ven. Ananda and Subhadda the Wanderer, and so he said to Ven. Ananda, 'Enough, Ananda. Do not stand in his way. Let him see the Tathagata. Whatever he asks me will all be for the sake of knowledge, and not to be bothersome. And whatever I answer when asked, he will quickly understand.'

So Ven. Ananda said to Subhadda the Wanderer, 'Go ahead, friend Subhadda. The Blessed One gives you his leave.'

Then Subhadda went to the Blessed One and exchanged courtesies, and after the exchange of courtesies sat to one side. As he was sitting there, he said to the Blessed One, 'Lord, these priests and contemplatives, each with his group, each with his community, each the teacher of his group, an honored leader, well-regarded by people at large — i.e., Purana Kassapa, Makkhali Gosala, Ajita Kesakambalin, Pakudha Kaccayana, Sañjaya Belatthaputta, and the Nigantha Nathaputta: Do they all have direct knowledge as they themselves claim, or do they all not have direct knowledge, or do some of them have direct knowledge and some of them not?' 'Enough, Subhadda. Put this question aside. I will teach you the Dhamma. Listen, and pay close attention. I will speak.'

'Yes, lord,' Subhadda answered, and the Blessed One said, 'In any doctrine and discipline where the noble eightfold path is not found, no contemplative of the first... second... third... fourth order [stream-winner, once-returner, non-returner, arahant] is found. But in any doctrine and discipline where the noble eightfold path *is* found, contemplatives of the first... second... third... fourth order *are* found. The noble eightfold path is found in this doctrine and discipline, and right here there are contemplatives of the first... second... third... fourth order. Other teachings are empty of knowledgeable contemplatives. And if the monks dwell rightly, this world will not be empty of arahants.

At age twenty-nine I went forth,
seeking what might be skillful,
and since my going forth
more than fifty years have past.
Outside of the realm
of methodical Dhamma,
there is no contemplative.

And no contemplative of the second... third... fourth order. Other teachings are empty of knowledgeable contemplatives. And if the monks dwell rightly, this world will not be empty of arahants.'

Then Subhadda the Wanderer said, 'Magnificent, lord, magnificent! In many ways has the Blessed One made the Dhamma clear — just as if one were to place upright what has been overturned, to reveal what has been hidden, to point out the way to one who is lost, or to set out a lamp in the darkness so that those with eyes might see forms. I go to the Blessed One for refuge, and to the Dhamma and to the community of monks. Let me obtain the going forth in the Blessed One's presence, let me obtain admission.'

'Anyone, Subhadda, who has previously belonged to another sect and who desires the going forth and admission in this doctrine and discipline must first undergo probation for four months. If, at the end of four months, the monks feel so moved, they give him the going forth and admit him to the monk's state. But I know distinctions among individuals in this matter.'

'Lord, if that is so, I am willing to undergo probation for four years. If, at the end of four years, the monks feel so moved, let them give me the going forth and admit me to the monk's state.'

Then the Blessed One said to Ven. Ananda, 'Very well then, Ananda, give Subhadda the going forth.'

'Yes, lord,' Ananda answered.

Then Subhadda said to Ven. Ananda, 'It is a gain for you, Ananda, a great gain, that you have been anointed here in the Teacher's presence with the pupil's anointing.'

Then Subhadda the Wanderer received the going forth and the admission in the Blessed One's presence. And not long after his admission — dwelling alone, secluded, heedful, ardent, and resolute — he in no long time reached and remained in the supreme goal of the holy life, for which clansmen rightly go forth from home into homelessness, knowing and realizing it for himself in the here and now. He knew: 'Birth is ended, the holy life fulfilled, the task done. There is nothing further for the sake of this world.' And thus Ven. Subhadda became another one of the arahants, the last of the Blessed One's face-to-face disciples...

Then the Blessed One addressed the monks, 'I exhort you, monks: All processes are subject to decay. Bring about completion by being heedful.' Those were the Tathagata's last words.

Then the Blessed One entered the first jhana. Emerging from that he entered the second. Emerging from that, he entered the third... the fourth... the dimension of the infinitude of space... the dimension of the infinitude of consciousness... the dimension of nothingness... the dimension of neither perception nor non-perception... the cessation of perception and feeling.

Then Ven. Ananda said to Ven. Anuruddha, "The Blessed One, sir, has entered total Unbinding."

"No, friend, the Blessed One has not entered total Unbinding. He has attained the cessation of perception and feeling."

Then emerging from the cessation of perception and feeling, the Blessed One entered the dimension of neither perception nor non-perception... the dimension of nothingness... the dimension of the infinitude of consciousness... the dimension of the infinitude of space... the fourth jhana... the third... the second... the first jhana. Emerging from the first jhana he entered the second... the third... the fourth jhana. Emerging from the fourth jhana, he entered total Unbinding in the interim...

When the Blessed One had attained total Unbinding, Sakka, ruler of the gods, uttered this stanza:

How inconstant are compounded things!

Their nature: to arise and pass away.

They disband as they are arising.

Their total stilling

is bliss.

— D 16

Dhamma

Basic Principles

Phenomena are preceded by the heart,

ruled by the heart,

made of the heart.

If you speak or act with a corrupted heart,

then suffering follows you —

as the wheel of the cart,

the track of the ox that pulls it.

Phenomena are preceded by the heart,

ruled by the heart,

made of the heart.

If you speak or act with a calm, bright heart,

happiness follows you,

like a shadow that never leaves.

— Dhp 1-2

Heedfulness: the path to the Deathless;

Heedlessness: the path to death.

The heedful do not die;

The heedless are as if already dead.

Knowing this as a true distinction,

those wise in heedfulness rejoice in heedfulness,

enjoying the range of the noble ones.

— Dhp 21-22

There are these five facts that one should reflect on often, whether one is a woman or a man, lay or ordained. Which five?

"I am subject to aging, have not gone beyond aging"...

"I am subject to illness, have not gone beyond illness"...

"I am subject to death, have not gone beyond death"...

"I will grow different, separate from all that is dear and appealing to me"...

"I am the owner of my actions (kamma), heir to my actions, born of my actions, related through my actions, and have my actions as my arbitrator. Whatever I do, for good or for evil, to that will I fall heir"...

These are the five facts that one should reflect on often, whether one is a woman or a man, lay or ordained.

Now, based on what line of reasoning should one often reflect that "I am subject to aging, have not gone beyond aging"? There are beings who are intoxicated with a [typical] youth's intoxication with youth. Because of that intoxication with youth, they conduct themselves in a bad way in body... in speech... and in mind. But when they often reflect on that fact, that youth's intoxication with youth will either be entirely abandoned or grow weaker...

Now, based on what line of reasoning should one often reflect... that "I am subject to illness, have not gone beyond illness"? There are beings who are intoxicated with a [typical] healthy person's intoxication with health. Because of that intoxication with health, they conduct themselves in a bad way in body... in speech... and in mind. But when they often reflect on that fact, that healthy person's intoxication with health will either be entirely abandoned or grow weaker...

Now, based on what line of reasoning should one often reflect... that "I am subject to death, have not gone beyond death"? There are beings who are intoxicated with a [typical] living person's intoxication with life. Because of that intoxication with life, they conduct themselves in a bad way in body... in speech... and in mind. But when they often reflect on that fact, that living person's intoxication with life will either be entirely abandoned or grow weaker...

Now, based on what line of reasoning should one often reflect... that "I will grow different, separate from all that is dear and appealing to me"? There are beings who feel desire and passion for the things they find dear and appealing. Because of that passion, they conduct themselves in a bad way in body... in speech... and in mind. But when they often reflect on that fact, that desire and passion for the things they find dear and appealing will either be entirely abandoned or grow weaker...

Now, based on what line of reasoning should one often reflect... that "I am the owner of my actions (kamma), heir to my actions, born of my actions, related through my actions, and have my actions as my arbitrator. Whatever I do, for good or for evil, to that will I fall heir"? There are beings who conduct themselves in a bad way in body... in speech... and in mind. But when they often reflect on that fact, that bad conduct in body, speech, and mind will either be entirely abandoned or grow weaker...

Now, a noble disciple considers this: "I am not the only one subject to aging, who has not gone beyond aging. To the extent that there are beings — past and future, passing away and re-arising — all beings are subject to aging, have not gone beyond aging." When he/she often reflects on this, the [factors of the] path take birth. He/she sticks with that path, develops it, cultivates it. As he/she sticks with that path, develops it and cultivates it, the fetters are abandoned, the latent tendencies destroyed. (Similarly with each of the other contemplations.) — A V.57

The non-doing of any evil,
the performance of what is skillful,
the cleansing of one's own mind:
This is the Buddhas' teaching.
Not disparaging, not injuring,
restraint in line with the Patimokkha,
moderation in food,
dwelling in seclusion,
commitment to the heightened mind:
This is the Buddhas' teaching.

— *Dhp 183, 185*

I do not see any one quality by which unarisen skillful qualities arise, and arisen unskillful qualities subside, like friendship with admirable people. When a person is friends with admirable people, unarisen skillful qualities arise, and arisen unskillful qualities subside. — A 1.72

Now what, TigerPaw (Byagghapajja), is friendship with admirable people? There is the case where a lay person, in whatever town or village he may dwell, spends time with householders or householders' sons, young or old, who are advanced in virtue. He talks with them, engages them in discussions.

He emulates consummate conviction [in the principle of kamma] in those who are consummate in conviction, consummate virtue in those who are consummate in virtue, consummate generosity in those who are consummate in generosity, and consummate discernment in those who are consummate in discernment. This is called friendship with admirable people. — A VIII.54

A female noble disciple who grows in terms of these five types of growth grows in the noble growth, grasps hold of what is essential, what is excellent in the body. Which five? She grows in terms of conviction, in terms of virtue, in terms of learning, in terms of generosity, in terms of discernment. Growing in terms of these five types of growth, the female noble disciple grows in the noble growth, grasps hold of what is essential, what is excellent in the body.

Growing in conviction and virtue
discernment, generosity, and learning,
a virtuous female lay disciple
such as this
takes hold of the essence within herself.

— *S XXXVII.34*

'Kamma should be known. The cause by which kamma comes into play should be known. The diversity in kamma should be known. The result of kamma should be known. The cessation of kamma should be known. The path of practice for the cessation of kamma should be known.' Thus it has been said. Why was it said?

Intention, I tell you, is kamma. Intending, one does kamma by way of body, speech, and intellect.

And what is the cause by which kamma comes into play? Contact...

And what is the diversity in kamma? There is kamma to be experienced in purgatory, kamma to be experienced in the realm of common animals, kamma to be experienced in the realm of the hungry shades, kamma to be experienced in the human world, kamma to be experienced in the celestial worlds... And what is the result of kamma? The result of kamma is of three sorts, I tell you: that which arises right here and now, that which arises later [in this lifetime], and that which arises following that...

And what is the cessation of kamma? From the cessation of contact is the cessation of kamma...

And what is the way leading to the cessation of kamma? Just this noble eightfold path: right view, right resolve, right speech, right action, right livelihood, right effort, right mindfulness, right concentration.

Now when a noble disciple discerns kamma in this way, the cause by which kamma comes into play in this way, the diversity of kamma in this way, the result of kamma in this way, the cessation of kamma in this way, and the path of practice leading to the cessation of kamma in this way, then he discerns this penetrative holy life as the cessation of kamma. — A VI.63

The Buddha: What do you think, Rahula: What is a mirror for?

Rahula: For reflection, sir.

The Buddha: In the same way, Rahula, bodily acts, verbal acts, and mental acts are to be done with repeated reflection.

Whenever you want to perform a bodily act, you should reflect on it: 'This bodily act I want to perform — would it lead to self-affliction, to the affliction of others, or to both? Is it an unskillful bodily act, with painful consequences, painful results?' If, on reflection, you know that it would lead to self-affliction, to the affliction of others, or to both; it would be an unskillful bodily act with painful consequences, painful results, then any bodily act of that sort is absolutely unfit for you to do. But if on reflection you know that it would not cause affliction... it would be a skillful bodily act with happy consequences, happy results, then any bodily act of that sort is fit for you to do. (Similarly with verbal acts and mental acts.)

While you are performing a bodily act, you should reflect on it: 'This bodily act I am doing — is it leading to self-affliction, to the affliction of others, or to both? Is it an unskillful bodily act, with painful consequences, painful results?' If, on reflection, you know that it is leading to self-affliction, to affliction of others, or both... you should give it up. But if on reflection you know that it is not... you may continue with it. (Similarly with verbal acts and mental acts.)

Having performed a bodily act, you should reflect on it... If, on reflection, you know that it led to self-affliction, to the affliction of others, or to both; it was an unskillful bodily act with painful consequences, painful results, then you should confess it, reveal it, lay it open to the Teacher r to a knowledgeable companion in the holy life. Having confessed it... you should exercise restraint in the future. But if on reflection you know that it did not lead to affliction... it was a skillful bodily act with happy consequences, happy results, then you should stay mentally refreshed and joyful, training day and night in skillful mental qualities (Similarly with verbal acts.)

Having performed a mental act, you should reflect on it... If, on reflection, you know that it led to self-affliction, to the affliction of others, or to both; it was an unskillful mental act with painful consequences, painful results, then you should feel horrified, humiliated, and disgusted with it. Feeling horrified... you should exercise restraint in the future. But if on reflection you know that it did not lead to affliction... it was a skillful mental act with happy consequences, happy results, then you should stay mentally refreshed and joyful, training day and night in skillful mental qualities.

Rahula, all the priests and contemplatives in the course of the past who purified their bodily acts, verbal acts, and mental acts, did it through repeated reflection on their bodily acts, verbal acts, and mental acts in just this way.

All the priests and contemplatives in the course of the future... All the priests and contemplatives at present who purify their bodily acts, verbal acts, and mental acts, do it through repeated reflection on their bodily acts, verbal acts, and mental acts in just this way.

Therefore, Rahula, you should train yourself: 'I will purify my bodily acts through repeated reflection. I will purify my verbal acts through repeated reflection. I will purify my mental acts through repeated reflection.' Thus you should train yourself.

That is what the Blessed One said. Pleased, Ven. Rahula delighted in the Blessed One's words. — M 61

These five things are welcome, agreeable, pleasant, and hard to obtain in the world. Which five? Long life... beauty... pleasure... status... rebirth in heaven... Now, I tell you, these five things are not to be obtained by reason of prayers or wishes. If they were to be obtained by reason of prayers or wishes, who here would lack them? It is not fitting for the noble disciple who desires long life to pray for it or to delight in doing so. Instead, the noble disciple who desires long life should follow the path of practice leading to long life. In so doing, he will attain long life, either human or divine. (Similarly with beauty, pleasure, status, and rebirth in heaven.) — A V.43

I have heard that at one time the Blessed One was staying in Savatthi at Jeta's Grove, Anathapindika's monastery. Then a certain deva, in the far extreme of the night, her extreme radiance lighting up the entirety of Jeta's Grove, approached the Blessed One. On approaching, having bowed down to the Blessed One, she stood to one side. As she was standing there, she addressed him with a verse.

"Many devas and human beings
give thought to protective charms,
desiring well-being.
Tell, then, the highest protective charm."
[The Buddha:]
"Not consorting with fools,
consorting with the wise,
homage to those deserving of homage:
This is the highest protective charm.
Living in a civilized land,
having made merit in the past,
directing oneself rightly:
This is the highest protective charm.
Broad knowledge, skill,
well-mastered discipline,
well-spoken words:
This is the highest protective charm.
Support for one's parents,
assistance to one's wife and children,
consistency in one's work:
This is the highest protective charm.
Giving, living in rectitude,
assistance to one's relatives,
deeds that are blameless:
This is the highest protective charm.

Avoiding, abstaining from evil;
refraining from intoxicants,
being heedful of the qualities of the mind:
This is the highest protective charm.
Respect, humility,
contentment, gratitude,
hearing the Dhamma on timely occasions:
This is the highest protective charm.
Patience, compliance,
seeing contemplatives,
discussing the Dhamma on timely occasions:
This is the highest protective charm.
Austerity, celibacy,
seeing the Noble Truths,
realizing Unbinding:
This is the highest protective charm.
A mind that, when touched
by the ways of the world,
is unshaken, sorrowless, dustless, secure:
This is the highest protective charm.
Everywhere undefeated
when acting in this way,
people go everywhere in well-being:
This is their highest protective charm." — Sn 2.4

Generosity

These are the five rewards of generosity: One is dear and appealing to people at large, one is admired by good people, one's good name is spread about, one does not stray from the rightful duties of the householder, and with the break-up of the body at death, one reappears in a good destination, in the heavenly worlds. — A V.35

What the miser fears,
that keeps him from giving,
is the very danger that comes
when he doesn't give. — S I.32

No misers go
to the world of the devas.
Those who don't praise giving
are fools.
The enlightened
express their approval for giving
and so finds ease
in the world beyond. — Dhp 177

If beings knew, as I know, the results of giving and sharing, they would not eat without having given, nor would the stain of miserliness overcome their minds. Even if it were their last bite, their last mouthful, they would not eat without having shared, if there were someone to receive their gift. But because beings do not know, as I know, the results of giving and sharing, they eat without having given. The stain of miserliness overcomes their minds. — Iti 26

Now on that occasion Princess Sumana — with an entourage of 500 ladies-in-waiting riding on 500 carriages — went to where the Buddha was staying. On arrival, having bowed down, she sat to one side. As she was sitting there, she said to the Blessed One, "Suppose there were two disciples of the Blessed One, equal in conviction, virtue, and discernment, but one was a giver of alms and the other was not. At the break-up of the body, after death, they would reappear in a good destination, in the heavenly world. Having become devas, would there be any distinction, any difference between the two?"

"Yes, there would," said the Blessed One. "The one who was a giver of alms, on becoming a deva, would surpass the other in five areas: in divine life span, divine beauty, divine pleasure, divine status, and divine power..."

"And if they were to fall from there and reappear in this world: Having become human beings, would there be any distinction, any difference between the two?"

"Yes, there would," said the Blessed One. "The one who was a giver of alms, on becoming a human being, would surpass the other in five areas: in human life span, human beauty, human pleasure, human status, and human power..."

"And if they were to go forth from home into the homeless life of a monk: Having gone forth, would there be any distinction, any difference between the two?"

"Yes, there would," said the Blessed One. "The one who was a giver of alms, on going forth, would surpass the other in five areas: He would often be asked to make use of robes; it would be rare that he wouldn't be asked. He would often be asked to take food... to make use of shelter... to make use of medicine; it would be rare that he wouldn't be asked. His companions in the holy life would often treat him with pleasing actions... pleasing words... pleasing thoughts... and present him with pleasing gifts, and rarely with unpleasing..."

"And if both were to attain arahantship, would there be any distinction, any difference between their attainments of arahantship?"

"In that case, I tell you that there would be no difference between the two as to their release."

"It is awesome, lord, and astounding. Just this is reason enough to give alms, to make merit, in that it benefits one as a deva, as a human being, and as a monk." A V.31

Virtue

There are these five gifts, five great gifts — original, long-standing, traditional, ancient, unadulterated, unadulterated from the beginning — are not open to suspicion, will never be open to suspicion, and are unfaulted by knowledgeable contemplatives and priests. Which five?

There is the case where a noble disciple, abandoning the taking of life, abstains from taking life. In doing so, he gives freedom from danger, freedom from animosity, freedom from oppression to limitless numbers of beings. In giving freedom from danger, freedom from animosity, freedom from oppression to limitless numbers of beings, he gains a share in limitless freedom from danger, freedom from animosity, and freedom from oppression...

Abandoning taking what is not given (stealing), he abstains from taking what is not given...

Abandoning illicit sex, he abstains from illicit sex...

Abandoning lying, he abstains from lying...

Abandoning the use of intoxicants, he abstains from taking intoxicants. In doing so, he gives freedom from danger, freedom from animosity, freedom from oppression to limitless numbers of beings. In giving freedom from danger, freedom from animosity, freedom from oppression to limitless numbers of beings, he gains a share in limitless freedom from danger, freedom from animosity, and freedom from oppression... This is the fifth gift, the fifth great gift — original, long-standing, traditional, ancient, unadulterated, unadulterated from the beginning — that is not open to suspicion, will never be open to suspicion, and is unfaulted by knowledgeable contemplatives and priests. — A VIII.39

Cleansing with regard to the body, Cunda, is threefold; cleansing with regard to speech is fourfold; and cleansing with regard to the mind, threefold. And how is cleansing with regard to the body threefold? There is the case where a certain person, abandoning the taking of life, abstains from the taking of life. He dwells with his rod laid down, his knife laid down, scrupulous, merciful, compassionate for the welfare of all living beings. Abandoning the taking of what is not given, he abstains from taking what is not given. He does not take the ungiven property of another, whether in a village or in the wilderness, with thievish intent. Abandoning sensual misconduct, he abstains from sensual misconduct. He does not get sexually involved with those who are protected by their mothers, their fathers, their brothers, their sisters, their relatives, or their Dhamma; those with husbands, those who entail punishments, or even those crowned with flowers by another man. This is how cleansing with regard to the body is threefold.

And how is cleansing with regard to speech fourfold? There is the case where a certain person, abandoning false speech, abstains from false speech. When he has been called to a town meeting, a group meeting, a gathering of his relatives, his guild, or of the royalty [i.e., a court proceeding], if he is asked as a witness, 'Come and tell, good man, what you know': If he doesn't know, he says, 'I don't know.' If he does know, he says, 'I know.' If he hasn't seen, he says, 'I haven't seen.' If he has seen, he says, 'I have seen.' Thus he doesn't consciously tell a lie for his own sake, for the sake of another, or for the sake of any reward. Abandoning divisive speech, he abstains from divisive speech. What he has heard here he does not tell there to break those people apart from these people here.

What he has heard there he does not tell here to break these people apart from those people there. Thus reconciling those who have broken apart or cementing those who are united, he loves concord, delights in concord, enjoys concord, speaks things that create concord. Abandoning abusive speech, he abstains from abusive speech. He speaks words that are soothing to the ear, that are affectionate, that go to the heart, that are polite, appealing & pleasing to people at large. Abandoning idle chatter, he abstains from idle chatter. He speaks in season, speaks what is factual, what is in accordance with the goal, the Dhamma, and the Vinaya. He speaks words worth treasuring, seasonable, reasonable, circumscribed, connected with the goal. This is how cleansing with regard to speech is fourfold.

And how is cleansing with regard to the mind threefold? There is the case where a certain person is not covetous. He does not covet the property of another, thinking, "O, if only what belongs to another were mine!" He is not malevolent at heart or destructive in his resolves. He thinks, "May these beings — free from animosity, free from oppression, and free from trouble — look after themselves with ease." He has right views and an unperverted outlook. He believes, "There is what is given, what is offered, what is sacrificed.

There are fruits and results of good and bad actions. There is this world and the next world. There is mother and father. There are spontaneously reborn beings; there are priests and contemplatives who, living rightly and practicing rightly, proclaim this world and the next after having directly known and realized it for themselves." This is how cleansing with regard to the mind is threefold. — A X.176

There are these five benefits in being virtuous, in being consummate in virtue. Which five? There is the case where a virtuous person, consummate in virtue, through not being heedless in his affairs amasses a great quantity of wealth... His good name is spread about... When approaching an assembly of nobles, priests, householders, or contemplatives, he does so unabashed and with assurance... He dies without becoming delirious... With the break-up of the body, after death, he reappears in a good destination, in the heavenly world. These are the five benefits in being virtuous, in being consummate in virtue. — D 16

This is to be done by one skilled in aims
who wants to break through to the state of peace:
Be capable, upright, and straightforward,
easy to instruct, gentle, and not proud,
content and easy to support,
with few duties, living lightly,
with peaceful faculties, masterful,
modest, and no greed for supporters.
Do not do the slightest thing
that the wise would later censure.
Think: Happy and secure,
may all beings be happy at heart.
Whatever beings there may be,
weak or strong, without exception,
long, large,
middling, short,
subtle, blatant,
seen & unseen,
near & far,
born & seeking birth:
May all beings be happy at heart.
Let no one deceive another
or despise anyone anywhere,
or through anger or irritation

wish for another to suffer.
As a mother would risk her life
to protect her child, her only child,
even so should one cultivate
a limitless heart
with regard to all beings.
With good will for the entire cosmos,
cultivate a limitless heart:
above, below, & all around,
unobstructed, without enmity or hate.
Whether standing, walking,
sitting, or lying down,
as long as one is alert,
one should be resolved on this mindfulness.
This is called a sublime abiding here & now.
Not taken with views,
but virtuous & consummate in vision,
having subdued desire for sensual pleasures,
one never again will lie in the womb. — Sn 1.8

Heaven

Blinded this world —
how few here see clearly!
Just as birds that have escaped from a net are
few, few are the people who make it to heaven.
— Dhp 174

The Buddha: "Suppose that a Universal Monarch possessed the seven treasures [the treasure of a divine wheel, the treasure of an ideal jewel, the treasure of an ideal elephant, the treasure of an ideal horse, the treasure of an ideal wife, the treasure of an ideal steward, and the treasure of an ideal counselor] and the four forms of prowess [he is surpassingly attractive, he has a surpassingly long life, he is surpassingly free from illness, and he loves his subjects and is loved by them]. Now what do you think? Would he... experience pleasure and joy?"

The monks: "Yes, lord."

Then, taking a small stone, the size of his hand, the Blessed One said, "What do you think? Which is larger, this small stone that I have taken, the size of my hand, or the Himalayas, king of mountains?"

"It is minuscule, the small stone... It does not count beside the Himalayas, the king of mountains. It is not even a small fraction. There is no comparison."

"In the same way, the pleasure and joy that the Universal Monarch experiences on account of his seven treasures and four forms of prowess do not count beside the pleasures of heaven. They are not even a small fraction. There is no comparison." — M 129

Drawbacks

Now what is the allure of sensuality? There are, monks, these five strings of sensuality. Which five? Forms cognizable via the eye — agreeable, pleasing, charming, endearing, fostering desire, enticing. Sounds cognizable via the ear... Aromas cognizable via the nose... Flavors cognizable via the tongue... Tactile sensations cognizable via the body — agreeable, pleasing, charming, endearing, fostering desire, enticing. Now whatever pleasure or joy arises in dependence on these five strings of sensuality, that is the allure of sensuality.

And what is the drawback of sensuality? There is the case where, on account of the occupation by which a clansman makes a living — whether checking or accounting or calculating or plowing or trading or cattle tending or archery or as a king's man, or whatever the occupation may be — he faces cold; he faces heat; being harassed by mosquitoes, flies, wind, sun, and creeping things; dying from hunger and thirst.

Now this drawback in the case of sensuality, this mass of stress visible here and now, has sensuality for its reason, sensuality for its source, sensuality for its cause, the reason being simply sensuality.

If the clansman gains no wealth while thus working and striving and making effort, he sorrows, grieves and laments, beats his breast, becomes distraught: 'My work is in vain, my efforts are fruitless!' Now this drawback too in the case of sensuality, this mass of stress visible here and now, has sensuality for its reason...

If the clansman gains wealth while thus working and striving and making effort, he experiences pain and distress in protecting it: 'How shall neither kings nor thieves make off with my property, nor fire burn it, nor water sweep it away nor hateful heirs make off with it?' And as he thus guards and watches over his property, kings or thieves make off with it, or fire burns it, or water sweeps it away, or hateful heirs make off with it. And he sorrows, grieves and laments, beats his breast, becomes distraught: 'What was mine is no more!' Now this drawback too in the case of sensuality, this mass of stress visible here and now, has sensuality for its reason...

Furthermore, it is with sensuality for the reason, sensuality for the source, sensuality for the cause, the reason being simply sensuality, that kings quarrel with kings, nobles with nobles, priests with priests, householders with householders, mother with child, child with mother, father with child, child with father, brother with brother, sister with sister, brother with sister, sister with brother, friend with friend. And then in their quarrels, brawls, and disputes, they attack one another with fists or with clods or with sticks or with knives, so that they incur death or deadly pain. Now this drawback too in the case of sensuality, this mass of stress visible here and now, has sensuality for its reason...

Furthermore, it is with sensuality for the reason, sensuality for the source... that (men), taking swords and shields and buckling on bows and quivers, charge into battle massed in double array while arrows and spears are flying and swords are flashing; and there they are wounded by arrows and spears, and their heads are cut off by swords, so that they incur death or deadly pain. Now this drawback too in the case of sensuality, this mass of stress visible here and now, has sensuality for its reason...

Furthermore, it is with sensuality for the reason, sensuality for the source... that (men), taking swords and shields and buckling on bows and quivers, charge slippery bastions while arrows and spears are flying and swords are flashing; and there they are splashed with boiling cow dung and crushed under heavy weights, and their heads are cut off by swords, so that they incur death or deadly pain. Now this drawback too in the case of sensuality, this mass of stress visible here and now, has sensuality for its reason, sensuality for its source, sensuality for its cause, the reason being simply sensuality.

And what is the emancipation from sensuality? Whatever is the subduing of passion and desire, the abandoning of passion and desire for sensuality, that is the emancipation from sensuality. — M 13

Which do you think is greater: the tears you have shed while transmigrating and wandering this long time — crying and weeping from being joined with what is displeasing, from being separated from what is pleasing — or the water in the four great oceans?... This is the greater: The tears you have shed... Why is that? From an inconceivable beginning comes transmigration. A beginning point is not evident, although beings hindered by ignorance and fettered by craving are transmigrating and wandering on. Long have you thus experienced stress, experienced pain, experienced loss, swelling the cemeteries — long enough to become disenchanted with all conditioned things, enough to become dispassionate, enough to be released. — S XV.3

Renunciation

Janussonin: I hold that there is no one who, subject to death, is not afraid or in terror of death.

The Buddha: There are those who, subject to death, are afraid and in terror of death. And there are those who, subject to death, are not afraid or in terror of death.

And who is the person who, subject to death, is afraid and in terror of death? There is the case of the person who has not abandoned passion, desire, fondness, thirst, fever, and craving for sensuality. When he comes down with a serious disease, the thought occurs to him, "O, those beloved sensual pleasures will be taken from me, and I will be taken from them!" He grieves and is tormented, weeps, beats his breast, and grows delirious...

Furthermore, there is the case of the person who has not abandoned passion, desire, fondness, thirst, fever, and craving for the body. When he is touched by a serious disease, the thought occurs to him, "O, my beloved body will be taken from me, and I will be taken from my body!" He grieves and is tormented, weeps, beats his breast, and grows delirious...

Furthermore, there is the case of the person who has not done what is good, has not done what is skillful, has not given protection to those in fear, and instead has done what is evil, savage, and cruel. When he comes down with a serious disease, the thought occurs to him, "...After death I am headed for the destination of those who have done what is evil, savage, and cruel." He grieves and is tormented, weeps, beats his breast, and grows delirious...

Furthermore, there is the case of the person in doubt and perplexity, who has not arrived at certainty with regard to the True Dhamma. When he comes down with a serious disease, the thought occurs to him, "How doubtful and perplexed I am! I have not arrived at any certainty with regard to the True Dhamma!" He grieves and is tormented, weeps, beats his breast, and grows delirious. This is another person who, subject to death, is afraid and in terror of death.

And who is the person who is not afraid or in terror of death? There is the case of the person who has abandoned passion, desire, fondness, thirst, fever, and craving for sensuality... who has abandoned passion, desire, fondness, thirst, fever, and craving for the body... who has done what is good, what is skillful, has given protection to those in fear, and has not done what is evil, savage, or cruel... who has no doubt or perplexity, who has arrived at certainty with regard to the True Dhamma. When he comes down with a serious disease... he does not grieve, is not tormented, does not weep or beat his breast or grow delirious. This is another person who, subject to death, is not afraid or in terror of death. — A IV.184

Now at that time, Ven. Bhaddiya Kaligodha, on going to a forest, to the foot of a tree, or to an empty dwelling, would repeatedly exclaim, "What bliss! What bliss!" Many monks heard him... repeatedly exclaim, "What bliss! What bliss!" and on hearing him, the thought occurred to them, "There's no doubt but that Ven. Bhaddiya Kaligodha is not enjoying the holy life, for when he was a householder he enjoyed royal pleasures, so that now, on recollecting them, he is exclaiming, "What bliss! What bliss!" They went to the Blessed One... and told him... and he told a certain monk, "Come, monk. In my name, call Bhaddiya, saying, "The Teacher calls you, my friend."

"Yes, lord," the monk answered...

Then Ven. Bhaddiya went to where the Blessed One was staying and, on arrival, having bowed down, sat to one side. As he was sitting there, the Blessed One said to him, "Is it true, Bhaddiya that, on going to a forest, to the foot of a tree, or to an empty dwelling, you repeatedly exclaim, "What bliss! What bliss!"

"Yes, lord."

"What do you have in mind that you repeatedly exclaim, "What bliss! What bliss!"

"Before, when I was a householder, maintaining my reign, I had guards posted within and without the royal apartments, within and without the city, within and without the countryside. But even though I was thus guarded, thus protected, I dwelled in fear — agitated, distrustful, and afraid. But now, on going alone to a forest, to the foot of a tree, or to an empty dwelling, I dwell without fear, unagitated, confident, and unafraid — unconcerned, unruffled, my wants satisfied, with my mind like a wild deer. This is what I have in mind that I repeatedly exclaim, "What bliss! What bliss!" — Ud 2.10

The Four Noble Truths

Now this, monks, is the noble truth of stress: Birth is stressful, aging is stressful, death is stressful; sorrow, lamentation, pain, distress, and despair are stressful; association with the unbeloved is stressful, separation from the loved is stressful, not getting what is wanted is stressful. In short, the five aggregates for sustenance are stressful.

And this, monks, is the noble truth of the origination of stress: the craving that makes for further becoming — accompanied by passion and delight, relishing now here and now there — i.e., craving for sensual pleasure, craving for becoming, craving for non-becoming.

And this, monks, is the noble truth of the cessation of stress: the remainderless fading and cessation, renunciation, relinquishment, release and letting go of that very craving.

And this, monks, is the noble truth of the way leading to the cessation of stress: precisely this Noble Eightfold Path — right view, right intention, right speech, right action, right livelihood, right effort, right mindfulness, right concentration.

Vision arose, insight arose, discernment arose, knowledge arose, illumination arose within me with regard to things never heard before: 'This is the noble truth of stress'...'This noble truth of stress is to be comprehended'...'This noble truth of stress has been comprehended'...

'This is the noble truth of the origination of stress'...'This noble truth of the origination of stress is to be abandoned'...'This noble truth of the origination of stress has been abandoned'...

'This is the noble truth of the cessation of stress'...'This noble truth of the cessation of stress is to be directly experienced'...'This noble truth of the cessation of stress has been directly experienced'...

'This is the noble truth of the way leading to the cessation of stress'...'This noble truth of the way leading to the cessation of stress is to be developed'...'This noble truth of the way leading to the cessation of stress has been developed.'

And, monks, as long as this knowledge and vision of mine — with its three rounds and twelve permutations concerning these four noble truths as they actually are — was not pure, I did not claim to have directly awakened to the unexcelled right self-awakening... But as soon as this knowledge and vision of mine — with its three rounds and twelve permutations concerning these four noble truths as they actually are — *was* truly pure, then did I claim to have directly awakened to the unexcelled right self-awakening... The knowledge and vision arose in me: 'Unshakable is my release. This is the last birth. There is now no further becoming.' — S LVI.11

The First Truth

I have heard that on one occasion the Blessed One was staying at Varanasi, in the Game Refuge at Isipatana. There he addressed the group of five monks:

'Physical form, monks, is not the self. If physical form were the self, this physical form (body) would not lend itself to dis-ease. One could get physical form to be like this and not be like that. But precisely because physical form is not the self, it lends itself to dis-ease. And one cannot get physical form to be like this and not be like that.

'Feeling is not the self... Perception is not the self... Mental fabrications are not the self...

'Consciousness is not the self. If consciousness were the self, this consciousness would not lend itself to dis-ease. One could get consciousness to be like this and not be like that. But precisely because consciousness is not the self, it lends itself to dis-ease. And one cannot get consciousness to be like this and not be like that.

'What do you think, monks — Is physical form constant or inconstant?' — 'Inconstant, Lord.' — 'And whatever is inconstant: Is it easeful or stressful?' — 'Stressful, Lord.' —

'And is it right to assume with regard to whatever is inconstant, stressful, subject to change, that "This is mine. This is my self. This is what I am"?' — 'No, Lord.'

'...Is feeling constant or inconstant?... Is perception constant or inconstant?... Are mental fabrications constant or inconstant?...

'Is consciousness constant or inconstant?' — 'Inconstant, Lord.' — 'And whatever is inconstant: Is it easeful or stressful?' — 'Stressful, Lord.' — 'And is it right to assume with regard to whatever is inconstant, stressful, subject to change, that "This is mine. This is my self. This is what I am"?' — 'No, Lord.'

'Thus, monks, any physical form whatsoever — past, future, or present; internal or external; blatant or subtle, common or sublime, far or near: every physical form — is to be seen as it actually is with right discernment as: "This is not mine. This is not my self. This is not what I am."

'Any feeling whatsoever... Any perception whatsoever... Any mental fabrications whatsoever...

'Any consciousness whatsoever — past, future, or present; internal or external; blatant or subtle, common or sublime, far or near: every consciousness — is to be seen as it actually is with right discernment as: "This is not mine. This is not my self. This is not what I am."

'Seeing thus, the instructed noble disciple grows disenchanted with the body, disenchanted with feeling, disenchanted with perception, disenchanted with mental processes, and disenchanted with consciousness. Disenchanted, he grows dispassionate. Through dispassion, he is released. With release, there is the knowledge, "Released." He discerns that "Birth is ended, the holy life fulfilled, the task done. There is nothing further for this world."'

That is what the Blessed One said. Glad at heart, the group of five monks delighted at his words. And while this explanation was being given, the hearts of the group of five monks, through not clinging (not being sustained), were released from the mental fermentations. — S XXII.59

The Second and Third Truths

If this sticky, uncouth craving
overcomes you in the world,
your sorrows grow like wild grass
after rain.
If, in the world, you overcome
this sticky, uncouth craving,
sorrows roll off you,
like water beads
off a lotus.
— Dhp 335-336

If its root remains
undamaged and strong,
a tree, even if cut,
will grow back.
So too if latent craving
is not rooted out,
this suffering returns
again
&
again. — Dhp 338

And what is the noble method that is rightly seen and rightly ferreted out by discernment? There is the case where a noble disciple notices:

When this is, that is.

From the arising of this comes the arising of that.

When this isn't, that isn't.

From the cessation of this comes the cessation of that.

In other words:

From ignorance as a requisite condition come fabrications.

From fabrications as a requisite condition comes consciousness.

From consciousness as a requisite condition comes name-and-form.

From name-and-form as a requisite condition come the six sense media.

From the six sense media as a requisite condition comes contact.

From contact as a requisite condition comes feeling.

From feeling as a requisite condition comes craving.

From craving as a requisite condition comes clinging/sustenance.

From clinging/sustenance as a requisite condition comes becoming.

From becoming as a requisite condition comes birth.

From birth as a requisite condition, then old age and death, sorrow, lamentation, pain, distress, and despair come into play. Such is the origination of this entire mass of stress and suffering.

Now from the remainderless fading and cessation of that very ignorance comes the cessation of fabrications. From the cessation of fabrications comes the cessation of consciousness. From the cessation of consciousness comes the cessation of name-and-form. From the cessation of name-and-form comes the cessation of the six sense media. From the cessation of the six sense media comes the cessation of contact. From the cessation of contact comes the cessation of feeling. From the cessation of feeling comes the cessation of craving. From the cessation of craving comes the cessation of clinging/sustenance.

From the cessation of clinging/sustenance comes the cessation of becoming. From the cessation of becoming comes the cessation of birth. From the cessation of birth, then old age and death, sorrow, lamentation, pain, distress, and despair all cease. Such is the cessation of this entire mass of stress and suffering.

This is the noble method that is rightly seen and rightly ferreted out by discernment. — A X.92

Stress and suffering have birth as their prerequisite,

conviction has stress and suffering as its prerequisite,

joy has conviction as its prerequisite,

rapture has joy as its prerequisite,

serenity has rapture as its prerequisite,

pleasure has serenity as its prerequisite,

concentration has pleasure as its prerequisite,

knowledge and vision of things as they actually are present has concentration as its prerequisite,

disenchantment has knowledge and vision of things as they actually are present as its prerequisite,

dispassion has disenchantment as its prerequisite,

release has dispassion as its prerequisite,

knowledge of ending has release as its prerequisite.

— S XII.23

The Fourth Truth

Monks, what is the noble eightfold path? Right view, right resolve, right speech, right action, right livelihood, right effort, right mindfulness, right concentration.

And what is right view? Knowledge with regard to stress, knowledge with regard to the origination of stress, knowledge with regard to the cessation of stress, knowledge with regard to the way of practice leading to the cessation of stress: This is called right view.

And what is right resolve? Being resolved on renunciation, on freedom from ill will, on harmlessness: This is called right resolve.

And what is right speech? Abstaining from lying, from divisive speech, from abusive speech, and from idle chatter: This is called right speech.

And what is right action? Abstaining from taking life, from stealing, and from unchastity. This is called right action.

And what is right livelihood? There is the case where a noble disciple, having abandoned dishonest livelihood, keeps his life going with right livelihood: This is called right livelihood.

And what is right effort? There is the case where a monk generates desire, endeavors, arouses persistence, upholds and exerts his intent for the sake of the non-arising of evil, unskillful qualities that have not yet arisen... for the sake of the abandoning of evil, unskillful qualities that have arisen... for the sake of the arising of skillful qualities that have not yet arisen...(and) for the maintenance, non-confusion, increase, plenitude, development, and culmination of skillful qualities that have arisen: This is called right effort. And what is right mindfulness? There is the case where a monk remains focused on the body in and of itself—

ardent, alert, and mindful — putting aside greed and distress with reference to the world. He remains focused on feelings in and of themselves... the mind in and of itself... mental qualities in and of themselves — ardent, alert, and mindful— putting aside greed and distress with reference to the world. This is called right mindfulness.

And what is right concentration? There is the case where a monk... enters and remains in the first jhana... the second jhana... the third jhana... the fourth jhana: purity of equanimity and mindfulness, neither pleasure nor pain. This is called right concentration. — S XLV.8

Right View

Then Anathapindika the householder went to where the wanderers of other persuasions were staying. On arrival he greeted them courteously. After an exchange of friendly greetings and courtesies, he sat to one side. As he was sitting there, the wanderers said to him, 'Tell us, householder, what views the contemplative Gotama has.'

'Venerable sirs, I don't know entirely what views the Blessed One has.'

'Well, well. So you don't know entirely what views the contemplative Gotama has. Then tell us what views the monks have.'

'I don't even know entirely what views the monks have.'

'So you don't know entirely what views the contemplative Gotama has or even that the monks have. Then tell us what views you have.'

'It wouldn't be difficult for me to expound to you what views I have. But please let the venerable ones expound each in line with his position, and then it won't be difficult for me to expound to you what views I have.'

When this had been said, one of the wanderers said to Anathapindika the householder, '*The cosmos is eternal.* Only this is true; anything otherwise is worthless. This is the sort of view I have.'

Another wanderer said to Anathapindika, '*The cosmos is not eternal.* Only this is true; anything otherwise is worthless. This is the sort of view I have.'

Another wanderer said, '*The cosmos is finite...'...'The cosmos is infinite...'...'The soul and the body are the same...'...'The soul is one thing and the body another...'...'After death a Tathagata exists...'...'After death a Tathagata does not exist...'...'After death a Tathagata both does and does not exist...'...'After death a Tathagata neither does nor does not exist.* Only this is true; anything otherwise is worthless. This is the sort of view I have.'

When this had been said, Anathapindika the householder said to the wanderers, 'As for the venerable one who says, "*The cosmos is eternal.* Only this is true; anything otherwise is worthless. This is the sort of view I have," his view arises from his own inappropriate attention or in dependence on the words of another. Now this view has been brought into being, is fabricated, willed, dependently originated. Whatever has been brought into being, is fabricated, willed, dependently originated, that is inconstant. Whatever is inconstant is stress. This venerable one thus adheres to that very stress, submits himself to that very stress.' (Similarly for the other positions.)

When this had been said, the wanderers said to Anathapindika the householder, 'We have each and every one expounded to you in line with our own positions. Now tell us what views you have.'

'Whatever has been brought into being, is fabricated, willed, dependently originated, that is inconstant. Whatever is inconstant is stress. Whatever is stress is not me, is not what I am, is not my self. This is the sort of view I have.'

'So, householder, whatever has been brought into being, is fabricated, willed, dependently originated, that is inconstant. Whatever is inconstant is stress. You thus adhere to that very stress, submit yourself to that very stress.'

'Venerable sirs, whatever has been brought into being, is fabricated, willed, dependently originated, that is inconstant. Whatever is inconstant is stress. Whatever is stress is not me, is not what I am, is not my self. Having seen this well with right discernment as it actually is present, I also discern the higher escape from it as it actually is present.'

When this had been said, the wanderers fell silent, abashed, sitting with their shoulders drooping, their heads down, brooding, at a loss for words. Anathapindika the householder, perceiving that the wanderers were silent, abashed... at a loss for words, got up and left. — A X.93

There is the case where an uninstructed, run-of-the-mill person... does not discern what ideas are fit for attention, or what ideas are unfit for attention. This being so, he does not attend to ideas fit for attention, and attends instead to ideas unfit for attention... This is how he attends inappropriately: 'Was I in the past? Was I not in the past? What was I in the past? How was I in the past? Having been what, what was I in the past? Shall I be in the future? Shall I not be in the future? What shall I be in the future? How shall I be in the future? Having been what, what shall I be in the future?' Or else he is inwardly perplexed about the immediate present: 'Am I? Am I not? What am I? How am I? Where has this being come from? Where is it bound?'

As this person attends inappropriately in this way, one of six kinds of view arises in him: The view *I have a self* arises in him as true and established, or the view *I have no self...* or the view *It is by means of self that I perceive self...* or the view *It is by means of self that I perceive not-*

self... or the view *It is by means of not-self that I perceive self* arises in him as true and established, or else he has a view like this: *This very self of mine — the knower that is sensitive here and there to the ripening of good and bad actions — is the self of mine that is constant, everlasting, eternal, not subject to change, and will endure as long as eternity.*

This is called a thicket of views, a wilderness of views, a contortion of views, a writhing of views, a fetter of views. Bound by a fetter of views, the uninstructed run-of-the-mill person is not freed from birth, aging, and death, from sorrow, lamentation, pain, distress, and despair. He is not freed from stress, I say.

The well-taught noble disciple... discerns what ideas are fit for attention, and what ideas are unfit for attention. This being so, he does not attend to ideas unfit for attention, and attends instead to ideas fit for attention... He attends appropriately, *This is stress... This is the origin of stress... This is the cessation of stress... This is the way leading to the cessation of stress.* As he attends appropriately in this way, three fetters are abandoned in him: identity-view, doubt, and grasping at precepts and practices. — M 2

Kaccayana: 'Lord, "Right view, right view," it is said. To what extent is there right view?'

The Buddha: 'By and large, Kaccayana, this cosmos is supported by (takes as its object) a polarity, that of existence and non-existence. But when one sees the origination of the cosmos as it actually is with right discernment, "non-existence" with reference to the cosmos does not occur to one. When one sees the cessation of the cosmos as it actually is with right discernment, "existence" with reference to the cosmos does not occur to one.

'By and large, Kaccayana, this cosmos is in bondage to attachments, clingings (sustenances), and biases. But one such as this does not get involved with or cling to these attachments, clingings, fixations of awareness, biases, and latent tendencies; nor is he resolved on "my self." He has no uncertainty or doubt that, when there is arising, only stress is arising; and that when there is passing away, stress is passing away. In this, one's knowledge is independent of others. It is to this extent, Kaccayana, that there is right view.' — S XII.15

Right Mindfulness & Concentration

Visakha: Now what is concentration, what qualities are its themes, what qualities are its requisites, and what is its development?

Sister Dhammadinna: Singleness of mind is concentration; the four frames of reference [= the objects of right mindfulness] are its themes; the four right exertions [= right effort] are its requisites; and any cultivation, development, and pursuit of these qualities is its development. — M 44

Mindfulness of in-and-out breathing, when developed and pursued, brings the four frames of reference to their culmination. The four frames of reference, when developed and pursued, bring the seven factors for Awakening to their culmination. The seven factors for Awakening, when developed and pursued, bring clear knowing and release to their culmination.

Now how is mindfulness of in-and-out breathing developed and pursuedso as to bring the four frames of reference to their culmination?

There is the case where a monk, having gone to the wilderness, to the shade of a tree, or to an empty building, sits down folding his legs crosswise, holding his body erect, and setting mindfulness to the fore. Always mindful, he breathes in; mindful he breathes out.

(1) Breathing in long, he discerns that he is breathing in long; or breathing out long, he discerns that he is breathing out long.

(2) Or breathing in short, he discerns that he is breathing in short; or breathing out short, he discerns that he is breathing out short.

(3) He trains himself to breathe in sensitive to the entire body, and to breathe out sensitive to the entire body.

(4) He trains himself to breathe in calming bodily fabrication, and to breathe out calming bodily fabrication.

(5) He trains himself to breathe in sensitive to rapture, and to breathe out sensitive to rapture.

(6) He trains himself to breathe in sensitive to pleasure, and to breathe out sensitive to pleasure.

(7) He trains himself to breathe in sensitive to mental fabrication, and to breathe out sensitive to mental fabrication.

(8) He trains himself to breathe in calming mental fabrication, and to breathe out calming mental fabrication.

(9) He trains himself to breathe in sensitive to the mind, and to breathe out sensitive to the mind.

(10) He trains himself to breathe in satisfying the mind, and to breathe out satisfying the mind.

(11) He trains himself to breathe in steadying the mind, and to breathe out steadying the mind.

(12) He trains himself to breathe in releasing the mind, and to breathe out releasing the mind.

(13) He trains himself to breathe in focusing on inconstancy, and to breathe out focusing on inconstancy.

(14) He trains himself to breathe in focusing on dispassion (*literally,* fading), and to breathe out focusing on dispassion.

(15) He trains himself to breathe in focusing on cessation, and to breathe out focusing on cessation.

(16) He trains himself to breathe in focusing on relinquishment, and to breathe out focusing on relinquishment.

Now, on whatever occasion a monk breathing in long discerns that he is breathing in long; or breathing out long, discerns that he is breathing out long; or breathing in short, discerns that he is breathing in short; or breathing out short, discerns that he is breathing out short; trains himself to breathe in... and... out sensitive to the entire body; trains himself to breathe in... and... out calming bodily fabrication: On that occasion the monk remains focused on the *body* in and of itself — ardent, alert, and mindful — putting aside greed and distress with reference to the world. I tell you, monks, that this — the in-and-out breath — is classed as a body among bodies, which is why the monk on that occasion remains focused on the body in and of itself — ardent, alert, and mindful — putting aside greed and distress with reference to the world.

On whatever occasion a monk trains himself to breathe in... and... out sensitive to rapture; trains himself to breathe in... and... out sensitive to pleasure; trains himself to breathe in... and... out sensitive to mental fabrication; trains himself to breathe in... and... out calming mental fabrication: On that occasion the monk remains focused on *feelings* in and of themselves — ardent, alert, and mindful — putting aside greed and distress with reference to the world. I tell you, monks, that this — close attention to in-and-out breaths — is classed as a feeling among feelings, which is why the monk on that occasion remains focused on feelings in and of themselves — ardent, alert, and mindful — putting aside greed and distress with reference to the world.

On whatever occasion a monk trains himself to breathe in... and... out sensitive to the mind; trains himself to breathe in... and... out satisfying the mind; trains himself to breathe in... and... out steadying the mind; trains himself to breathe in... and... out releasing the mind: On that occasion the monk remains focused on the *mind* in and of itself — ardent, alert, and mindful — putting aside greed and distress with reference to the world. I don't say that there is mindfulness of in-and-out breathing in one of confused mindfulness and no alertness, which is why the monk on that occasion remains focused on the mind in and of itself — ardent, alert, and mindful — putting aside greed and distress with reference to the world.

On whatever occasion a monk trains himself to breathe in... and... out focusing on inconstancy; trains himself to breathe in... and... out focusing on dispassion; trains himself to breathe in... and... out focusing on cessation; trains himself to breathe in... and... out focusing on relinquishment: On that occasion the monk remains focused on *mental qualities* in and of themselves — ardent, alert, and mindful — putting aside greed and distress with reference to the world. He who sees clearly with discernment the abandoning of greed and distress is one who oversees with equanimity, which is why the monk on that occasion remains focused on mental qualities in and of themselves — ardent, alert, and mindful— putting aside greed and distress with reference to the world.

This is how mindfulness of in-and-out breathing is developed and pursued so as to bring the four frames of reference to their culmination.

And how are the four frames of reference developed and pursued so as to bring the seven factors for Awakening to their culmination?

(1) On whatever occasion the monk remains focused on the *body* in and of itself — ardent, alert, and mindful— putting aside greed and distress with reference to the world, on that occasion his mindfulness is steady and without lapse. When his mindfulness is steady and without lapse, then *mindfulness* as a factor for Awakening becomes aroused. He develops it, and for him it goes to the culmination of its development.

(2) Remaining mindful in this way, he examines, analyzes, and comes to a comprehension of that quality with discernment. When he remains mindful in this way, examining, analyzing, and coming to a comprehension of that quality with discernment, then *analysis of qualities* as a factor for Awakening becomes aroused. He develops it, and for him it goes to the culmination of its development.

(3) In one who examines, analyzes, and comes to a comprehension of that quality with discernment, unflagging persistence is aroused. When unflagging persistence is aroused in one who examines, analyzes, and comes to a comprehension of that quality with discernment, then *persistence* as a factor for Awakening becomes aroused. He develops it, and for him it goes to the culmination of its development.

(4) In one whose persistence is aroused, a rapture not-of-the-flesh arises. When a rapture not-of-the-flesh arises in one whose persistence is aroused, then *rapture* as a factor for Awakening becomes aroused. He develops it, and for him it goes to the culmination of its development.

(5) For one who is enraptured, the body grows calm and the mind grows calm. When the body and mind of an enraptured monk grow calm, then *serenity* as a factor for Awakening becomes aroused. He develops

it, and for him it goes to the culmination of its development.

(6) For one who is at ease — his body calmed — the mind becomes concentrated. When the mind of one who is at ease — his body calmed — becomes concentrated, then *concentration* as a factor for Awakening becomes aroused. He develops it, and for him it goes to the culmination of its development.

(7) He oversees the mind thus concentrated with equanimity. When he oversees the mind thus concentrated with equanimity, *equanimity* as a factor for Awakening becomes aroused. He develops it, and for him it goes to the culmination of its development.

(Similarly with the other three frames of reference: feelings, mind, and mental qualities.)

This is how the four frames of reference are developed and pursued so as to bring the seven factors for Awakening to their culmination.

And how are the seven factors for Awakening developed and pursued so as to bring clear knowing and release to their culmination? There is the case where a monk develops *mindfulness* as a factor for Awakening dependent on seclusion... dispassion... cessation, resulting in relinquishment. He develops *analysis of qualities* as a factor for Awakening...*persistence* as a factor for Awakening...*rapture* as a factor for Awakening...*serenity* as a factor for Awakening... *concentration* as a factor for Awakening... *equanimity* as a factor for Awakening dependent on seclusion... dispassion... cessation, resulting in relinquishment.

This is how the seven factors for Awakening are developed and pursued so as to bring clear knowing and release to their culmination. — M 118

[On attaining the fourth level of jhana] there remains only equanimity: pure and bright, pliant, malleable and luminous. Just as if a skilled goldsmith or goldsmith's apprentice were to prepare a furnace, heat up a crucible, and, taking gold with a pair of tongs, place it in the crucible. He would blow on it periodically, sprinkle water on it periodically, examine it periodically, so that the gold would become refined, well-refined, thoroughly refined, flawless, free from dross, pliant, malleable and luminous.

Then whatever sort of ornament he had in mind — whether a belt, an earring, a necklace, or a gold chain — it would serve his purpose. In the same way, there remains only equanimity: pure and bright, pliant, malleable, and luminous. He (the meditator) discerns that 'If I were to direct equanimity as pure and bright as this toward the dimension of the infinitude of space, I would develop the mind along those lines, and thus this equanimity of mine— thus supported, thus sustained — would last for a long time. (Similarly with the dimensions of the infinitude of consciousness, nothingness, and neither perception nor non-perception.)'

He discerns that 'If I were to direct equanimity as pure and bright as this toward the dimension of the infinitude of space and to develop the mind along those lines, that would be fabricated. (Similarly with the dimensions of the infinitude of consciousness, nothingness, and neither perception nor non-perception.)'

He neither fabricates nor wills for the sake of becoming or un-becoming. This being the case, he is not sustained by anything in the world (does not cling to anything in the world). Unsustained, he is not agitated. Unagitated, he is totally unbound right within. He discerns that 'Birth is ended, the holy life fulfilled, the task done. There is nothing further for this world.' — M 140

Liberation

There is that dimension where there is neither earth, nor water, nor fire, nor wind; neither dimension of the infinitude of space, nor dimension of the infinitude of consciousness, nor dimension of nothingness, nor dimension of neither perception nor non-perception; neither this world, nor the next world, nor sun, nor moon. And there, I say, there is neither coming, nor going, nor stasis; neither passing away nor arising: without stance, without foundation, without support (mental object). This, just this, is the end of stress. — Ud 8.1

Where water, earth, fire, and wind have no footing:

There the stars do not shine,

the sun is not visible,

the moon does not appear,

darkness is not found.

And when a sage, a worthy one, through sagacity

has known (this) for himself,

then from form and formless,

from pleasure and pain,

he is freed. — Ud 1.10

Aggivessana Vacchagotta: 'But, Venerable Gotama the monk whose mind is thus released: Where does he reappear?'

Buddha: '"Reappear," Vaccha, doesn't apply.'

'In that case, Venerable Gotama, he does not reappear.'

'"Does not reappear," Vaccha, doesn't apply.'

'...both does and does not reappear.'

'...doesn't apply.'

'...Neither does nor does not reappear.'

'...doesn't apply.'...

'At this point, Venerable Gotama, I am befuddled; at this point, confused. The modicum of clarity coming to me from your earlier conversation is now obscured.'

'Of course you're befuddled, Vaccha. Of course you're confused. Deep, Vaccha, is this phenomenon, hard to see, hard to realize, tranquil, refined, beyond the scope of conjecture, subtle, to-be-experienced by the wise. For those with other views, other satisfactions, other aims, other teachers, it is difficult to know. That being the case, I will now put some questions to you. Answer as you see fit. What do you think, Vaccha: If a fire were burning in front of you, would you know that, "This fire is burning in front of me"?'

'...yes...'

'And suppose someone were to ask you, Vaccha, "This fire burning in front of you, dependent on what is it burning?" Thus asked, how would you reply?'

'...I would reply, "This fire burning in front of me is burning dependent on grass and timber as its sustenance."'

'If the fire burning in front of you were to go out, would you know that, "This fire burning in front of me has gone out"?'

'...yes...'

'And suppose someone were to ask you, "This fire that has gone out in front of you, in which direction from here has it gone? East? West? North? Or south?" Thus asked, how would you reply?'

'That doesn't apply, Venerable Gotama. Any fire burning dependent on a sustenance of grass and timber, being unnourished — from having consumed that sustenance and not being offered any other — is classified simply as "out."'

'Even so, Vaccha, any physical form by which one describing the Tathagata would describe him: That the

Tathagata has abandoned, its root destroyed, like an uprooted palm tree, deprived of the conditions of existence, not destined for future arising. Freed from the classification of form, Vaccha, the Tathagata is deep, boundless, hard-to-fathom, like the sea. "Reappears" does not apply. "Does not reappear" does not apply. "Both does and does not reappear" does not apply. "Neither reappears nor does not reappear" does not apply.

'Any feeling... Any perception... Any mental fabrication...

'Any [act of] consciousness by which one describing the Tathagata would describe him: That the Tathagata has abandoned... Freed from the classification of consciousness, Vaccha, the Tathagata is deep, boundless, hard-to-fathom, like the sea.' — M 72

Sangha

The Rewards of the Contemplative Life

There is the case where a Tathagata appears in the world, worthy and rightly self-awakened. He teaches the Dhamma admirable in its beginning, admirable in its middle, admirable in its end. He proclaims the holy life both in its particulars and in its essence, entirely perfect, surpassingly pure.

A householder or householder's son, hearing the Dhamma, gains conviction in the Tathagata and reflects: 'Household life is confining, a dusty path. The life gone forth is like the open air. It is not easy living at home to practice the holy life totally perfect, totally pure, like a polished shell. Suppose I were to go forth?'

So after some time he abandons his mass of wealth, large or small; leaves his circle of relatives, large or small; shaves off his hair and beard, puts on the saffron robes, and goes forth from the household life into homelessness.

When he has thus gone forth, he lives restrained by the rules of the monastic code, seeing danger in the slightest faults. Consummate in his virtue, he guards the doors of his senses, is possessed of mindfulness and presence of mind, and is content...

Now, how does a monk guard the doors of his senses? On seeing a form with the eye, he does not grasp at any theme or variations by which — if he were to dwell without restraint over the faculty of the eye — evil, unskillful qualities such as greed or distress might assail him. (Similarly with the ear, nose, tongue, body, and intellect.)

And how is a monk possessed of mindfulness and alertness? When going forward and returning, he acts with alertness. When looking toward and looking away... when bending and extending his limbs... when carrying his outer cloak, his upper robe, and his bowl... when eating, drinking, chewing, and tasting... when urinating and defecating... when walking, standing, sitting, falling asleep, waking up, talking, and remaining silent, he acts with alertness.

And how is a monk content? Just as a bird, wherever it goes, flies with its wings as its only burden; so too is he content with a set of robes to provide for his body and alms food to provide for his hunger. Wherever he goes, he takes only his barest necessities along.

He seeks out a secluded dwelling: a forest, the shade of a tree, a mountain, a glen, a hillside cave, a charnel ground, a jungle grove, the open air, a heap of straw. After his meal, returning from his alms round, he sits down, crosses his legs, holds his body erect, and brings mindfulness to the fore. He purifies his mind from greed, ill will, sloth and torpor, restlessness and anxiety, and uncertainty. As long as these five hindrances are not abandoned within him, he regards it as a debt, a sickness, a prison, slavery, a road through desolate country. But when these five hindrances are abandoned within him, he regards it as unindebtedness, good health, release from prison, freedom, a place of security. Seeing that they have been abandoned within him, he becomes glad, enraptured, tranquil, sensitive to pleasure. Feeling pleasure, his mind becomes concentrated.

Quite withdrawn from sensuality, withdrawn from unskillful mental qualities, he enters and remains in the first jhana: rapture and pleasure born from withdrawal, accompanied by directed thought and evaluation. He permeates and pervades, suffuses and fills this very body with the rapture and pleasure born from withdrawal. Just as if a skilled bathman or bathman's apprentice would pour bath powder into a brass basin and knead it together, sprinkling it again and again with water, so that his ball of bath powder — saturated, moisture-laden, permeated within and without — would nevertheless not drip; even so, the monk permeates... this very body with the rapture and pleasure born of withdrawal. There is nothing of his entire body unpervaded by rapture and pleasure born from withdrawal. This is a reward of the contemplative life, visible here and now, more excellent than the previous ones and more sublime.

Furthermore, with the stilling of directed thoughts & evaluations, he enters and remains in the second jhana: rapture and pleasure born of composure, unification of awareness free from directed thought and evaluation — internal assurance. He permeates and pervades, suffuses and fills this very body with the rapture and pleasure born of composure.

Just like a lake with spring-water welling up from within, having no inflow from the east, west, north, or south, and with the skies supplying abundant showers time and again, so that the cool fount of water welling up from within the lake would permeate and pervade, suffuse and fill it with cool waters, there being no part of the lake unpervaded by the cool waters; even so, the monk permeates... this very body with the rapture and pleasure born of composure. There is nothing of his entire body unpervaded by rapture and pleasure born of composure. This, too, is a reward of the contemplative life, visible here and now, more excellent than the previous ones and more sublime.

And furthermore, with the fading of rapture, he remains in equanimity, is mindful & alert, and senses pleasure with the body. He enters & remains in the third jhana, of which the Noble Ones declare, 'Equanimous & mindful, he has a pleasurable abiding.' He permeates and pervades, suffuses and fills this very body with the pleasure divested of rapture.

Just as in a lotus pond, some of the lotuses, born and growing in the water, stay immersed in the water and flourish without standing up out of the water, so that they are permeated and pervaded, suffused and filled with cool water from their roots to their tips, and nothing of those lotuses would be unpervaded with cool water; even so, the monk permeates... this very body with the pleasure divested of rapture. There is nothing of his entire body unpervaded with pleasure divested of rapture. This, too, is a reward of the contemplative life, visible here and now, more excellent than the previous ones and more sublime.

And furthermore, with the abandoning of pleasure and stress — as with the earlier disappearance of elation and distress — he enters and remains in the fourth jhana: purity of equanimity and mindfulness, neither-pleasure nor stress. He sits, permeating the body with a pure, bright awareness. Just as if a man were sitting covered from head to foot with a white cloth so that there would be no part of his body to which the white cloth did not extend; even so, the monk sits, permeating the body with a pure, bright awareness. There is nothing of his entire body unpervaded by pure, bright awareness. This, too, is a reward of the contemplative life, visible here and now, more excellent than the previous ones and more sublime...

With his mind thus concentrated, purified, and bright, he directs it to the knowledge of the ending of the mental fermentations. Just as if there were a pool of water in a mountain glen — clear, limpid, and unsullied — where a man with good eyesight standing on the bank could see shells, gravel, and pebbles, and also shoals of fish swimming about and resting, and it would occur to him, 'This pool of water is clear, limpid, and unsullied. Here are these shells, gravel, and pebbles, and also these shoals of fish swimming about and resting.' In the same way, the monk discerns, as it has come to be, that 'This is stress... This is the origination of stress... This is the cessation of stress... This is the way leading to the cessation of stress... These are mental fermentations... This is the origination of fermentations... This is the cessation of fermentations... This is the way leading to the cessation of fermentations.' His heart, thus knowing, thus seeing, is released from the fermentations of sensuality, becoming, and ignorance. With release, there is the knowledge, 'Released.' He discerns that 'Birth is ended, the holy life fulfilled, the task done. There is nothing further for this world.' This, too, is a reward of the contemplative life, visible here and now, more excellent than the previous ones and more sublime. And as for another visible fruit of the contemplative life, higher and more sublime than this, there is none. — D 2

Aids to Awakening

Then Ven. Assaji, arising early in the morning, taking his robe and bowl, entered Rajagaha for alms: gracious in the way he approached and departed, looked forward and behind, drew in and stretched out his arm; his eyes downcast, his every movement consummate. Sariputta the wanderer saw Ven. Assaji going for alms in Rajagaha: gracious... his eyes downcast, his every movement consummate. On seeing him, the thought occurred to him: "Surely, of those in this world who are arahants or have entered the path to arahantship, this is one. What if I were to approach him and question him: 'On whose account have you gone forth? Who is your teacher? Of whose Dhamma do you approve?'"

But then the thought occurred to Sariputta the wanderer: "This is the wrong time to question him. He is going for alms in the town. What if I were to follow behind this monk who has found the path for those who seek it?"

Then Ven. Assaji, having gone for alms in Rajagaha, left, taking the alms he had received. Sariputta the wanderer approached him and, on arrival, having exchanged friendly greetings and courtesies, stood to one side. As he stood there he said, "Your faculties are bright, my friend, your complexion pure and clear. On whose account have you gone forth? Who is your teacher? Of whose Dhamma do you approve?"

"There is, my friend, the Great Contemplative, a son of the Sakyans, gone forth from a Sakyan family. I have gone forth on account of that Blessed One. That Blessed One is my teacher. It is of that Blessed One's Dhamma that I approve."

"But what is your teacher's teaching? What does he proclaim?"

"I am new, my friend, not long gone forth, only recently come to this doctrine and discipline. I cannot explain the doctrine in detail, but I can give you the gist in brief."

Then Sariputta the wanderer spoke thus to the Ven. Assaji:

Speak a little or a lot,
but tell me just the gist.

The gist is what I want.

What use is a lot of rhetoric?

Then Ven. Assaji gave this Dhamma exposition to Sariputta the Wanderer:

Whatever phenomena arise from cause:

their cause

& their cessation.

Such is the teaching of the Tathagata,

the Great Contemplative.

Then to Sariputta the Wanderer, as he heard this Dhamma exposition, there arose the dustless, stainless Dhamma eye: *Whatever is subject to origination is all subject to cessation.* — Mv 1.23.5

Then Mahapajapati Gotami [the first nun, and the Buddha's foster mother] approached the Blessed One and on arrival, having bowed down, stood to one side. As she was standing there, she said, "It would be good if the Blessed One would teach me the Dhamma in brief so that I, having heard the Dhamma, might dwell alone, secluded, heedful, ardent, and resolute."

> *"...Gotami, the qualities of which you may know, 'These qualities lead to dispassion, not to passion; to being unfettered and not to being fettered; to self-effacement and not to self-aggrandizement; to modesty and not to ambition; to contentment and not to discontent; to seclusion and not to entanglement; to the arousing of persistence and not to laziness; to being unburdensome and not to being burdensome': You may definitely hold, 'This is the Dhamma, this is the Vinaya, this is the Teacher's instruction.'"*

[According to the commentaries, Mahapajapati Gotami gained arahantship soon after receiving this instruction.] — Cv X 5

Sister Sona on Aging

Ten children I bore
from this physical heap.
Then weak from that, aged,
I went to a nun.
She taught me the Dhamma:
aggregates, sense spheres, elements.
Hearing the Dhamma,
I cut off my hair and ordained.
Having purified the divine eye
while still a probationer,
I know my previous lives,
where I lived in the past.
I develop the theme-less meditation:
well-focused singleness.
I gain the liberation of immediacy —
from lack of clinging, unbound.
The five aggregates, comprehended,
stand like a tree with its root cut through.
I spit on old age.
There is now no further becoming.

— Thig 5.8

Punna on Death

Punna: "Lord, I am going to live in the Sunaparanta country."

The Buddha: "Punna, the Sunaparanta people are fierce. They are rough. If they insult and ridicule you, what will you think?"

"...I will think, 'These Sunaparanta people are civilized, very civilized, in that they don't hit me with their hands.' That is what I will think..."

"But if they hit you with their hands...?"

"...I will think, 'These Sunaparanta people are civilized, very civilized, in that they don't hit me with a clod'..."

"But if they hit you with a clod...?"

"...I will think, 'These Sunaparanta people are civilized, very civilized, in that they don't hit me with a stick'..."

"But if they hit you with a stick...?"

"...I will think, 'These Sunaparanta people are civilized, very civilized, in that they don't hit me with a knife'..."

"But if they hit you with a knife...?"

"...I will think, 'These Sunaparanta people are civilized, very civilized, in that they don't take my life with a sharp knife'..."

"But if they take your life with a sharp knife...?"

"...I will think, 'There are disciples of the Blessed One who — horrified, humiliated, and disgusted by the body and by life — have sought for an assassin, but here I have met my assassin without searching for him.' That is what I will think..."

"Good, Punna, very good. Possessing such calm and self-control you are fit to dwell among the Sunaparantans. Now it is time to do as you see fit."

Then Ven. Punna, delighting and rejoicing in the Blessed One's words, rising from his seat, bowed down to the Blessed One and left, keeping him on his right side. Setting his dwelling in order and taking his robe and bowl, he set out for the Sunaparanta country and, after wandering stage by stage, he arrived there. There he lived. During that Rains retreat he established 500 male and 500 female lay followers in the practice, while he realized the three knowledges. At a later time, he attained total (final) Unbinding. — M 145

Sister Patacara on Awakening

Washing my feet, I noticed
the water.
And in watching it flow from high
to low,
my heart was composed
like a fine thoroughbred steed.
Then taking a lamp, I entered the hut,
checked the bedding,
sat down on the bed.
And taking a pin, I pulled out the wick:
Like the flame's unbinding
was the liberation
of awareness. — *Thig 5.10*

4

BUDDHA AND MEANING OF THE BUDDHA'S AWAKENING

The two crucial aspects of the Buddha's Awakening are the *what* and the *how:* what he awakened to and how he did it. His Awakening is special in that the two aspects come together. He awakened to the fact that there is an undying happiness, and that it can be attained through human effort. The human effort involved in this process ultimately focuses on the question of understanding the nature of human effort itself — in terms of skillful kamma and dependent co-arising — what its powers and limitations are, and what kind of right effort (i.e., the Noble Path) can take one beyond its limitations and bring one to the threshold of the Deathless.

As the Buddha described the Awakening experience in one of his discourses, first there is the knowledge of the regularity of the Dhamma — which in this context means dependent co-arising — then there is the knowledge of nibbana. In other passages, he describes the three stages that led to insight into dependent co-arising: knowledge of his own previous lifetimes, knowledge of the passing away and rebirth of all living beings, and finally insight into the four Noble Truths. The first two forms of knowledge were not new with the Buddha. They have been reported by other seers throughout history, although the Buddha's insight into the second knowledge had a special twist: He saw that beings are reborn according to the ethical quality of their thoughts, words, and deeds, and that this quality is essentially a factor of the mind. The quality of one's views and intentions determines the experienced result of one's actions.

This insight had a double impact on his mind. On the one hand, it made him realize the futility of the round of rebirth — that even the best efforts aimed at winning pleasure and fulfillment within the round could have only temporary effects. On the other hand, his realization of the importance of the mind in determining the round is what led him to focus directly on his own mind in the present to see how the processes in the mind that kept the round going could be disbanded.

This was how he gained insight into the four noble truths and dependent co-arising — seeing how the aggregates that made up his "person" were also the impelling factors in the experience of the world at large, and how the whole show could be brought to cessation. With its cessation, there remained the experience of the unconditioned, which he also termed nibbana (Unbinding), consciousness without surface or feature, the Deathless.

When we address the question of how other "enlightenment" experiences recorded in world history relate to the Buddha's, we have to keep in mind the Buddha's own dictum: First there is the knowledge of dependent co-arising, then there is the knowledge of nibbana. Without the first— which includes not only an understanding of kamma, but also of how kamma leads to the understanding itself — no realization, no matter how calm or boundless, that doesn't result from these sorts of understanding can count as an Awakening in the Buddhist sense. True Awakening necessarily involves both ethics and insight into causality.

As for what the Buddha's Awakening means for us now, four points stand out.

1) The role that kamma plays in the Awakening is empowering. It means that what each of us does, says, and thinks *does* matter — this, in opposition to the sense of futility that can come from reading, say, world history, geology, or astronomy and realizing the fleeting nature of the entire human enterprise. The Awakening lets us see that the choices we make in each moment of our lives have consequences. The fact that we are empowered also means that we are responsible for our experiences. We are not strangers in a strange land. We have formed and are continuing to form the world we experience.This helps us to face the events we encounter in life with greater equanimity, for we know that we had a hand in creating them, and yet at the same time we can avoid any debilitating sense of guilt because with each new choice we can always make a fresh start.

2) The Awakening also tells us that good and bad are not mere social conventions, but are built into the mechanics of how the world is constructed. We may be free to design our lives, but we are not free to change the underlying rules that determine what good and bad actions are, and how the process of kamma works itself out. Thus cultural relativism — even though it may have paved the way for many of us to leave our earlier religious orientations and enter the Buddhist fold — has no place once we are within that fold. There are certain ways of acting that are inherently unskillful, and we are fools if we insist on our right to behave in those ways.

3) As the Buddha says at one point in describing his Awakening, "Ignorance was destroyed; knowledge arose; darkness was destroyed; light arose — as

happens in one who is heedful, ardent, and resolute." In other words, he gained liberating knowledge through qualities that we can all develop: heedfulness, ardency, resolution. If we are willing to face the implications of this fact, we realize that the Buddha's Awakening is a challenge to our entire set of values. The fact that the Unconditioned can be attained forces us to re-evaluate any other goals we may set for ourselves, any worlds we may want to create, in our lives. On an obvious level, it points out the spiritual poverty of a life devoted to wealth, status, or sensual pursuits; but it also forces us to take a hard look at other more "worthwhile" goals that our culture and its sub-cultures tend to exalt, such as social acceptance, meaningful relationships, stewardship of the planet, etc. These, too, will inevitably lead to suffering. The interdependence of all things cannot be, for any truly sensitive mind, a source of security or comfort. If the Unconditioned is available, and it's the only trustworthy happiness around, the most sensible course is to invest our efforts and whatever mental and spiritual resources we have in its direction.

4) Even for those who are not ready to make that kind of investment, the Awakening assures us that happiness comes from developing qualities within ourselves that we can be proud of, such as kindness, sensitivity, equanimity, mindfulness, conviction, determination, and discernment. Again, this is a very different message from the one we pick up from the world telling us that in order to gain happiness we have to develop qualities we can't take any genuine pride in: aggressiveness, self-aggrandizement, dishonesty, etc. Just this much can give an entirely new orientation to our lives and our ideas of what is worthwhile investment of our time and efforts.

The news of the Buddha's Awakening sets the standards for judging the culture we were brought up in, and not the other way around. This is not a question of choosing Asian culture over American. The Buddha's Awakening challenged many of the presuppositions of Indian culture in his day; and even in so-called Buddhist countries, the true practice of the Buddha's teachings is always counter-cultural. It's a question of evaluating our normal concerns — conditioned by time, space, and the limitations of aging, illness, and death — against the possibility of a timeless, spaceless, limitless happiness. All cultures are tied up in the limited, conditioned side of things, while the Buddha's Awakening points beyond all cultures. It offers the challenge of the Deathless that his contemporaries found liberating and that we, if we are willing to accept the challenge, may find liberating ourselves.

DHAMMA

Life Isn't Just Suffering

You've probably heard the rumor that Buddhism is pessimistic, that "Life is suffering" is the Buddha's first noble truth. It's a rumor with good credentials, spread by well-respected academics and meditation teachers alike, but a rumor nonetheless. The real truth about the noble truths is far more interesting. The Buddha taught four truths — not one — about life: There is suffering, there is a cause for suffering, there is an end of suffering, and there is a path of practice that puts an end to suffering. These truths, taken as a whole, are far from pessimistic. They're a practical, problem-solving approach — the way a doctor approaches an illness, or a mechanic a faulty engine. You identify a problem and look for its cause. You then put an end to the problem by eliminating the cause.

What's special about the Buddha's approach is that the problem he attacks is the whole of human suffering, and the solution he offers is something human beings can do for themselves. Just as a doctor with a surefire cure for measles isn't afraid of measles, the Buddha isn't afraid of any aspect of human suffering. And, having experienced a happiness that's totally unconditional, he's not afraid to point out the suffering and stress inherent in places where most of us would rather not see it — in the conditioned pleasures we cling to. He teaches us not to deny that suffering and stress, or to run away from it, but to stand still and face up to it. To examine it carefully. That way — by understanding it — we can ferret out its cause and put an end to it. Totally. How confident can you get?

A fair number of writers have pointed out the basic confidence inherent in the four noble truths, and yet the rumor of Buddhism's pessimism persists. I wonder why. One possible explanation is that, in coming to Buddhism, we sub-consciously expect it to address issues that have a long history in our own culture. By starting out with suffering as his first truth, the Buddha seems to be offering his position on a question with a long history in the West: is the world basically good or bad?

According to Genesis, this was the first question that occurred to God after he had finished his creation: had he done a good job? So he looked at the world and saw that it was good. Ever since then, people in the West have sided with or against God on his answer, but in doing so they have affirmed that the question was worth asking to begin with. When Theravada — the only form of Buddhism to take on Christianity when Europe colonized Asia — was looking for ways to head off what it saw as the missionary menace, Buddhists who had received their education from the missionaries assumed that the question was valid and pressed the first noble truth into service as a refutation of the Christian God: look at how miserable life is, they said, and it's hard to accept God's verdict on his handiwork.

This debating strategy may have scored a few points at the time, and it's easy to find Buddhist apologists who — still living in the colonial past — keep trying to score the same points. The real issue, though, is whether the Buddha intended for his first noble truth to be an answer to God's question in the first place and — more importantly — whether we're getting the most out of the first noble truth if we see it in that light.

It's hard to imagine what you could accomplish by saying that life is suffering. You'd have to spend your time arguing with people who see more than just suffering in life. The Buddha himself says as much in one of his discourses. A brahman named Long-nails (Dighanakha) comes to him and announces that he doesn't approve of anything. This would have been a perfect time for the Buddha, if he had wanted, to chime in with the truth that life is suffering. Instead, he attacks the whole notion of taking a stand on whether life is worthy of approval. There are three possible answers to this question: (1) nothing is worthy of approval, (2) everything is, and (3) some things are and some things aren't. If you take any of these three positions, you end up arguing with the people who take either of the other two positions. And where does that get you?

The Buddha then teaches Long-nails to look at his body and feelings as instances of the first noble truth: they're stressful, inconstant, and don't deserve to be clung to as self. Long-nails follows the Buddha's instructions and, in letting go of his attachment to body and feelings, gains his first glimpse of the Deathless, of what it's like to be totally free from suffering. •

The point of this story is that trying to answer God's question, passing judgment on the world, is a waste of time. And it offers a better use for the first noble truth: looking at things, not in terms of "world" or "life," but simply identifying suffering so that you can comprehend it, let it go, and attain release. Rather than asking us to make a blanket judgment — which, in effect, would be asking us to be blind partisans — the first noble truth asks us to look and see precisely where the problem of suffering lies.

Other discourses make the point that the problem isn't with body and feelings in and of themselves. They themselves aren't suffering. The suffering lies in clinging to them. In his definition of the first noble truth, the Buddha summarizes all types of suffering under the phrase, "the five aggregates of clinging": clinging to physical form (including the body), feelings, perceptions, thought constructs, and consciousness. However, when the five aggregates are free from clinging, he tells us, they lead to long-term benefit and happiness. Of course, by "happiness" he isn't here referring to the arts, food, travel, sports, family life, or any of the other sections of the Sunday newspaper. He's talking about the solid well-being that comes when we treat the aggregates as factors in the path to the Deathless. The aggregates in themselves are neutral. The role they play in leading to true happiness or suffering lies in whether or not we cling.

So the first noble truth, simply put, is that *clinging* is suffering. It's because of clinging that physical pain becomes mental pain. It's because of clinging that aging, illness, and death cause mental distress. How do we cling? The texts list four ways: the clinging of sensual passion, the clinging of views, the clinging of precepts and practices, and the clinging of doctrines of the self. It's rare that a moment passes in the ordinary mind without some form of clinging. Even when we abandon a particular form of clinging, it's usually because it gets in the way of another form. We may abandon a puritanical view because it interferes with sensual pleasure; or a sensual pleasure because it conflicts with a view about what we should do to stay healthy. Our views of who we are may expand and contract depending on which of our many senses of "I" is feeling the most pain, expanding into a sense of cosmic oneness when we feel confined by the limitations of our small mind-body complex, shrinking into a small shell when we feel wounded from identifying with a cosmos so filled with cruelty, thoughtlessness, and waste. When the insignificance of our finite self becomes oppressive again, we may jump at the idea that we have no self, but then *that* becomes oppressive.

So our minds jump from clinging to clinging like a bird trapped in a cage. And when we realize we're captive, we naturally search for a way out. This is where it's so important that the first noble truth *not* say that "Life is suffering," for if life were suffering, where would we look for an end to suffering? We'd be left with nothing but death and annihilation. But when the actual truth is that clinging is suffering, we simply have to look to see precisely where clinging is and learn not to cling.

This is where we encounter the Buddha's great skill as a strategist: He tells us to take the clingings we'll have to abandon and transform them into the path to their abandoning. We'll need a certain amount of sensory pleasure — in terms of adequate food, clothing, and shelter — to find the strength to go beyond sensual passion. We'll need right view — seeing all things, including views, in terms of the four noble truths — to undermine our clinging to views. And we'll need a regimen of the five ethical precepts and the practice of meditation to put the mind in a solid position where it can drop its clinging to precepts and practices. Underlying all this, we'll need a strong sense of self-responsibility and self-discipline to master the practices leading to the insight that cuts through our clinging to doctrines of the self.

So we start the path to the end of suffering, not by trying to drop our clingings immediately, but by learning to cling more strategically. In other words, we start where we are and make the best use of the habits we've already got. We progress along the path by finding better and better things to cling to, and more skillful ways to cling, in the same way you climb a ladder to the top of a roof: grab hold of a higher rung so that you can let go of a lower rung, and then grab onto a rung still higher. As the rungs get further off the ground, you find that the mind grows clearer and can see precisely where its clingings are. It gets a sharper sense of which parts of experience belong to which noble truth and what should be done with them: the parts that are suffering should be comprehended, the parts that cause of suffering — craving and ignorance — should be abandoned; the parts that form the path to the end of suffering should be developed; and the parts that belong to the end of suffering should be verified. This helps you get higher and higher on the ladder until you find yourself securely on the roof. That's when you can finally let go of the ladder and be totally free.

So the real question we face isn't God's question, passing judgment on how skillfully he created life or the world. It's *our* question: how skillfully are we handling the raw stuff of life? Are we clinging in ways that serve only to continue the round of suffering, or are we learning to cling in ways that will reduce suffering so that ultimately we can grow up and won't have to cling. If we negotiate life armed with all four noble truths, realizing that life contains both suffering and an end to suffering, there's hope: hope that we'll be able to sort out which parts of life belong to which truth; hope that someday, in this life, we'll come to the point where we agree with the Buddha, "Oh. Yes. This is the end of suffering and stress."

No-self or Not-self?

One of the first stumbling blocks that Westerners often encounter when they learn about Buddhism is the teaching on *anatta,* often translated as no-self. This teaching is a stumbling block for two reasons. First, the idea of there being no self doesn't fit well with other Buddhist teachings, such as the doctrine of kamma and rebirth: If there's no self, what experiences the results of kamma and takes rebirth? Second, it doesn't fit well with our own Judeo-Christian background, which assumes the existence of an eternal soul or self as a basic presupposition: If there's no self, what's the purpose of a spiritual life?

Many books try to answer these questions, but if you look at the Pali canon — the earliest extant record of the Buddha's teachings — you won't find them addressed at all. In fact, the one place where the Buddha was asked point-blank whether or not there was a self, he refused to answer. When later asked why, he said that to hold either that there is a self or that there is no self is to fall into extreme forms of wrong view that make the path of Buddhist practice impossible. Thus the question should be put aside. To understand what his silence on this question says about the meaning of anatta, we first have to look at his teachings on how questions should be asked and answered, and how to interpret his answers.

The Buddha divided all questions into four classes: those that deserve a categorical (straight yes or no) answer; those that deserve an analytical answer, defining and qualifying the terms of the question; those that deserve a counter-question, putting the ball back in the questioner's court; and those that deserve to be put aside. The last class of question consists of those that don't lead to the end of suffering and stress. The first duty of a teacher, when asked a question, is to figure out which class the question belongs to, and then to respond in the appropriate way. You don't, for example, say yes or no to a question that should be put aside. If you are the person asking the question and you get an answer, you should then determine how far the answer should be interpreted. The Buddha said that there are two types of people who misrepresent him: those who draw inferences from statements that shouldn't have inferences drawn from them, and those who don't draw inferences from those that should.

These are the basic ground rules for interpreting the Buddha's teachings, but if we look at the way most writers treat the anatta doctrine, we find these ground rules ignored. Some writers try to qualify the no-self interpretation by saying that the Buddha denied the existence of an *eternal* self or a *separate* self, but this is to give an analytical answer to a question that the Buddha showed should be put aside. Others try to draw inferences from the few statements in the discourse that seem to imply that there is no self, but it seems safe to assume that if one forces those statements to give an answer to a question that should be put aside, one is drawing inferences where they shouldn't be drawn.

So, instead of answering "no" to the question of whether or not there is a self — interconnected or separate, eternal or not — the Buddha felt that the question was misguided to begin with. Why? No matter how you define the line between "self" and "other," the notion of self involves an element of self-identification and clinging, and thus suffering and stress. This holds as much for an interconnected self, which recognizes no "other," as it does for a separate self. If one identifies with all of nature, one is pained by every felled tree. It also holds for an entirely "other" universe, in which the sense of alienation and futility would become so debilitating as to make the quest for happiness — one's own or that of others — impossible. For these reasons, the Buddha advised paying no attention to such questions as "Do I exist?" or "Don't I exist?" for however you answer them, they lead to suffering and stress.

To avoid the suffering implicit in questions of "self" and "other," he offered an alternative way of dividing up experience: the four Noble Truths of stress, its cause, its cessation, and the path to its cessation. Rather than viewing these truths as pertaining to self or other, he said, one should recognize them simply for what they are, in and of themselves, as they are directly experienced, and then perform the duty appropriate to each. Stress should be comprehended, its cause abandoned, its cessation realized, and the path to its cessation developed. These duties form the context in which the anatta doctrine is best understood. If you develop the path of virtue, concentration, and discernment to a state of calm well-being and use that calm state to look at experience in terms of the Noble Truths, the questions that occur to the mind are not "Is there a self? What is my self?" but rather "Am I suffering stress because I'm holding onto this particular phenomenon? Is it really me, myself, or mine? If it's stressful but not really me or mine, why hold on?" These last questions merit straightforward answers, as they then help you to comprehend stress and to chip away at the attachment and clinging — the residual sense of self-identification — that cause it, until ultimately all traces of self-identification are gone and all that's left is limitless freedom.

In this sense, the anatta teaching is not a doctrine of no-self, but a not-self strategy for shedding suffering by letting go of its cause, leading to the highest, undying happiness. At that point, questions of self, no-self, and not-self fall aside. Once there's the experience of such total freedom, where would there be any concern about what's experiencing it, or whether or not it's a self?

Nibbana

We all know what happens when a fire goes out. The flames die down and the fire is gone for good. So when we first learn that the name for the goal of Buddhist practice, nibbana (nirvana), literally means the extinguishing of a fire, it's hard to imagine a deadlier image for a spiritual goal: utter annihilation. It turns out, though, that this reading of the concept is a mistake in translation, not so much of a word as of an image. What did an extinguished fire represent to the Indians of the Buddha's day? Anything but annihilation.

According to the ancient Brahmins, when a fire was extinguished it went into a state of latency. Rather than ceasing to exist, it became dormant and in that state — unbound from any particular fuel — it became diffused throughout the cosmos. When the Buddha used the image to explain nibbana to the Indian Brahmins of his day, he bypassed the question of whether an extinguished fire continues to exist or not, and focused instead on the impossibility of defining a fire that doesn't burn: thus his statement that the person who has gone totally "out" can't be described.

However, when teaching his own disciples, the Buddha used nibbana more as an image of freedom. Apparently, all Indians at the time saw burning fire as agitated, dependent, and trapped, both clinging and being stuck to its fuel as it burned. To ignite a fire, one had to "seize" it. When fire let go of its fuel, it was "freed," released from its agitation, dependence, and entrapment — calm and unconfined. This is why Pali poetry repeatedly uses the image of extinguished fire as a metaphor for freedom. In fact, this metaphor is part of a pattern of fire imagery that involves two other related terms as well. *Upadana*, or clinging, also refers to the sustenance a fire takes from its fuel. *Khandha* means not only one of the five "heaps" (form, feeling, perception, thought processes, and consciousness) that define all conditioned experience, but also the trunk of a tree. Just as fire goes out when it stops clinging and taking sustenance from wood, so the mind is freed when it stops clinging to the khandhas.

Thus the image underlying nibbana is one of freedom. The Pali commentaries support this point by tracing the word nibbana to its verbal root, which means "unbinding." What kind of unbinding? The texts describe two levels. One is the unbinding in this lifetime, symbolized by a fire that has gone out but whose embers are still warm. This stands for the enlightened arahant, who is conscious of sights and sounds, sensitive to pleasure and pain, but freed from passion, aversion, and delusion. The second level of unbinding, symbolized by a fire so totally out that its embers have grown cold, is what the arahant experiences after this life. All input from the senses cools away and he/she is totally freed from even the subtlest stresses and limitations of existence in space and time.

The Buddha insists that this level is indescribable, even in terms of existence or nonexistence, because words work only for things that have limits. All he really says about it — apart from images and metaphors — is that one can have foretastes of the experience in this lifetime, and that it's the ultimate happiness, something truly worth knowing.

So the next time you watch a fire going out, see it not as a case of annihilation, but as a lesson in how freedom is to be found in letting go.

SANGHA

The Economy of Gifts

According to the Buddhist monastic code, monks and nuns are not allowed to accept money or even to engage in barter or trade with lay people. They live entirely in an economy of gifts. Lay supporters provide gifts of material requisites for the monastics, while the monastics provide their supporters with the gift of the teaching. Ideally — and to a great extent in actual practice — this is an exchange that comes from the heart, something totally voluntary. There are many stories in the texts that emphasize the point that returns in this economy — it might also be called an economy of merit — depend not on the material value of the object given, but on the purity of heart of the donor and recipient. You give what is appropriate to the occasion and to your means, when and wherever your heart feels inspired. For the monastics, this means that you teach, out of compassion, what should be taught, regardless of whether it will sell. For the laity, this means that you give what you have to spare and feel inclined to share. There is no price for the teachings, nor even a "suggested donation." Anyone who regards the act of teaching or the act of giving requisites as a repayment for a particular favor is ridiculed as mercenary. Instead, you give because giving is good for the heart and because the survival of the Dhamma as a living principle depends on daily acts of generosity.

The primary symbol of this economy is the alms bowl. If you are a monastic, it represents your dependence on others, your need to accept generosity no matter what form it takes. You may not get what you want in the bowl, but you realize that you always get what you need, even if it's a hard-earned lesson in doing without. One of my students in Thailand once went to the mountains in the northern part of the country to practice in solitude. His hillside shack was an ideal place to meditate, but he had to depend on a nearby hilltribe village for alms, and the diet was mostly plain rice with some occasional boiled vegetables. After two months on this diet, his meditation theme became the conflict in his mind over whether he should go or stay.

One rainy morning, as he was on his alms round, he came to a shack just as the morning rice was ready. The wife of the house called out, asking him to wait while she got some rice from the pot. As he was waiting there in the pouring rain, he couldn't help grumbling inwardly about the fact that there would be nothing to go with the rice. It so happened that the woman had an infant son who was sitting near the kitchen fire, crying from hunger. So as she scooped some rice out of the pot, she stuck a small lump of rice in his mouth. Immediately, the boy stopped crying and began to grin.

My student saw this, and it was like a light bulb turning on in his head. "Here you are, complaining about what people are giving you for free," he told himself. "You're no match for a little kid. If he can be happy with just a lump of rice, why can't you?" As a result, the lesson that came with his scoop of rice that day gave my student the strength he needed to stay on in the mountains for another three years.

For a monastic the bowl also represents the opportunity you give others to practice the Dhamma in accordance with their means. In Thailand, this is reflected in one of the idioms used to describe going for alms: *proad sat,* doing a favor for living beings. There were times on my alms round in rural Thailand when, as I walked past a tiny grass shack, someone would come running out to put rice in my bowl. Years earlier, as lay person, my reaction on seeing such a bare, tiny shack would have been to want to give monetary help to them. But now I was on the receiving end of *their* generosity. In my new position I may have been doing less for them in material terms than I could have done as a lay person, but at least I was giving them the opportunity to have the dignity that comes with being a donor.

For the donors, the monk's alms bowl becomes a symbol of the good they have done. On several occasions in Thailand people would tell me that they had dreamed of a monk standing before them, opening the lid to his bowl. The details would differ as to what the dreamer saw in the bowl, but in each case the interpretation of the dream was the same: the dreamer's merit was about to bear fruit in an especially positive way.

The alms round itself is also a gift that goes both ways. On the one hand, daily contact with lay donors reminds the monastics that their practice is not just an individual matter, but a concern of the entire community. They are indebted to others for the right and opportunity to practice, and should do their best to practice diligently as a way of repaying that debt. At the same time, the opportunity to walk through a village early in the morning, passing by the houses of the rich and poor, the happy and unhappy, gives plenty of opportunities to reflect on the human condition and the need to find a way out of the grinding cycle of death and rebirth.

For the donors, the alms round is a reminder that the monetary economy is not the only way to happiness. It helps to keep a society sane when there are monastics infiltrating the towns every morning, embodying an ethos very different from the dominant monetary economy. The gently subversive quality of this custom helps people to keep their values straight.

Above all, the economy of gifts symbolized by the alms bowl and the alms round allows for specialization, a division of labor, from which both sides benefit. Those who are willing can give up many of the privileges of home life and in return receive the free time, the basic support, and the communal training needed to devote themselves fully to Dhamma practice. Those who stay at home can benefit from having full-time Dhamma practitioners around on a daily basis. I have always found it ironic that the modern world honors specialization in almost every area — even in things like running, jumping, and throwing a ball — but not in the Dhamma, where it is denounced as "dualism," "elitism," or worse. The Buddha began the monastic order on the first day of his teaching career because he saw the benefits that come with specialization. Without it, the practice tends to become limited and diluted, negotiated into the demands of the monetary economy. The Dhamma becomes limited to what will sell and what will fit into a schedule dictated by the demands of family and job. In this sort of situation, everyone ends up poorer in things of the heart.

The fact that tangible goods run only one way in the economy of gifts means that the exchange is open to all sorts of abuses. This is why there are so many rules in the monastic code to keep the monastics from taking unfair advantage of the generosity of lay donors. There are rules against asking for donations in inappropriate circumstances, from making claims as to one's spiritual attainments, and even from covering up the good foods in one's bowl with rice, in hopes that donors will then feel inclined to provide something more substantial. Most of the rules, in fact, were instituted at the request of lay supporters or in response to their complaints. They had made their investment in the merit economy and were interested in protecting their investment.

This observation applies not only to ancient India, but also to the modern-day West. On their first contact with the Sangha, most people tend to see little reason for the disciplinary rules, and regard them as quaint holdovers from ancient Indian prejudices. When, however, they come to see the rules in the context of the economy of gifts and begin to participate in that economy themselves, they also tend to become avid advocates of the rules and active protectors of "their" monastics.

The arrangement may limit the freedom of the monastics in certain ways, but it means that the lay supporters take an active interest not only in what the monastic teaches, but also in how the monastic lives — a useful safeguard to make sure that teachers walk their talk. This, again, insures that the practice remains a communal concern. As the Buddha said,

> Monks, householders are very helpful to you, as they provide you with the requisites of robes, alms food, lodgings, and medicine. And you, monks, are very helpful to householders, as you teach them the Dhamma admirable in the beginning, admirable in the middle, and admirable in the end, as you expound the holy life both in its particulars and in its essence, entirely complete, surpassingly pure. In this way the holy life is lived in mutual dependence, for the purpose of crossing over the flood, for making a right end to suffering and stress. — Iti 107

Periodically, throughout the history of Buddhism, the economy of gifts has broken down, usually when one side or the other gets fixated on the tangible side of the exchange and forgets the qualities of the heart that are its reason for being. And periodically it has been revived when people are sensitive to its rewards in terms of the living Dhamma. By its very nature, the economy of gifts is something of a hothouse creation that requires careful nurture and a sensitive discernment of its benefits. I find it amazing that such an economy has lasted for more than 2,600 years. It will never be more than an alternative to the dominant monetary economy, largely because its rewards are so intangible and require so much patience, trust, and discipline in order to be appreciated.

Those who demand immediate return for specific services and goods will always require a monetary system. Sincere Buddhist lay people, however, have the chance to play an amphibious role, engaging in the monetary economy in order to maintain their livelihood, and contributing to the economy of gifts whenever they feel so inclined. In this way they can maintain direct contact with teachers, insuring the best possible instruction for their own practice, in an atmosphere where mutual compassion and concern are the medium of exchange; and purity of heart, the bottom line.

SUMMARY

A Refuge in Skillful Action

Is human action real or illusory? If real, is it effective? If it is effective, does one have a choice in what one does? If one has a choice, can one choose to act in a way that will lead to genuine happiness? If so, what is that way? These are questions that lie at the heart of the way we conduct our lives. The way we answer them will determine whether we look for happiness through our own abilities, seek happiness through outside help, or abandon the quest for a higher-than-ordinary happiness altogether.

These questions were precisely the ones that led Siddhattha Gotama — the Bodhisatta, or Buddha-to-be — to undertake his quest for Awakening. He felt that there was no honor, no value in life, if true happiness could not be found through one's own efforts. Thus he put his life on the line to see how far human effort could go. Eventually he found that effort, skillfully applied, could lead to an Awakening to the Deathless. The lessons he learned about action and effort in the course of developing that skill, and which were confirmed by the experience of his Awakening, formed the basis of his doctrine of kamma (in Sanskrit: *karma).* This doctrine lies at the heart of his teaching, and forms the essence of the Triple Refuge. Put briefly, it states that action is real, effective, and the result of one's own choice. If one chooses to act skillfully and works to develop that skill, one's actions can lead to happiness, not only on the ordinary sensory level, but also on a level that transcends all the dimensions of time and the present. To understand this doctrine and get a sense of its full implications, we must first have some background on how the Buddha arrived at it. This will help us to see how kamma can act as a refuge, and what kind of refuge it provides.

People often believe that the Buddha simply picked up the doctrine of kamma from his environment, but nothing could be further from the truth. Northern India at his time was a place of great intellectual activity, and — as science made new advances and called many of the old, established beliefs into question — all of the great philosophical and religious issues of human life were up for grabs. The foremost science at that time was astronomy. New, precise observations of planetary movements, combined with new advances in mathematics, had led astronomers to conclude that time was measured in eons, incomprehensibly long cycles that repeat themselves endlessly. Philosophers of the time tried to work out the implications of this vast temporal frame for the drama of human life and the quest for ultimate happiness. These philosophers fell into two broad camps: those who conducted their speculations within the traditions of the Vedas, orthodox religious and ritual texts; and other, unorthodox groups, called the Samanas (contemplatives), who questioned the authority of the Vedas.

By the time of Siddhattḥa Gotama, philosophers of the Vedic and Samana schools had developed widely differing views of the laws of nature and how they affected the pursuit of true happiness. Their main points of disagreement were two:

1) *Personal identity.* Most Vedic and Samana philosophers assumed that a person's identity extended beyond this lifetime, eons before birth back into the past, and after death on into the future. There was some disagreement, however, as to whether one's identity from life to life would change or remain

the same. The Vedas had viewed rebirth in a positive light, but by the time of Prince Siddhattha the influence of the newly discovered astronomical cycles had led those who believed in rebirth to regard the cycles as pointless and confining, and release as the only possibility for true happiness. There was, however, a Samana school of hedonist materialists, called Lokayatans, who denied the existence of any identity beyond death and insisted that happiness could be found only by indulging in sensual pleasures here and now.

2) *Action and causality*. The ancient Vedas had formulated a doctrine of kamma, or action, which stated that correctly performed actions played a causal role in providing for one's happiness in the life after death. The primary actions recognized by these texts, though, were ritualistic: ritually performed sacrifices, often involving the slaughter of animals, and gifts to priests. To be effective, the ritual actions had to be correctly performed. This concern for correct performance led the Vedists to compose ritual manuals prescribing in minute detail the proper things to do and say in the course of their rituals. They even included special chants and spellsto compensate for any inadvertent mistakes in the course of a particular ritual, so great was their conviction that the quality of an act depend on its physical expression.

The Samana schools rejected the Vedic teachings on kamma, but for a variety of different reasons. One set of Samana schools, called the Ajivakas, asserted that an individual's actions were not in the least bit responsible for the course of his/her life. One branch of the Ajivakas taught that all action in the cosmos is illusory, as the only truly existing things are the unchanging substances of which the cosmos is made. Thus there is no such thing as right or wrong, good or evil, for in the ultimate sense there is no such thing as action.

Another branch of the Ajivakas taught that action was real but totally subject to fate: deterministic causal laws that left no room for free will. Thus they insisted that release from the round of rebirth came only when the round worked itself out. Peace of mind could be found by accepting one's fate and patiently waiting for the cycle, like a ball of string unwinding, to come to its end. Although these two positions derived from two very different pictures of the cosmos, they both led to the same conclusion: good and evil were illusory social conventions, human beings were not responsible for their acts, and human action had no role in shaping one's experience of the cosmos.

The Lokayatans came to a similar conclusion, but for different reasons. They agreed with the Vedists that physical action was real, but they maintained that it bore no results. There was no way to observe any invariable cause-effect relationship between events, they said; as a result, all events were spontaneous and self-caused. This meant that human actions had no consequences, and thus there were no such things as good and evil because no action could have a good or evil effect on anything else. They concluded that one could safely ignore moral rules in one's pursuit of sensual pleasure, and would be a fool to deny oneself immediate gratification of one's desires whenever the opportunity appeared.

Another school, the Jains, accepted the Vedic premise that one's actions shaped one's experience of the cosmos, but they differed from the Vedas in the way they conceived of action. All action, according to them, was a form of violence. The more violent the act, the more it produced effluents, conceived as sticky substances that bound the soul to the round of rebirth. Thus they rejected the Vedic assertion that ritual sacrifice produced good kamma, for the violence involved in killing the sacrificial animals was actually a form of very sticky bad kamma. In their eyes, the only way to true happiness was to try to escape the round of kamma entirely.

This was to be done by violence against themselves: various forms of self-torture that were supposed to burn away the effluents, the "heat" of pain being a sign that the effluents were burning. At the same time, they tried to create as little new kamma as possible. This practice would culminate in total abstinence from physical action, resulting in suicide by starvation, the theory being that if old kamma were completely burned away, and no new kamma created, there would be no more effluents to bind the soul to the cosmos. Thus the soul would be released.

Despite the differences between the Vedic and Jain views of action, they shared some important similarities: Both believed that the physical performance of an action, rather than the mental attitude behind it, determined its kammic result. And, both saw kamma as acting under deterministic, linear laws. Kamma performed in the present would not bear fruit until the future, and the relationship between a particular action and its result was predictable and fixed.

These divergent viewpoints on the nature of action formed the backdrop for the Bodhisatta's quest for ultimate happiness. On the one side stood the Ajivakas and Lokayatans, who insisted for various reasons that human action was ineffective: either non-existent, chaotic, or totally pre-determined. On the other side stood the Vedic and Jain thinkers, who taught that physical action was effective, but that it was subject to deterministic and linear laws, and could not lead to true happiness beyond the round of rebirth.

The Buddha's position on kamma broke from both sides of the issue, largely because he approached the question from a radically new direction.

The Principle of Skillful Action

Instead of arguing from abstract science, the Bodhisatta focused directly on the level of immediate experience and explored the implications of truths that both sides overlooked. Instead of fixing on the content of the views expressed, he considered the actions of those who were expressing the views. If views of determinism and total chaos were followed to their logical end, there would be no point in purposeful action, and yet the proponents of both theories continued to act in purposeful ways. If only physical acts bore consequences, there would be no point in teaching a proper understanding of the nature of action — for the mental act of understanding, right or wrong, would have no consequences — and yet all sides agreed that it was important to understand reality in the right way. The fact that each side insisted that the other used unskillful forms of observation and argumentation to advance its views implied that mental skills were crucial in determining the truth. Thus the Bodhisatta looked directly at skillful mental action in and of itseif, followed its implications in developing knowledge itself as a skill — rather than as a body of facts— and found that those implications carried him all the way to release.

The most basic lesson he learned was that mental skills can be developed. As one of the Pali discourses notes, he found that thoughts imbued with passion, aversion, and delusion were harmful; thoughts devoid of these qualities were not harmful; and he could shepherd his thoughts in such a way to avoid harm. The fact that he could develop this skill meant that mental action is not illusory, that it actually gives results. Otherwise, there would be no such thing as skill, for no actions would be more effective than others. The fact of skillfulness also implies that some results are preferable to others, for otherwise there would be no point in trying to develop skills. In addition, the fact that it is possible to learn from mistakes in the course of developing a skill — so that one's future actions may be more skillful — implies that the cycle of action, result, and reaction is not entirely deterministic. Acts of perception, attention, and intention can actually provide new input as the cycle goes through successive turns.

The important element in this input is attention. Anyone who has mastered a skill will realize that the process of attaining mastery requires attention to three things: (1) to pre-existing conditions, (2) to what one is doing in relation to those conditions, and (3) to the results that come from one's actions. This threefold focus enables one to monitor one's actions and adjust them accordingly. In this way, attention to conditions, actions, and effects allows the results of an action to feed back into future action, thus allowing for refinement in one's skill.

In the first stage of his practice, the Bodhisatta refined the skillfulness of his mind until it reached a state of jhana, or concentrated mental absorption, marked by perfect equanimity and mindfulness. The question that occurred at that point was how much further the principle of skillful action could be applied. Did intentional action directly or indirectly explain all experience in the world, or only some of it? If all of it, could the same principle be used to gain escape from the suffering inherent in the world, or were the Jains right in saying that action could only keep one bound to the cycle of suffering?

As the texts tell us, the Bodhisatta's first attempt to answer these questions was to direct his mind — now stable, bright, clear, and malleable — to knowledge of previous lifetimes. If it were true that he had been born before, his actions from past lives might explain experiences in this life— such as the circumstances into which he was born — for which no actions in this life could account. He found that he could indeed remember previous lives, many thousands of them: what he had been born as, where, what his experience of pleasure and pain, how he had died and then experienced rebirth as something else.

This first insight, however, did not fully answer his question. He needed to know if kamma was indeed the principle that shaped life, not only in terms of the narrative of his own lives, but also as a cosmic principle effecting the lives of all beings. So he directed his mind to knowledge of the passing away and arising of beings throughout the cosmos, and found that he could indeed see beings dying and gaining rebirth, that the pleasure and pain of their new lives was shaped by the quality of their kamma, and the kamma in turn was dependent on the views that gave rise to it. Right views — believing that good kamma, based on skillful intentions, gave rise to happiness — lay behind good kamma, while wrong views — not believing these principles— lay behind bad.

Even this second insight, however, didn't fully answer his question. To begin with, there was no guarantee that the visions providing this knowledge were true or complete. And, even if they were, they did not tell whether there was a form of right view that would underlie a level of skillful kamma that would lead, not simply to a pleasant rebirth within the cycle of rebirth, but to release from the cycle altogether.

Here was where the Bodhisatta turned to look again at the events in the mind, in and of themselves in the present, and in particular at the process of developing of skillfulness, to see if it offered any clues as to what a right view leading out of the cycle of rebirth might be. As we noted above, the process of skillfulness implies two things: a non-linear principle of cause and effect, involving feedback loops to allow for greater skillfulness; and the fact that some results are preferable to others. The Bodhisatta used these principles, in their most basic form, to divide experience into four categories based on two sets of variables: cause and effect on one hand, and stress and its cessation on the other. He then dropped the categories in which the first two knowledges had been expressed. In other words, he dropped the sense of "self" and "others" in which the narrative of the first knowledge had been expressed; and the sense of "beings" inhabiting a "world" in which the cosmology of the second knowledge had been expressed. In his place, he analyzed experience in categories empty of those concepts, simply in terms of the direct experience of stress, its cause, its cessation, and the path of mental factors leading to its cessation.

In the first round of this new insight, he was able to identify each of these categories: stress, in ultimate terms, was attachment to anything that might be identified as a "self." The cause of stress was craving, which in turn was based on ignorance about the true nature of stress. The cessation of stress was the total abandoning of craving, while the path to the cessation of stress was a cluster of eight factors: right view, right resolve, right speech, right action, right livelihood, right effort, right mindfulness, and right concentration. In the second round of this insight, he realized the duties that had to be performed with regard to each of these categories. Stress was to be comprehended, its cause abandoned, its cessation realized, and the path developed. He then pursued those duties until the mental powers of the path were so fully developed that stress was totally comprehended. This meant that there were no more objects on which craving could land, and so it was naturally abandoned. Thus in the third round of this insight he realized that the duties with regard to all four truths had been fulfilled. At that point there was nothing further for the mind to do — there was nothing more it *could* do in these terms. Right view and concentration — the mental qualities lying at the heart of the path — had done such a thorough job of ferreting out stress and craving that, as their final act, they detected the subtle stress and craving inherent in the act of right view and right concentration themselves. Thus, as its final act, the mind let go even of these path factors, just as a carpenter would let go of his tools when they had finished their job.

As a result, all present mental input into the processes of experience naturally came to a halt in a state of non-fashioning. This state opened onto an experience of total liberation, called Unbinding *(nibbana;* in Sanskrit, *nirvana).* Realizing that this Unbinding was the total cessation of suffering and of the processes of death and rebirth as generated in the mind, the Bodhisatta, now the Buddha, knew that his questions had been answered. Skillful action, based on right view in the form of the four categories based around stress — which he termed the four noble truths — could indeed bring about a total happiness free from the limitations of birth, aging, illness, and death.

The Teaching of Right View

The texts tell us that the Buddha spent the first seven weeks after his Awakening experiencing that happiness and freedom. Then he decided to teach the way to that happiness to others. His teachings were based on the three insights that had led to his own experience of Awakening. Because right view lay at the heart of his analysis of kamma and the way out of kamma, his teachings focused in particular on the two forms of right view that he learned in the course of those insights: the form he learned in the second insight, which led to a favorable rebirth; and the form he learned in the third insight, which led out from the cycle of death and rebirth once and for all.

The first level of right view the Buddha termed mundane right view. He expressed it in these terms:

There is what is given, what is offered, what is sacrificed. There are fruits and results of good and bad actions. There is this world and the next world. There is mother and father. There are spontaneously reborn beings; there are priests and contemplatives who, faring rightly and practicing rightly, proclaim this world and the next after having directly known and realized it for themselves. — M 117

This passage means that there is merit in generosity; that the moral qualities of good and bad are inherent in the universe, and not simply social conventions; that there is life after death; that one has a true moral debt to one's parents; and that there are people who have lived the renunciate's life properly in such a way that they have gained true and direct knowledge of these matters. These beliefs form the minimum prerequisite for following the path of skillful action that will lead to happy results within the cycle of rebirth. Thus this might be termed right view for the purpose of a happy rebirth.

The second level of right view, which the Buddha termed transcendent right view, he expressed simply as:

Knowledge in terms of stress, knowledge in terms of the origination of stress, knowledge in terms of the cessation of stress, knowledge in terms of the way of practice leading to the cessation of stress. — D 22

In other words, this level of right view consists of knowledge in terms of the four noble truths, and might be called right view for the purpose of escaping from rebirth altogether.

Just as the third insight grew out of the first two insights, the second level of right view grows out of the first. Its purpose is impossible to fathom if taken outside of the context of mundane good and bad kamma and their good and bad results. Together, the two levels of right view provide a complete and complementary picture of the nature of kamma as viewed from two different perspectives. The first level views kamma as a cosmic principle at work in the narrative of each individual's many lives. The second form views kamma as a principle at work in the present moment, approached from a frame of mind empty of the categories of self and other, being and non-being, which lie at the essence of narratives and cosmologies.

To see how these two levels of right view complement one another in shaping the form and content of the Buddha's teachings, we can look at his most common mode of presenting his teachings: the "graduated discourse" *(anupubbi-katha)*, beginning with the principle of good and bad kamma and gradually building up through the topics of generosity, virtue, heaven, drawbacks, and renunciation, ending with the topic of the four noble truths. There were several reasons for this gradual approach, but primarily they came down to the fact that the four truths were too abstract to appear immediately relevant, and the goal of escape from rebirth made no sense unless viewed in the proper context. The role of the graduated discourse was to provide that sense of relevance and context.

Starting with the first level of right view, the Buddha would describe good actions under two main categories: generosity and virtue. Together, the two categories could be stretched to cover almost any type of good physical, verbal, or mental deeds. For example, generosity covers not only the giving of material gifts, but also generosity with one's time, knowledge, gratitude, and forgiveness. Virtue begins with the five precepts — against killing, stealing, illicit sex, lying, and taking intoxicants — includes prohibitions against five forms of wrong livelihood — selling slaves, intoxicants, poisons, weapons, and animals to be killed for food — and goes on to cover abstention from all forms of harmful behavior. Thus good behavior, taken under the categories of generosity and virtue, means both refraining from harmful behavior and performing actions that are beneficial.

Having described good actions, the Buddha would describe their rewards, as results of the cosmic principle of kamma. The rewards here include both those visible in this world and those to be anticipated in the next. The Buddhist texts contain glowing descriptions both of the sense of well-being in the immediate present that results from good actions, and of the exquisite pleasures that rebirth in heaven entails. Implicit in these descriptions is the dark side of the principle of kamma: the inherent punishments that come from bad behavior, again both in this world and in the next: in the various levels of hell and other lower births — such as a common animal — and again in this world on one's return to the human state.

However — because finite actions can't produce infinite results — the rewards of kamma, good or bad, are not eternal. This point led naturally to the next topic in the discourse: the drawbacks of the cycle of rebirth as a whole. No happiness within the cycle is permanent; even the most refined heavenly pleasures must end when the force of one's good kamma ends, and one is forced to return to the rough and tumble of lower realms of being.

The changeablility of the mind lying behind the creation of kamma means that the course of an individual's life through the realms of rebirth is not necessarily ever upward. In fact, as the Buddha saw from his remembrance of his own lives, the course leading from one rebirth to another is filled with aimless ups and downs, like a stick thrown into the air: sometimes landing on this end, sometimes on the other end, sometimes in the middle. The amount of suffering and stress suffered in the course of these many throws is more than can be measured.

These considerations led naturally to the next topic of the discourse: renunciation. Having realized the fleeting nature of even the most refined pleasures in the round of rebirth, the sensitive listener would be prepared to look favorably on the idea of renouncing any aspiration for happiness within the round, and cultivating the path to release. The texts compare this mental preparation to the act of washing a cloth so that it would be ready to take dye. This was when the Buddha would take the listener beyond the level of mundane right view and broach the transcendent level.

The texts describing the steps of the graduated discourse describe this step simply as "the teaching special to the Buddhas: stress, its origination, its cessation, and the path," i.e., the four noble truths. However, the four noble truths are simply one out of three interrelated versions of transcendent right view taught in the texts:

(1) this/that conditionality *(idappaccayatã),*

(2) dependent co-arising *(paticca samuppãda),* and

(3) the four noble truths *(ariya sacca).* In order to gain a full picture of the Buddha's teachings on the nature of kamma, we should look at all three.

This/That Conditionality

The most basic version of right view is simply the causal principle of feedback loops that the Buddha found in the process of developing skillful action. He called this principle "this/that conditionality" because it explains experience in terms that are immediately present to awareness — events that can be pointed to in the mind as "this" or "that" —

rather than principles hidden from awareness. He expressed this principle in a simple-looking formula:

"(1) When this is, that is.

(2) From the arising of this comes the arising of that.

(3) When this isn't, that isn't.

(4) From the stopping of this comes the stopping of that."

— A X.92

Of the many possible ways of interpreting this formula, only one does justice both to the way the formula is worded and to the complex, fluid manner in which specific examples of causal relationships are described in the texts. That way is to view the formula as the interplay of two causal principles: one *diachronic,* acting over time; and the other *synchronic,* acting in a single instant of time. The two principles combine to form a non-linear pattern. The diachronic principle — taking (2) and (4) as a pair — connects events over time; the synchronic principle — (1) and (3) — connects objects and events in the present moment. The two principles intersect, so that any given event is influenced by two sets of conditions: input from the past and input from the present.

Although each principle seems simple, their interaction makes their consequences very complex. To begin with, every act has repercussions in the present moment together with reverberations extending into the future. Depending on the intensity of the act, these reverberations can last for a very short or a very long time. Thus every event takes place in a context determined by the combined effects of past events coming from a wide range in time, together with the effects of present acts. These effects can intensify one another, can coexist with little interaction, or can cancel one another out. Thus, even though it is possible to predict that a certain type of act will tend to give a certain type of result— for example, acting on anger will lead to pain — there is no way to predict when or where that result will make itself felt.

The complexity of the system is further enhanced by the fact that both causal principles meet at the mind. Through its views and intentions, the mind keeps both principles active. Through its sensory powers, it is affected by the results of the causes it has set in motion. This allows for the causal principles to feed back into themselves, as the mind reacts to the results of its own actions. These reactions can form positive feedback loops, intensifying the original input and its results, much like the howl in a speaker placed next to the microphone feeding into it. They can also create negative feedback loops, counteracting the original input, in the same way that a thermostat turns off a heater when the temperature in a room is too high, and turns it on again when it gets too low. Because the results of actions can be immediate, and the mind can react to them immediately, these feedback loops can sometimes quickly spin out of control; at other times, they may provide skillful checks on one's behavior.

For example, a man may act out of anger, which gives him an immediate sense of dis-ease to which he may react with further anger, thus creating a snowballing effect. On the other hand, he may come to understand that the anger is causing his dis-ease, and so immediately attempt to stop it. However, there can also be times when the results of his past actions may obscure his present dis-ease, so that he doesn't immediately react to it at all. This means that, although there are general patterns relating habitual acts to their results, there is no set one-for-one, tit-for-tat, relationship between a particular action and its results. Instead, the results are determined by the entire context of the act, shaped by the actions that preceded or followed it, and by one's state of mind at the time of acting or experiencing the result.

In this way, the combination of two causal principles — influences from the past interacting with those in the immediate present — accounts for the complexity of causal relationships on the level of immediate experience. However, the combination of the two principles also opens the possibility for finding a systematic way to break the causal web. If causes and effects were entirely linear, the cosmos would be totally deterministic, and nothing could be done to escape from the machinations of the causal process. If they were entirely synchronic, there would be no relationship from one moment to the next, and all events would be arbitrary. The web could break down totally or reform spontaneously for no reason at all. However, with the two modes working together, one can learn from causal patterns observed from the past and apply one's insights to disentangling the same causal patterns acting in the present. If one's insights are true, one can then gain freedom from those patterns. This allows for escape from the cycle of kamma altogether by developing kamma at a heightened level of skill by pursuing the noble eightfold path.

In addition, the non-linearity of this/that conditionality explains why heightened skillfulness, when focused on the present moment, can succeed in leading to the end of the kamma that has formed the experience of the entire cosmos. All non-linear processes exhibit what is called scale invariance, meaning that the behavior of the process on any one scale is similar to its behavior on smaller or larger scales. To understand, say, the large-scale pattern of a particular non-linear process, one need only focus on its behavior on a smaller scale that is easier to observe, and one will see the same pattern at work. In the case of kamma, one need only focus on the process of kamma in the immediate present, in the course of developing heightened skillfulness, and the large-scale issues over the expanses of space and time will become clear as one gains release from them.

DEPENDENT CO-ARISING

The teaching on dependent co-arising helps to provide more detailed instructions on this point, showing precisely where the cycle of kamma provides openings for more skillful present input. In doing so, it both explains the importance of the act of attention in developing heightened skillfulness, and acts as a guide for focusing attention on present experience in appropriate ways.

Dependent co-arising shows how the cosmos, when viewed in the context of how it is directly experienced by a person developing skillfulness, is subsumed entirely under factors immediately present to awareness: the five aggregates of form, feeling, perception, mental fabrication, and consciousness, and the six sense media — i.e., the five senses plus the mind. The standard list of causal factors runs as follows: the suffering and stress of aging, illness, and death depend on birth; birth in turn depends on becoming; and so on down through clinging, craving, feeling, sensory contact, the six senses, name and form (mental and physical phenomena), sensory consciousness, mental fabrications, and ignorance. Although the list reads like a linear pattern, the precise definitions of the terms show that it is filled with many feedback loops. Because it is non-linear, it thus functions on several scales: "birth," for instance, refers both to the birth of a physical organism and to the birth of a sense of being in the mind.

Included in this list is the Buddha's ultimate analysis of kamma and rebirth. For instance, the nexus of kamma, clinging, becoming, and birth accounts for the realm in which birth takes place. Kamma (covered under the factors of name and form) gives rise to the five aggregates, which form the objects for craving and clinging. Once there is clinging, there is a "coming-into-being" in any of three realms: the sensual realm, the realm of form, and the formless realm. These realms refer not only to levels of being on the cosmic scale, but also to levels of mental states. Some mental states are concerned with sensual images, others with forms, and still others with formless abstractions. The relationship between birth and becoming can be compared to the process of falling asleep and dreaming. As drowsiness leads the mind to lose contact with waking reality, a dream image of another place and time will appear in it. The appearance of this image is called becoming. The act of entering into this image and taking on a role or identity within it — and thus entering the world of the dream and falling asleep — is birth. The commentaries to the Pali texts maintain that precisely the same process is what enables rebirth to follow the death of the body. At the same time, the analogy between falling asleep and taking birth explains why release from the cycle of becoming is called Awakening.

Once there is birth in a particular realm, the nexus of name-and-form with consciousness accounts for the arising and survival of the active organism within that realm. Without consciousness, the mental and physical organism would die. Without the mental and physical organism, consciousness would have no place to land and develop. This nexus also explains the feedback loops that can lead to skillful action. "Name" includes the sub-factors of attention, intention, feeling, perception, and contact, which are precisely the factors at work in the process of kamma and its result. The first lesson of skillfulness is that the essence of an action lies in the intention motivating it: an act motivated by the intention for greater skillfulness will give results different from those of an act motivated by greed, aversion, or delusion.

Intention, in turn, is influenced by the appropriateness or inappropriateness of the act of attention to one's circumstances. The less an act of attention is clouded by delusion, the more clearly it will see things in appropriate terms. The combination of attention and intention in turn determines the quality of the feeling and the physical events ("form") that result from the act. The more skilled the action, the more refined these results will be. Perceptions arise with regard to those results, some more appropriate than others. The act of attention selects which ones to focus on, thus feeding back into another round in the cycle of action. Underlying the entire cycle is the fact that all its factors are in contact with consciousness.

This interplay of name, form, and consciousness provides an answer to the quandary of how the stress and suffering inherent in the cycle of action can be ended. If one tried simply to stop the cycle through a direct intention, the intention itself would count as kamma, and thus as a factor to keep the cycle going.

This double bind can be dissolved, however, if one can watch as the contact between consciousness and the cycle naturally falls away. This requires, not inaction, but more and more appropriate attention to the process of kamma itself. When one's attention to and mastery of the process becomes fully complete, there occurs a point of equipoise called "non-fashioning" *(atammayata)*, in which the contact between the processes of kamma and consciousness — still fully conscious — naturally becomes disengaged. One modern teacher has compared this disengagement to that of a fruit naturally falling, when fully ripened, from the tree. This is how the cycle of action comes to an end in the moment of Awakening.

As this analysis shows, the most important obstacle to release is the ignorance that keeps attention from being fully perceptive. As the Buddha traced the element of ignorance that underlay the processes of mental fabrication, he found that it came down to ignorance of the four noble truths: the identity of the truths, the duties appropriate to each, and the mastery of those duties. When this ignorance is fully overcome, the craving that keeps the cycle going will have nothing to fasten on, for all its possible objects are seen for what they are: suffering and stress. With no place to land, craving disappears, and the cycle can come to an end.

The Four Noble Truths

Because knowledge in terms of the four noble truths is what ends ignorance and craving, the Buddha most often expressed transcendent right view in their terms. These truths focus the analysis of kamma directly on the question of stress and suffering: issues at the heart of the narratives that people make of their own life experiences. As the Buddha noted in his second insight, his memory of previous lives included his experience of pleasure and pain in each life, and most people — when recounting their own lives — tend to focus on these issues as well.

The four truths, however, do not stop simply with tales about stress: they approach it from the problem-solving perspective of a person engaged in developing a skill. What this means for the meditator trying to master heightened skillfulness is that these truths cannot be fully comprehended by passive observation. Only by participating sensitively in the process of developing skillful powers of mindfulness, concentration, and discernment — and gaining a practical feel for the relationship of cause and effect among the mental factors that shape that process — can one eradicate the ignorance that obstructs the ending of kamma. Thus, only through developing skillfulness to the ultimate degree can the cycle be brought to equilibrium and, as a result, disband.

The Knowledge of Unbinding

The truth of the Buddha's understanding of the processes of kamma — as informed by this/that conditionality, dependent co-arising, and the four noble truths — was confirmed by the knowledge of Unbinding that followed immediately on his mastery of heightened skillfulness.

He found that when skillfulness is intentionally brought to a point of full consummation, as expressed in the direct awareness of this/that conditionality, it leads to a state of non-fashioning that opens to a level of consciousness in which all experience of the cosmos has fallen away. When one's experience of the cosmos resumes after the experience of Awakening, one sees clearly that it is composed entirely of the results of old kamma; with no new kamma added to the process, all experience of the cosmos will eventually run out — or, in the words of the texts, "will grow cold right here."

This discovery confirmed the basic premise that kamma not only plays a role in shaping experience of the cosmos, it plays the primary role.

If this were not so, then even when kamma was ended there would still remain the types of experience that came from other sources. But because none of the limitations of the cosmos — time, space, etc. — remain when all present kamma disbands, and none resume after all old kamma runs out, kamma must be the factor accounting for all experience of those limitations. This fact implies that even the limiting factors that one encounters in terms of sights, sounds, etc., are actually the fruit of past kamma in thought, word, and deed — committed not only in this, but also in many preceding lifetimes. Thus, even though the Buddha's development of heightened skillfulness focused on the present moment, the resulting Awakening gave insights that encompassed all of time.

Faith in the Principle of Kamma

From this discussion it should become clear why kamma, as an article of faith, is a necessary factor in the path of Buddhist practice. The teaching on kamma, in its narrative and cosmological forms, provides the context for the practice, giving it direction and urgency.

Because the cosmos is governed by the laws of kamma, those laws provide the only mechanism by which happiness can be found. But because good and bad kamma, consisting of good and bad intentions, simply perpetuate the ups and downs of experience in the cosmos, a way must be found out of the mechanism of kamma by mastering it in a way that allows it to disband in an attentive state of non-intention. And, because there is no telling what sudden surprises the results of one's past kamma may still hold in store, one should try to develop that mastery as quickly as possible.

In its "empty" mode — i.e., focusing on the process of action, without referring to questions of whether or not there is a self or a being behind the processes — the teaching on kamma accounts for the *focus* and the *terms of analysis* used in the practice. It also accounts for the *mental qualities* needed to attain and maintain that level of focus and analysis.

In terms of focus, the principle of scale invariance means that the complexities of kamma can be mastered by giving total attention to phenomena in and of themselves in the immediate present.

These phenomena are then analyzed in terms of the four noble truths, the terms used in observing and directing the experience of developing the qualities of skillful action. The most immediate skillful kamma that can be observed on this level is the mastery of the very same mental qualities that are supporting this refined level of focus and analysis:

mindfulness, concentration, and discernment, together with the more basic qualities on which they are based. Thus, these mental qualities act not only as supports to the focus and analysis, but also as their object. Ultimately, discernment becomes so refined that the focus and analysis take as their object the act of focusing and analyzing, in and of themselves. The cycle of action then short-circuits as it reaches culmination, and Unbinding occurs.

It is entirely possible that a person with no firm conviction in the principle of kamma can follow parts of the Buddhist path, including mindfulness and concentration practices, and gain positive results from them. For instance, one can pursue mindfulness practice for the sense of balance, equanimity, and peace it gives to one's daily life, or for the sake of bringing the mind to the present for the purpose of spontaneity and "going with the flow."

The full practice of the path, however, is a skillful diverting of the flow of the mind from its habitual kammic streams to the stream of Unbinding. As the Buddha said, this practice requires a willingness to "develop and abandon" to an extreme degree. The *developing* requires a supreme effort aimed at full and conscious mastery of mindfulness, concentration, and discernment to the point of non-fashioning and on to release.

A lack of conviction in the principle of kamma would undercut the patience and commitment, the desire, persistence, intent, and refined powers of discrimination needed to pursue concentration and discernment to the most heightened levels, beyond what is needed for a general sense of peace or spontaneity.

The *abandoning* involves uprooting the most deeply buried forms of clinging and attachment that maintain bondage to the cycle of rebirth. Some of these forms of clinging — such as views and theories about self-identity—

are so entrenched in the narrative and cosmological modes in which most people function that only firm conviction in the benefits to be had by abandoning them will be able to pry them loose.

This is why the Buddha insisted repeatedly that conviction in the fact of his Awakening necessarily involves conviction in the principle of kamma, and that both forms of conviction are needed for the full mastery of the kamma of heightened skillfulness leading to release.

There are many well-known passages in the Canon where the Buddha asks his listeners not to accept his teachings simply on faith, but these remarks were directed to people just beginning the practice. Beginners need only accept the general principles of skillful action on a trial basis, focusing on the input that their intentions are putting into the causal system at the present moment, and exploring the connection between skillful intentions and favorable results.

The more complex issues of kamma come into play at this level only in forcing one to be patient with the practice. Many times skillful intentions do not produce their favorable results immediately, aside from the sense of well-being — sometimes clearly perceptible, sometimes barely — that comes with acting skillfully. Were it not for this delay, the principle of kamma would be self-evident, no one would dare act on unskillful intentions, and there would be no need to take the principle on faith. The complexity of this/that conditionality is the major cause of the confusion and lack of skill with which most people live their lives. The ability to master this process takes time.

As one progresses on the path, however — and as the process of developing skillfulness in and of itself gradually comes to take center stage in one's awareness — the actual results of developing skillfulness should give greater and greater reason for conviction in the principle of kamma. Except in cases where people fall into the trap of heedlessness or complacency, these results can spur and inspire one to hold to the principle of kamma with the increasing levels of firmness, focus, and refinement needed for Awakening.

This, then, is the sense in which kamma, or intentional action, forms the basic refuge for the person on the path. On the one hand, as a doctrine, it provides guidance to the proper path of action, and encouragement to muster the energy needed to follow the path. On the other hand, as the actual principle by which skillful action is brought to a pitch of non-fashioning on the threshold of the Deathless, it provides the mechanism by which human effort and action can bring about the ultimate in genuine happiness.

5

THE PATH OF CONCENTRATION AND MINDFULNESS

Many people tell us that the Buddha taught two different types of meditation — mindfulness meditation and concentration meditation. Mindfulness meditation, they say, is the direct path, while concentration practice is the scenic route that you take at your own risk because it's very easy to get caught there and you may never get out. But when you actually look at what the Buddha taught, he never separates these two practices. They are both parts of a single whole. Every time he explains mindfulness and its place in the path, he makes it clear that the purpose of mindfulness practice is to lead the mind into a state of Right Concentration — to get the mind to settle down and to find a place where it can really feel stable, at home, where it can look at things steadily and see them for what they are.

Part of the "two practices" issue centers on how we understand the word *jhana,* which is a synonym for Right Concentration. Many of us have heard that jhana is a very intense trance-like state that requires intense staring and shutting out the rest of the world. It sounds nothing like mindfulness at all. But if you look in the Canon where the Buddha describes jhana, that's not the kind of state he's talking about. To be in jhana is to be absorbed, very pleasurably, in the sense of the whole body altogether. A very broad sense of awareness fills the entire body. One of the images the Buddha used to describe this state is that of a person kneading water into dough so that the water permeates throughout the flour. Another is a lake in which a cool spring comes welling up and suffuses the entire lake.

Now, when you're with the body as a whole, you're very much in the present moment. You're right there all the time. As the Buddha says, the fourth jhana — in which the body is filled with bright awareness — is the point where mindfulness and equanimity become pure. So there should be no problem in combining mindfulness practice with the whole-body awareness that gets very settled and still. In fact, the Buddha himself combines them in his description of the first four steps of breath meditation: (1) being aware of long breathing, (2) being aware of short breathing, (3) being aware of the whole body as you breathe in and breathe out, and then (4) calming the sensation of the breath within the body. This, as the texts tell us, is basic mindfulness practice. It's also a basic concentration practice. You're getting into the first jhana — Right Concentration — right there, at the same time that you're practicing Right Mindfulness.

To see how Right Mindfulness and Right Concentration help each other in the practice, we can look at the three stages of mindfulness practice given in the Foundations of Mindfulness Sutta. Take the body as an example. The first stage is to keep focused on the body in and of itself, putting aside greed and distress with reference to the world. What this means is taking the body as a body without thinking about it in terms of what it means or what it can do in the world. It could be either good or bad looking. It could be strong or weak. It could be agile or clumsy — all the issues we tend to worry about when we think about ourselves. The Buddha says to put those issues aside.

Just be with the body in and of itself, sitting right here. You close your eyes — what do you have? There's the sensation of "bodiness" that you're sitting with. That's your frame of reference. Try to stay with it. Keep bringing the mind back to this sense of the body until it gets the message and begins to settle down. In the beginning of the practice you find the mind going out to grasp this or that, so you note it enough to tell it to let go, return to the body, and hold on there. Then it goes out to grasp something else, so you tell it to let go, come back, and latch onto the body again. Eventually, though, you reach a point where you can actually grasp hold of the breath and you don't let go, okay? You keep holding onto it. From that point on, whatever else that happens to come into your awareness is like something coming up and brushing the back of your hand. You don't have to note it. You stay with the body as your basic frame of reference. Other things come and go, you're aware of them, but you don't drop the breath and go grasping after them. This is when you really have established the body as a solid frame of reference.

As you do this, you develop three qualities of mind. One is mindfulness *(sati)*. The term mindfulness means being able to remember, to keep something in mind. In the case of establishing the body as a frame of reference, it means being able to remember where you're supposed to be — with the body — and you don't let yourself forget. The second quality, alertness *(sampajañña)*, means being aware of what is actually going on in the present. Are you with the body? Are you with the breath? Is the breath comfortable? Simply notice what's actually happening in the present moment. We tend to confuse mindfulness with alertness, but actually they are two separate things: mindfulness means being able to remember where you want to keep your awareness; alertness means being aware of what's actually happening. The third quality, ardency *(atappa)*, means two things. One, if you realize that the mind has wandered off, you bring it right back. Immediately. You don't let it wander around, sniffing the flowers. Two, when the mind is with its proper frame of reference, ardency means trying to be as sensitive as possible to what's going on — not just drifting in the present moment, but really trying to penetrate more and more into the subtle details of what's actually happening with the breath or the mind.

When you have these three qualities focused on the body in and of itself, you can't help but settle down and get really comfortable with the body in the present moment. That's when you're ready for the second stage in the practice, which is described as being aware of the phenomenon of origination and the phenomenon of passing away. This is a stage where you're trying to understand cause and effect as they happen in the present. In terms of concentration practice, once you've got the mind to settle down, you want to understand the interaction of cause and effect in the process of concentration so that you can get it to settle down more solidly for longer periods of time in all sorts of situations, on the cushion and off. To do this, you have to learn about how things arise and pass away in the mind, not by simply watching them, but by actually getting involved in their arising and passing away.

You can see this in the Buddha's instructions for dealing with the hindrances. In the first stage, he says to be aware of the hindrances as they come and go. Some people think that this is an exercise in "choiceless awareness," where you don't try to will the mind in any direction, where you simply sit and watch willy-nilly whatever comes into the mind. In actual practice, though, the mind isn't yet ready for that. What you need at this stage is a fixed point of reference for evaluating the events in the mind, just as when you're trying to gauge the motion of clouds through the sky: You need to choose a fixed point — like a roof gable or a light pole — at which to stare so that you can get a sense of which direction and how fast the clouds are moving. The same with the coming and going of sensual desire, ill will, etc., in the mind: You have to try to maintain a fixed reference point for the mind — like the breath — if you want to be really sensitive to when there are hindrances in the mind—getting in the way of your reference point — and when there are not.

Suppose that anger is interfering with your concentration. Instead of getting involved in the anger, you try simply to be aware of when it's there and when it's not. You look at the anger as an event in and of itself — as it comes, as it goes. But you don't stop there. The next step—as you're still working at focusing on the breath — is recognizing how anger can be made to go away. Sometimes simply watching it is enough to make it go away; sometimes it's not, and you have to deal with it in other ways, such as arguing with the reasoning behind the anger or reminding yourself of the drawbacks of anger. In the course of dealing with it, you have to get your hands dirty. You've got to try and figure out why the anger is coming, why it's going, how you can get it out of there, because you realize that it's an unskillful state. And this requires that you improvise. Experiment. You've got to chase your ego and impatience out of the way so that you can have the space to make mistakes and learn from them, so that you can develop a skill in dealing with the anger. It's not just a question of hating the anger and trying to push it away, or of loving the anger and welcoming it. These approaches may give results in the short run, but in the long run they're not especially skillful. What's called for here is the ability to see what the anger is composed of; how can you take it apart.

One technique I like to use — when anger is present and you're in a situation where you don't immediately have to react to people — is simply to ask yourself in a good-natured way, "Okay, why are you angry?" Listen to what the mind has to say. Then pursue the matter: "But why are you angry at *that?*" "Of course, I'm angry. After all..." "Well, why are you angry at that?" If you keep this up, the mind will eventually admit to something stupid, like the assumption that people shouldn't be that way — even though they blatantly *are* that way — or that people should act in line with your standards, or whatever the mind is so embarrassed about that it tries to hide from you. But finally, if you keep probing, it'll fess up. You gain a lot of understanding of the anger that way, and this can really weaken its power over you.

In terms of the positive qualities like mindfulness, serenity, and concentration, it's a similar sort of thing. First, you're aware of when they're there and when they're not, and then you realize that when they're there it's much nicer than when they're not. So you try to figure out *how* they come, how they go. You do this by consciously trying to maintain that state of mindfulness and concentration. If you're really observant — and this is what it's all about, being observant — you begin to see that there are skillful ways of maintaining the state without getting all tied up in failure or success in doing it, without letting the desire for a settled state of mind actually get in the way of the mind's settling down.

You do want to succeed, but you need a balanced attitude toward failure and success so that you can learn from them. Nobody's keeping score or taking grades. You're here to understand for your own sake. So this process of developing your foundation of mindfulness or developing your frame of reference is not "just watching." It's more a participation in the process of arising and passing away — actually playing with the process — so that you can learn from experience how cause and effect work in the mind.

Once, when I was in college, I wrote home complaining about the food, and my mother sent me a Julia Child cookbook. In the book was a section on dealing with eggs in which she said that the sign of a really good cook is knowing eggs. And so I took an egg out. You can watch an egg — you can learn certain things just by watching it, but you don't learn very much. To learn about eggs you have to put them in a pan and try to make something out of them. If you do this long enough you begin to understand that there are variations in eggs, and there are certain ways that they react to heat and ways that they react to oil or butter or whatever. And so by actually working with the egg and trying to make something out of it, you really come to understand eggs. It's similar with clay: you really don't know clay until you become a potter and actually try to make something out of the clay.

And it's the same with the mind: unless you actually try to make something out of the mind, try to get a mental state going and keep it going, you don't really know your own mind. You don't know the processes of cause and effect within the mind. There has to be a factor of actual participation in the process. That way you can understand it. This all comes down to being observant and developing a skill. The essence of developing a skill means two things. One, you're aware of a situation as it is given and, two, you're aware of what you put into it. When the Buddha talks about causation, he says that every situation is shaped from two directions — the causes coming in from the past and the causes you're putting into the present. You need to be sensitive to both. If you aren't sensitive to what you're putting into a situation, you'll never develop any kind of skill. As you're aware of what you're doing, you also look at the results. If something isn't right, you go back and change what you've done — keeping at this until you get the results you want. And in the process, you learn a great deal from the clay, the eggs, or whatever you're trying to deal with skillfully.

The same holds true with the mind. Of course, you could learn something about the mind by trying to get it into any sort of a state, but for the purpose of developing really penetrating insight, a state of stable, balanced, mindful concentration is the best kind of soufflé or pot you want to make with the mind. The factors of pleasure, ease, and sometimes even rapture that arise when the mind really settles down help you stay comfortably in the present moment, with a low center of gravity. Once the mind is firmly settled there, you have something to look at for a long period of time so that you can see what it's made up of. In the typical unbalanced state of the mind, things are appearing and disappearing too fast for you to notice them clearly.

But as the Buddha notes, when you get really skilled at jhana, you can step back a bit and really see what you've got. You can see, say, where there's an element of attachment, where there's an element of stress, or even where there's inconstancy within your balanced state. This is where you begin to gain insight, as you see the natural cleavage lines among the different factors of the mind, and in particular, the cleavage line between awareness and the objects of awareness.

Another advantage to this mindful, concentrated state is that as you feel more and more at home in it, you begin to realize that it's possible to have happiness and pleasure in life without depending on things outside of yourself — people, relationships, approval from others, or any of the issues that come from being part of the world. This realization helps pry loose your attachments to things outside. Some people are afraid of getting attached to a state of calm, but actually, it's very important that you get attached here, so that you begin to settle down and begin to undo your other attachments. Only when this attachment to calm is the only one left do you begin work on loosening it up as well.

Still another reason why solid concentration is necessary for insight is that when discernment comes to the mind, the basic lesson it will teach you is that you've been stupid. You've held onto things even though deep down inside you should have known better. Now, try telling that to people when they're hungry and tired. They'll come right back with, "You're stupid, too," and that's the end of the discussion. Nothing gets accomplished. But if you talk to someone who has had a full meal and feels rested, you can broach all kinds of topics without risking a fight. It's the same with the mind. When it has been well fed with the rapture and ease coming from concentration, it's ready to learn. It can accept your criticisms without feeling threatened or abused.

So. This is the role that concentration practice plays in this second stage of mindfulness practice: It gives you something to play with, a skill to develop so you can begin to understand the factors of cause and effect within the mind. You begin to see the mind as just a flux of causes with their effects coming back at you. Your ideas are part of this flux of cause and effect, your emotions, your sense of who you are. This insight begins to loosen your attachments to the whole process.

What finally happens is that the mind reaches a third level of mindfulness practice where the mind comes to a state of perfect equilibrium — where you've developed this state of concentration, this state of equilibrium to the point where you don't have to put anything more into it. In the Foundations of Mindfulness Sutta this is described as simply being aware — if you are using the body as your frame of reference, being aware that "There is a body," just enough for knowledge and mindfulness, without being attached to anything in the world. Other texts call this the state of "non-fashioning." The mind reaches the point where you begin to realize that all causal processes in the mind — including the processes of concentration and insight — are like tar babies. If you like them, you get stuck; if you don't like them, you get stuck. So what are you going to do? You have to get to the point where you're not really contributing anything more to the present moment. You unravel your participation in it. That's when things open up in the mind.

Many people want to jump right in and begin at this level of not adding anything to the present moment, but it doesn't work that way. You can't be sensitive to the subtle things the mind is habitually adding to the present until you've consciously tried to alter what you're adding. As you get more and more skilled, you get more sensitive to the subtle things you didn't realize you were doing. You reach a point of disenchantment, where you realize that the most skillful way of dealing with the present is to strip away all levels of participation that cause even the slightest bit of stress in the mind. You start dismantling the levels of participation that you learned in the second stage of the practice, to the point where things reach equilibrium on their own, where there's letting go and release.

So it's important to realize that there are these three stages to mindfulness practice, and to understand the role that deliberate concentration practice plays in taking you through the first two. Without aiming at Right Concentration, you can't develop the skills needed for understanding the mind — for it's in the process of mastering the skill of mindful concentration that true insight arises. Just as you don't really understand a herd of cattle until you've successfully herded them — learning from all your failures along the way — you can't get a sense of all the cause-and-effect currents running through the mind until you've learned from your failures and successes in getting them to gather in a state of concentrated mindfulness and mindful concentration. And only when you've really understood and mastered these currents — the currents of craving that cause suffering and stress, and the currents of mindfulness and concentration that form the Path — can you let them go and find freedom from them.

THE BUDDHIST ATTITUDE TOWARDS NATURE

Modern man in his search for pleasure and affluence has exploited nature without any moral restraint to such an extent that nature has been rendered almost incapable of sustaining healthy life. Invaluable gifts of nature, such as air and water, have been polluted with severely disastrous consequences. Man is now searching for ways and means of overcoming the pollution problem as his health too is alarmingly threatened. He also feels that it is irresponsible and morally wrong on his part to commit the future generations to a polluted planet.

If man is to act with a sense of responsibility to the natural world, to his fellow human beings and to unborn future generations, he has to find an appropriate environmental ethic today to prevent further aggravation of the present pollution problem. Hence his search for wisdom and attitudes in a hitherto neglected area of knowledge, namely, religion.

Buddhism strictly limits itself to the delineation of a way of life designed to eradicate human suffering. The Buddha refused to answer questions which did not directly or indirectly bear on the central problem of human suffering and its ending. Furthermore, environmental pollution is a problem of the modern age, unheard of and unsuspected during the time of the Buddha. Therefore it is difficult to find any specific discourse which deals with the topic we are interested in here. Nevertheless, as Buddhism is a full-fledged philosophy of life reflecting all aspects of experience, it is possible to find enough material in the Pali canon to delineate the Buddhist attitude towards nature.

The word "nature" means everything in the world which is not organized and constructed by man. The Pali equivalents which come closest to "nature" are *loka* and *yathabhūta*. The former is usually translated as "world" while the latter literally means "things as they really are." The words *dhammata* and *niyama* are used in the Pali canon to mean "natural law or way."

Nature as Dynamic

According to Buddhism changeability is one of the perennial principles of nature. Everything changes in nature and nothing remains static. This concept is expressed by the Pali term *aniccā*. Everything formed is in a constant process of change *(sabbe sankhara anicca)*. The world is therefore defined as that which disintegrates *(lujjati ti loko)*; the world is so called because it is dynamic and kinetic, it is constantly in a process of undergoing change. In nature there are no static and stable "things"; there are only ever-changing, ever-moving processes. Rain is a good example to illustrate this point. Though we use a noun called "rain" which appears to denote a "thing," rain is nothing but the process of drops of water falling from the skies. Apart from this process, the activity of raining, there is no rain as such which could be expressed by a seemingly static nominal concept. The very elements of solidity *(paṭhavi)*, liquidity *(āpo)*, heat *(tejo)* and mobility *(vāyo)*, recognized as the building material of nature, are all ever-changing phenomena. Even the most solid looking mountains and the very earth that supports everything on it are not beyond this inexorable law of change. One sutta explains how the massive king of mountains — Mount Sineru, which is rooted in the great ocean to a depth of 84,000 leagues and which rises above sea level to another great height of 84,000 leagues and which is very classical symbol of stability and steadfastness — also gets destroyed by heat, without leaving even ashes, with the appearance of multiple suns. Thus change is the very essence of nature.

Morality and Nature

The world passes through alternating cycles of evolution and dissolution, each of which endures for a long period of time. Though change is inherent in nature, Buddhism believes that natural processes are affected by the morals of man.

According to the *Aggañña Sutta,* which relates the Buddhist legend regarding the evolution of the world, the appearance of greed in the primordial beings — who at that time were self-luminous, subsisting on joy, and traversing in the skies — caused the gradual loss of their radiance and their ability to subsist on joy and to move about in the sky. The moral degradation had effects on the external environment too. At that time the entire earth was covered over by a very flavorsome fragrant substance similar to butter. When beings started partaking of this substance with more and more greed, on the one hand their subtle bodies became coarser and coarser. On the other hand the flavorsome substance itself started gradually diminishing. With the solidification of bodies differences of form appeared; some were beautiful while others were homely. Thereupon conceit manifested itself in those beings, and the beautiful ones started looking down upon the others. As a result of these moral blemishes the delicious edible earth-substance completely disappeared. In its place there appeared edible mushrooms and later another kind of edible creeper. In the beings who subsisted on them successively sex differentiation became manifest and the former method of spontaneous birth was replaced by sexual reproduction.

Self-growing rice appeared on earth and through laziness to collect each meal man grew accustomed to hoarding food. As a result of this hoarding habit, the growth rate of food could not keep pace with the rate of demand. Therupon land had to be divided among families. After private ownership of land became the order of the day, those who were of a more greedy disposition started robbing from others' plots of land. When they were detected they denied that they had stolen. Thus through greed vices such as stealing and lying became manifest in society. To curb the wrong doers and punish them a king was elected by the people and thus the original simple society became much more complex and complicated. It is said that this moral degeneration of man had adverse effects on nature. The richness of the earth diminished and self-growing rice disappeared. Man had to till the land and cultivate rice for food. This rice grain was enveloped in chaff; it needed cleaning before consumption.

The point I wish to emphasize by citing this evolutionary legend is that Buddhism believes that though change is a factor inherent in nature, man's moral deterioration accelerates the process of change and brings about changes which are adverse to human well being and happiness.

The *Cakkavattisihanada Sutta* of the Digha Nikaya predicts the future course of events when human morals undergo further degeneration. Gradually man's health will deteriorate so much that life expectancy will diminish until at last the average human life-span is reduced to ten years and marriageable age to five years. At that time all delicacies such as ghee, butter, honey, etc. will have disappeared from the earth; what is considered the poorest coarse food today will become a delicacy of that day. Thus Buddhism maintains that there is a close link between man's morals and the natural resources available to him.

According to a discourse in the Anguttara Nikaya, when

profligate lust, wanton greed, and wrong values grip the heart of man and immorality becomes widespread in society, timely rain does not fall. When timely rain does not fall crops get adversely affected with various kinds of pests and plant diseases. Through lack of nourishing food the human mortality rate rises.

Thus several suttas from the Pali canon show that early Buddhism believes there to be a close relationship between human morality and the natural environment. This idea has been systematized in the theory of the five natural laws *(pañca niyamadhamma)* in the later commentaries. According to this theory, in the cosmos there are five natural laws or forces at work, namely *utuniyama* (lit. "season-law"), *bijaniyama* (lit. "seed-law"), *cittaniyama, kammaniyama,* and *dhammaniyama.* They can be translated as physical laws, biological laws, psychological laws, moral laws, and causal laws, respectively. While the first four laws operate within their respective spheres, the last-mentioned law of causality operates *within* each of them as well as *among* them.

This means that the physical environment of any given area conditions the growth and development of its biological component, i.e. flora and fauna. These in turn influence the thought pattern of the people interacting with them. Modes of thinking determine moral standards. The opposite process of interaction is also possible. The morals of man influence not only the psychological makeup of the people but the biological and physical environment of the area as well. Thus the five laws demonstrate that man and nature are bound together in a reciprocal causal relationship with changes in one necessarily bringing about changes in the other.

The commentary on the *Cakkavattisihanada Sutta* goes on to explain the pattern of mutual interaction further.

When mankind is demoralized through greed, famine is the natural outcome; when moral degeneration is due to ignorance, epidemic is the inevitable result; when hatred is the demoralizing force, widespread violence is the ultimate outcome. If and when mankind realizes that large-scale devastation has taken place as a result of his moral degeneration, a change of heart takes place among the few surviving human beings. With gradual moral regeneration conditions improve through a long period of cause and effect and mankind again starts to enjoy gradually increasing prosperity and longer life. The world, including nature and mankind, stands or falls with the type of moral force at work. If immorality grips society, man and nature deteriorate; if morality reigns, the quality of human life and nature improves. Thus greed, hatred, and delusion produce pollution within and without. Generosity, compassion, and wisdom produce purity within and without. This is one reason the Buddha has pronounced that the world is led by the mind, *cittena niyati loko.* Thus man and nature, according to the ideas expressed in early Buddhism, are interdependent.

Human Use of Natural Resources

For survival mankind has to depend on nature for his food, clothing, shelter, medicine, and other requisites.

For optimum benefits man has to understand nature so that he can utilize natural resources and live harmoniously with nature. By understanding the working of nature — for example, the seasonal rainfall pattern, methods of conserving water by irrigation, the soil types, the physical conditions required for growth of various food crops, etc. — man can learn to get better returns from his agricultural pursuits. But this learning has to be accompanied by moral restraint if he is to enjoy the benefits of natural resources for a long time. Man must learn to satisfy his needs and not feed his greeds. The resources of the world are not unlimited whereas man's greed knows neither limit nor satiation. Modern man in his unbridled voracious greed for pleasure and acquisition of wealth has exploited nature to the point of near impoverishment.

Ostentatious consumerism is accepted as the order of the day. One writer says that within forty years Americans alone have consumed natural resources to the quantity of what all mankind has consumed for the last 4000 years. The vast non-replenishable resources of fossil fuels which took millions of years to form have been consumed within a couple of centuries to the point of near exhaustion. This consumerism has given rise to an energy crisis on the one hand and a pollution problem on the other. Man's unrestrained exploitation of nature to gratify his insatiate greed reminds one of the traditional parable of the goose that laid the golden eggs.

Buddhism tirelessly advocates the virtues of non-greed, non-hatred and non-delusion in all human pursuits. Greed breeds sorrow and unhealthy consequences. Contentment *(santutthi)* is a much praised virtue in Buddhism. The man leading a simple life with few wants easily satisfied is upheld and appreciated as an exemplary character. Miserliness and wastefulness are equally deplored in Buddhism as two degenerate extremes. Wealth has only instrumental value; it is to be utilized for the satisfaction of man's needs. Hoarding is a senseless anti-social habit comparable to the attitude of the dog in the manger. The vast hoarding of wealth in some countries and the methodical destruction of large quantities of agricultural produce to keep the market prices from falling, while half the world is dying of hunger and starvation, is really a sad paradox of the present affluent age.

Buddhism commends frugality as a virtue in its own right. Once Ananda explained to King Udena the thrifty economic use of robes by the monks in the following order. When new robes are received the old robes are used as coverlets, the old coverlets as mattress covers, the old mattress covers as rugs, the old rugs as dusters, and the old tattered dusters are kneaded with clay and used to repair cracked floors and walls. Thus nothing is wasted. Those who waste are derided as "wood-apple eaters." A man shakes the branch of a wood-apple tree and all the fruits, ripe as well as unripe, fall. The man would collect only what he wants and walk away leaving the rest to rot. Such a wasteful attitude is certainly deplored in Buddhism as not only anti-social but criminal. The excessive exploitation of nature as is done today would certainly be condemned by Buddhism in the strongest possible terms.

Buddhism advocates a gentle non-aggressive attitude towards nature. According to the *Sigalovada Sutta* a householder should accumulate wealth as a bee collects pollen from a flower. The bee harms neither the fragrance nor the beauty of the flower, but gathers pollen to turn it into sweet honey. Similarly, man is expected to make legitimate use of nature so that he can rise above nature and realize his innate spiritual potential.

Attitude towards Animal and Plant Life

The well-known Five Precepts *(pañca sila)* form the minimum code of ethics that every lay Buddhist is expected to adhere to. Its first precept involves abstention from injury to life. It is explained as the casting aside of all forms of weapons, being conscientious about depriving a living being of life. In its positive sense it means the cultivation of compassion and sympathy for all living things. The Buddhist layman is expected to abstain from trading in meat too.

The Buddhist monk has to abide by an even stricter code of ethics than the layman. He has to abstain from practices which would involve even unintentional injury to living creatures.

For instance, the Buddha promulgated the rule against going on a journey during the rainy season because of possible injury to worms and insects that come to the surface in wet weather. The same concern for non-violence prevents a monk from digging the ground. Once a monk who was a potter prior to ordination built for himself a clay hut and set it on fire to give it a fine finish.

The Buddha strongly objected to this as so many living creatures would have been burnt in the process. The hut was broken down on the Buddha's instructions to prevent it from creating a bad precedent for later generations.

The scrupulous nonviolent attitude towards even the smallest living creatures prevents the monks from drinking unstrained water. It is no doubt a sound hygienic habit, but what is noteworthy is the reason which prompts the practice, namely sympathy for living creatures.

Buddhism also prescribes the practice of *metta,* "loving-kindness" towards all creatures of all quarters without restriction.

The *Karaniyametta Sutta* enjoins the cultivation of loving-kindness towards all creatures timid and steady, long and short, big and small, minute and great, visible and invisible, near and far, born and awaiting birth. All quarters are to be suffused with this loving attitude. Just as one's own life is precious to oneself, so is the life of the other precious to himself. Therefore a reverential attitude must be cultivated towards all forms of life.

The *Nandivisala Jataka* illustrates how kindness should be shown to animals domesticated for human service. Even a wild animal can be tamed with kind words. Parileyya was a wild elephant who attended on the Buddha when he spent time in the forest away from the monks.

The infuriated elephant Nalagiri was tamed by the Buddha with no other miraculous power than the power of loving-kindness. Man and beast can live and let live without fear of one another if only man cultivates sympathy and regards all life with compassion.

The understanding of kamma and rebirth, too, prepares the Buddhist to adopt a sympathetic attitude towards animals.

According to this belief it is possible for human beings to be reborn in subhuman states among animals. The *Kukkuravatika Sutta* can be cited as a canonical reference which substantiates this view.

The Jatakas provide ample testimony to this view from commentarial literature. It is possible that our own close relatives have been reborn as animals. Therefore it is only right that we should treat animals with kindness and sympathy.

The Buddhist notion of merit also engenders a gentle non-violent attitude towards living creatures. It is said that if one throws dish-washing water into a pool where there are insects and living creatures, intending that they feed on the tiny particles of food thus washed away, one accumulates merit even by such trivial generosity. According to the *Macchuddana Jataka* the Bodhisatta threw his leftover food into a river in order to feed the fish, and by the power of that merit he was saved from an impending disaster.

Thus kindness to animals, be they big or small, is a source of merit — merit needed for human beings to improve their lot in the cycle of rebirths and to approach the final goal of Nibbana. Buddhism expresses a gentle non-violent attitude towards the vegetable kingdom as well. It is said that one should not even break the branch of a tree that has given one shelter.

Plants are so helpful to us in providing us with all necessities of life that we are expected not to adopt a callous attitude towards them. The more strict monastic rules prevent the monks from injuring plant life.

Prior to the rise of Buddhism people regarded natural phenomena such as mountains, forests, groves, and trees with a sense of awe and reverence.

They considered them as the abode of powerful non-human beings who could assist human beings at times of need. Though Buddhism gave man a far superior Triple Refuge *(tisarana)* in the Buddha, Dhamma, and Sangha, these places continued to enjoy public patronage at a popular level, as the acceptance of terrestrial non-human beings such as *devatas* and *yakkhas* did not violate the belief system of Buddhism.

Therefore among the Buddhists there is a reverential attitude towards specially long-standing gigantic trees. They are *vanaspati* in Pali, meaning "lords of the forests."

As huge trees such as the ironwood, the sala, and the fig are also recognized as the Bodhi trees of former Buddhas, the deferential attitude towards trees is further strengthened. It is well known that the *ficus religiosa* is held as an object of great veneration in the Buddhist world today as the tree under which the Buddha attained Enlightenment.

The construction of parks and pleasure groves for public use is considered a great meritorious deed. Sakka the lord of gods is said to have reached his status as a result of social services such as the construction of parks, pleasure groves, ponds, wells, and roads. The open air, natural habitats and forest trees have a special fascination for the Eastern mind as symbols of spiritual freedom.

The home life is regarded as a fetter *(sambadha)* that keeps man in bondage and misery. Renunciation is like the open air *(abbhokasa),* nature unhampered by man's activity. The chief events in the life of the Buddha too took place in the open air. He was born in a park at the foot of a tree in Kapilavatthu; he attained Enlightenment in the open air at the foot of the Bodhi tree in Bodhgaya; he inaugurated his missionary activity in the open air in the sala grove of the Malas in Pava.

The Buddha's constant advice to his disciples also was to resort to natural habitats such as forest groves and glades. There, undisturbed by human activity, they could zealously engage themselves in meditation.

Attitude towards Pollution

Environmental pollution has assumed such vast proportions today that man has been forced to recognize the presence of an ecological crisis.

He can no longer turn a blind eye to the situation as he is already threatened with new pollution-related diseases. Pollution to this extent was unheard of during the time of the Buddha. But there is sufficient evidence in the Pali canon to give us insight into the Buddhist attitude towards the pollution problem.

Several Vinaya rules prohibit monks from polluting green grass and water with saliva, urine, and feces. These were the common agents of pollution known during the Buddha's day and rules were promulgated against causing such pollution. Cleanliness was highly commended by the Buddhists both in the person and in the environment. They were much concerned about keeping water clean, be it in the river, pond, or well. These sources of water were for public use and each individual had to use them with proper public-spirited caution so that others after him could use them with the same degree of cleanliness.

Rules regarding the cleanliness of green grass were prompted by ethical and aesthetic considerations. Moreover, grass is food for most animals and it is man's duty to refrain from polluting it by his activities.

Noise is today recognized as a serious personal and environmental pollutant troubling everyone to some extent. It causes deafness, stress, and irritation, breeds resentment, saps energy, and inevitably lowers efficiency.

The Buddha's attitude to noise is very clear from the Pali canon. He was critical of noise and did not hesitate to voice his stern disapproval whenever occasion arose. Once he ordered a group of monks to leave the monastery for noisy behavior.

He enjoyed solitude and silence immensely and spoke in praise of silence as it is most appropriate for mental culture. Noise is described as a thorn to one engaged in the first step of meditation, but thereafter noise ceases to be a disturbance as the meditator passes beyond the possibility of being disturbed by sound.

The Buddha and his disciples reveled in the silent solitary natural habitats unencumbered by human activity. Even in the choice of monasteries the presence of undisturbed silence was an important quality they looked for. Silence invigorates those who are pure at heart and raises their efficiency for meditation.

But silence overawes those who are impure with ignoble impulses of greed, hatred, and delusion. The *Bhayabherava Sutta* beautifully illustrates how even the rustle of leaves by a falling twig in the forest sends tremors through an impure heart. This may perhaps account for the present craze for constant auditory stimulation with transistors and cassettes.

The moral impurity caused by greed, avarice, acquisitive instincts, and aggression has rendered man so timid that he cannot bear silence which lays bare the reality of self-awareness. He therefore prefers to drown himself in loud music. Unlike classical music, which tends to soothe nerves and induce relaxation, rock music excites the senses. Constant exposure to it actually renders man incapable of relaxation and sound sleep without tranquilizers.

As to the question of the Buddhist attitude to music, it is recorded that the Buddha has spoken quite appreciatively of music on one occasion.

When Pañcasikha the divine musician sang a song while playing the lute in front of the Buddha, the Buddha praised his musical ability saying that the instrumental music blended well with his song. Again, the remark of an Arahant that the joy of seeing the real nature of things is far more exquisite than orchestral music shows the recognition that music affords a certain amount of pleasure even if it is inferior to higher kinds of pleasure.

But it is stressed that the ear is a powerful sensory channel through which man gets addicted to sense pleasures. Therefore, to dissuade monks from getting addicted to melodious sounds, the monastic discipline describes music as a lament.

The psychological training of the monks is so advanced that they are expected to cultivate a taste not only for external silence, but for inner silence of speech, desire, and thought as well.

The sub-vocal speech, the inner chatter that goes on constantly within us in our waking life is expected to be silenced through meditation. The sage who succeeded in quelling this inner speech completely is described as a *muni*, a silent one. His inner silence is maintained even when he speaks!

It is not inappropriate to pay passing notice to the Buddhist attitude to speech as well. Moderation in speech is considered a virtue, as one can avoid four unwholesome vocal activities thereby, namely, falsehood, slander, harsh speech, and frivolous talk. In its positive aspect moderation in speech paves the path to self-awareness.

Buddhism commends speaking at the appropriate time, speaking the truth, speaking gently, speaking what is useful, and speaking out of loving-kindness; the opposite modes of speech are condemned.

The Buddha's general advice to the monks regarding speech is to be engaged in discussing the Dhamma or maintain noble silence. The silence that reigned in vast congregations of monks during the Buddha's day was indeed a surprise even to the kings of the time. Silence is serene and noble as it is conducive to the spiritual progress of those who are pure at heart.

Even Buddhist laymen were reputed to have appreciated quietude and silence. Pañcangika Thapati can be cited as a conspicuous example. Once Mahanama the Sakyan complained to the Buddha that he is disturbed by the hustle of the busy city of Kapilavatthu.

He explained that he experiences calm serenity when he visits the Buddha in the quiet salubrious surroundings of the monastery and his peace of mind gets disturbed when he goes to the city. Though noise to the extent of being a pollutant causing health hazards was not known during the Buddha's day, we have adduced enough material from the Pali canon to illustrate the Buddha's attitude to the problem.

Quietude is much appreciated as spiritually rewarding, while noise condemned as a personal and social nuisance.

Nature as Beautiful

The Buddha and his disciples regarded natural beauty as a source of great joy and aesthetic satisfaction. The saints who purged themselves of sensuous worldly pleasures responded to natural beauty with a detached sense of appreciation.

The average poet looks at nature and derives inspiration mostly by the sentiments it evokes in his own heart; he becomes emotionally involved with nature. For instance, he may compare the sun's rays passing over the mountain tops to the blush on a sensitive face, he may see a tear in a dew drop, the lips of his beloved in a rose petal, etc.

But the appreciation of the saint is quite different. He appreciates nature's beauty for its own sake and derives joy unsullied by sensuous associations and self-projected ideas. The simple spontaneous appreciation of nature's exquisite beauty is expressed by the Elder Mahakassapa in the following words:

Those upland glades delightful to the soul,
Where the Kaveri spreads its wildering wreaths,
Where sound the trumpet-calls of elephants:
Those are the hills where my soul delights.
Those rocky heights with hue of dark blue clouds
Where lies embossed many a shining lake
Of crystal-clear, cool waters, and whose slopes
The 'herds of Indra' cover and bedeck:
Those are the hills wherein my soul delights.
Fair uplands rain-refreshed, and resonant
With crested creatures' cries antiphonal,

Lone heights where silent Rishis oft resort:

Those are the hills wherein my soul delights.

Again the poem of Kaludayi, inviting the Buddha to visit Kapilavatthu, contains a beautiful description of spring:

Now crimson glow the trees, dear Lord, and cast

Their ancient foliage in quest of fruit,

Like crests of flame they shine irradiant

And rich in hope, great Hero, is the hour.

Verdure and blossom-time in every tree

Wherever we look delightful to the eye,

And every quarter breathing fragrant airs,

While petals falling, yearning comes fruit:

It is time, O Hero, that we set out hence.

The long poem of Talaputa is a fascinating soliloquy. His religious aspirations are beautifully blended with a profound knowledge of the teachings of the Buddha against the background of a sylvan resort.

Many more poems could be cited for saintly appreciation of nature, but it is not necessary to burden the essay with any more quotations. Suffice it to know that the saints, too, were sensitive to the beauties and harmony of nature and that their appreciation is colored by spontaneity, simplicity, and a non-sensuous spirituality.

CONCLUSION

In the modern age man has become alienated from himself and nature. When science started opening new vistas of knowledge revealing the secrets of nature one by one, man gradually lost faith in theistic religions. Consequently, he developed scanty respect for moral and spiritual values as well. With the advent of the Industrial Revolution and the acquisition of wealth by mechanical exploitation of natural resources, man has become more and more materialistic in his attitudes and values. The pursuit of sense pleasures and the acquisition of possessions have become ends in themselves.

Man's sense faculties dominate him to an unrelenting degree and man has become a slave to his insatiable passions. (Incidentally the sense faculties are in Pali *indriyas* or lords, because they control man unless he is sufficiently vigilant to become their master.) Thus man has become alienated from himself as he abandoned himself to the influence of sense pleasures and acquisitive instincts.

In his greed for more and more possessions he has adopted a violent and aggressive attitude towards nature. Forgetting that he is a part and parcel of nature, he exploits it with unrestrained greed, thus alienating himself from nature as well.

The net result is the deterioration of man's physical and mental health on the one hand, and the rapid depletion of non-replenishable natural resources and environmental pollution on the other.

These results remind us of the Buddhist teachings in the suttas discussed above, which maintain that the moral degeneration of man leads to the decrease of his life-span and the depletion of natural resources.

Moral degeneration is a double-edged weapon, it exercises adverse effects on man's psycho-physical well being as well as on nature.

Already killer diseases such as heart ailments, cancer, diabetes, AIDS, etc., are claiming victims on an unprecedented scale. In the final analysis these can all be traced to man's moral deterioration. Depletion of vast resources of fossil fuels and forests has given rise to a very severe energy crisis.

It cannot be emphasized too strongly that such rapid depletion of non-renewable natural resources within less than two centuries, an infinitesimal fraction of the millions of years taken for them to form, is due to modern man's inordinate greed and acquisitiveness.

A number of simple ancient societies had advanced technological skills, as is evident by their vast sophisticated irrigation schemes designed to feed the fundamental needs of several millions. Yet they survived in some countries over 2000 years without such problems as environmental pollution and depletion of natural resources. This was no doubt due to to validity of the philosophy which inspired and formed the basis of these civilizations.

In the present ecocrisis man has to look for radical solutions. "Pollution cannot be dealt with in the long term on a remedial or cosmetic basis or by tackling symptoms: all measures should deal with basic causes. These are determined largely by our values, priorities, and choices." Man must reappraise his value system.

The materialism that has guided his lifestyle has landed him in very severe problems. Buddhism teaches that mind is the forerunner of all things, mind is supreme. If one acts with an impure mind, i.e. a mind sullied with greed, hatred and delusion, suffering is the inevitable result.

If one acts with a pure mind, i.e. with the opposite qualities of contentment, compassion, and wisdom, happiness will follow like a shadow. Man has to understand that pollution in the environment has been caused because there has been psychological pollution within himself. If he wants a clean environment he has to adopt a lifestyle that springs from a moral and spiritual dimension.

Buddhism offers man a simple moderate lifestyle eschewing both extremes of self-deprivation and self-indulgence. Satisfaction of basic human necessities, reduction of wants to the minimum, frugality, and contentment are its important characteristics. Each man has to order his life on normal principles, exercise self-control in the enjoyment of the senses, discharge his duties in his various social roles, and conduct himself with wisdom and self-awareness in all activities. It is only when each man adopts a simple moderate lifestyle that mankind as a whole will stop polluting the environment. This seems to be the only way of overcoming the present ecocrisis and the problem of alienation. With such a lifestyle, man will adopt a non-exploitative, non-aggressive, gentle attitude towards nature. He can then live in harmony with nature, utilizing its resources for the satisfaction of his basic needs. The Buddhist admonition is to utilize nature in the same way as a bee collects pollen from the flower, neither polluting its beauty nor depleting its fragrance. Just as the bee manufactures honey out of pollen, so man should be able to find happiness and fulfillment in life without harming the natural world in which he lives.

BIBLIOGRAPHY

Batchelor, Martine and Kerry Brown: *Buddhism and Ecology,* London, Cassell, 1992.

Bell, Sir Charles: *Portrait of a Dalai Lama: The Life and Times of the Great Thirteenth,* Boston, Wisdom Publications, 1987.

Cook, Elizabeth: *Holy Places of the Buddha,* Berkeley, Dharma Publishing, 1994.

Dargyay, Eva M.: *The Rise of Esoteric Buddhism in Tibet,* Delhi, Motilal Banarsidass, 1977.

Dayal, Har: *The Bodhisattva Doctrine in Buddhist Sanskrit Literature,* London, Kegan Paul, 1932.

Eppsteiner, Fred: *The Path of Compassion: Writings on Socially Engaged Buddhism,* Berkeley, Parallax Press, 1988.

Eppsteiner, Fred: *The Path of Compassion: Writings on Socially Engaged Buddhism,* Berkeley, Parallax Press, 1988.

Gombrich, Richard F.: *Buddhist Precept and Practice,* Delhi, Motilal Banarsidass, 1991.

Gonda, Jan: *Vedic Literature: Samhitas and Brahmanas,* Wiesbaden, 1975.

Hakeda, Yoshito S.: *Kukai, Major Works,* New York, Columbia University Press, 1972.

Jones, Ken: *Beyond Optimism: A Buddhist Political Ecology,* Oxford, Jon Carpenter, 1993.

Keown, Damien: *The Nature of Buddhist Ethics,* New York, St. Martin's Press, 1992.

Khoroche, Peter: *Once the Buddha Was a Monkey: Arya Sura's Jatakamala,* Chicago, University of Chicago Press, 1989.

Lalwani. K.C.: *Kalpa Sutra of Badrabahu Svami,* Delhi, Motilal Banarsidass. 1979.

Lamotte, Etienne: *The Suramgamasamadhi Sutra,* London, Curzon, 1998.

Mookerjee, Satkari: *Buddhist Philosophy of Universal Flux,* Delhi, Motilal Banarsidass, 1980.

Nyanatiloka, *A.: Guide through the Abhidhamma Pitaka,* Kandy, Buddhist Publication Society, 1971.

Payutto, Prayudh: *Buddhist Economics: A Middle Way for the Marketplace,* Bangkok, Buddhadhamma Foundation, 1994.

Poppe, Nicholas: *The Twelve Deeds of Buddha,* Seattle, University of Washington Press, 1967.

Powers, John: *Wisdom of Buddha: The Samdhinirmocana Sutra,* Berkeley, Dharma Publishing, 1994.

Sarkisyanz, E.: *Buddhist Backgrounds of the Burmese Revolution,* The Hague, Martinus Nijhoff, 1965.

Sotoshu Shumucho: *International Symposium: The Future of the Earth and Zen Buddhism,* Tokyo, Sotoshu Shumucho, 1991.

Sprung, Mervyn: *The Problem of Two Truths in Buddhism and Vedanta,* Boston, Reidel, 1973.

Strong, John: *The Legend of King Asoka,* Princeton, Princeton University Press, 1983.

Thomas, E. J.: *The Life of the Buddha as Legend and History,* London, Routledge & Kegan Paul, 1927.

Titmuss, Christopher: *The Green Buddha,* Devon, Insights, 1995.

Wells, Kenneth E.: *Thai Buddhism, Its Rites and Activities,* Bangkok, Christian Bookstore, 1960.

Williams, Paul: *The Reflexive Nature of Awareness,* London, Curzon, 1997.

INDEX

□□□